11/01

STORIES
THAT
CHANGED
AMERICA

STORIES THAT CHANGED AMERICA

Muckrakers of the 20th Century

CARL JENSEN, PH.D.

SEVEN STORIES PRESS

New York | Toronto | London | Sydney

Copyright © 2000 by Carl Jensen

A Seven Stories Press First Edition

Seven Stories Press
140 Watts Street
New York, NY 10013
http://www.sevenstories.com

In Canada: Hushion House, 36 Northline Road, Toronto, Ontario M4B 3E2

In the U.K.: Turnaround Publisher Services Ltd., Unit 3, Olympia Trading Estate, Coburg Road, Wood Green, London N22 6TZ

In Australia: Tower Books, 9/19 Rodborough Road, Frenchs Forest NSW 2086

Library of Congress Cataloging-in-Publication Data

Jensen, Carl
    Stories that changed America: muckrakers of the 20th century/Carl Jensen.—A Seven Stories Press 1st ed.
    p. cm.
    Includes bibliographical references.
    ISBN 1-58322-027-5
    1. Journalists—United States—Biography. 2. Investigative reporting—United States—History—20th century. 3. Reportage literature, American—History and criticism. I. Title.

PN4871.J46 2000
070'.92'273—dc21
[B]
                                                        00-020365

9 8 7 6 5 4 3 2 1

College professors may order examination copies of Seven Stories Press titles for a free six-month trial period. To order, visit www.sevenstories.com/textbook, or fax on school letterhead to (212) 226-1411.

Book design by Cindy LaBreacht

Printed in the U.S.A.

Dedicated
to my children,
John, Pia, Lisa, and Sherman
in hopes they will
continue the struggle
to make the world
a better place.

It can happen.

ACKNOWLEDGMENTS

My greatest appreciation goes to the twenty-one authors cited in this book and to their original publishers. Their efforts and their stories rocked the boat and made the United States—and, in some cases, the world—a better place for all of us. They have given us a lasting example of what one person can do. We are all in their debt. Authors still living were given an opportunity to review their brief biographies for accuracy. I appreciate the suggestions from Paul Brodeur, Paul Ehrlich, Ralph Nader, and Frances Moore Lappé to help keep the record straight. I am also indebted to Dan Simon, owner of Seven Stories Press (SSP) and publisher of this book, for his advice, support, faith and friendship. Special thanks are eagerly offered Nicole Dewey for her reassuring updates during the publishing process and her marketing talents, Kera Bolonik for her sensitive editing skills, Cindy LaBreacht for the book design, and Jon Gilbert for keeping it all together. Thanks also go to the reference librarians at the Ruben Salazar Library, Sonoma State University, California, for their patience and assistance in locating obscure sources. Finally I want to especially thank my wife, Sandra Scott Jensen, for the many hours she spent reviewing early versions of this book and for all the support and encouragement she has given me the past 25 years.

Carl Jensen
Cotati, California

9

CONTENTS

Introduction
MUCKRAKING
IN THE
TWENTIETH
CENTURY

Every society has stories to tell. Stories about its heroes, history, and achievements. Some of these tales enliven the spirit and inspire the reader to want to make a difference. This is a book of stories that changed America, written by storytellers who have at times been dubbed "muckrakers."

For more than two thousand years, a muckrake was a harmless three-pronged pitchfork-like tool used on farms to clean up stables and barns. Its first recorded use was in Mesopotamia in 750 B.C. But in 1906, it became a term used to vilify some of the most prominent and effective writers of the time.

The end of the nineteenth century was a time of prosperity and excess for the power elite in America. In 1860, there were three American millionaires. By 1901, just forty years later, there were about 3,800. Corporate America ruled the country with few regulations and little monitoring by the government. Everyone else, it seemed, was at the mercy of the "Robber Barons," an apt term used by author Matthew Josephson to describe the leading businessmen of the time. This formidable and wealthy rogues' gallery included John D. Rockefeller, J.P. Morgan, Cornelius Vanderbilt, Jay Gould, John Jacob Astor, and Andrew Carnegie—names that are familiar to this day.

It didn't take great insight to recognize that poverty, vice, electoral fraud, unsafe foods, monopolistic practices, segregation, child labor exploitation, and civil rights violations were leading to the disintegration of society. But it did take some courageous individuals who saw the problems to dedicate their lives and talents to solving them.

In reaction to the corruption of the time, a group of men and women made their voices heard as they successfully challenged the Robber Barons. They exposed the political and economic corruption and social hardships caused by greedy businessmen and corrupt politicians.

One of these individuals was a slim young man in his twenties who took on one of the largest, most profitable, and most harmful industries of the time. For seven weeks, in 1904, he carefully observed the working conditions and the way meat was processed at the Chicago stockyards. Wearing well-worn working clothes, carrying a lunch pail, he blended in well with the other workers. But he wasn't a worker. His name was Upton Sinclair, an undercover investigative author and one of the greatest storytellers of the century.

In February 1906, Sinclair published his research in a fact-based novel entitled *The Jungle*. The book quickly became a best seller and came to be heralded as a landmark example of the Golden Age of Muckraking, an era that spanned the first decade of the twentieth century. Following the book's publication, there was a national uproar over the safety of the nation's meat supply.

President Theodore Roosevelt and other politicians responded to the public outrage. In short order, there were newspaper reports and editorials followed by congressional hearings. On June 30, 1906, President Roosevelt signed the Pure Food and Drug Act into law, the first enforceable national legislation dealing with the safety of our food products. The meat packers and the beef trust fought Sinclair and his book but were defeated by overwhelming public support for the author.

The meatpacking industry was just one of many institutions targeted by investigative journalists during the first ten years of the twentieth century. In a series of devastating exposés, the muckrakers took on political and corporate corruption in the oil industry, insurance, banking, railroads, mining, prisons, and municipal, state, and federal governments. Their words led to a nation-wide public revolt against social evils and a decade of reforms in anti-trust legislation, the electoral process, banking regulations, and a host of other social programs.

It was also the peak of Progressive Era politics when journalists, publishers, and some legislators complemented one another, investigating, exposing, and correcting the social problems that plagued most Americans.

One particular series of exposés, entitled "The Treason of the Senate," by David Graham Phillips, targeted Congress. Phillips accused powerful Senators —including some of President Roosevelt's own supporters—of drafting legislation benefiting corporations in which they had a personal financial stake. As a result, pressure was brought to bear on Roosevelt to do something about these journalistic troublemakers. At the time, Roosevelt was in a precarious position in his presidency and needed the support of Congress to implement his programs. While he had previously supported investigative journalists like Sinclair, he suddenly found it necessary to undercut their efforts.

Shortly after the "treason" series began in *Cosmopolitan* in March 1906, Roosevelt spoke before the Gridiron Club of newspapermen in Washington, D.C. He charged that the writers who were engaging in the exposure of corruption were "muckrakers," and likened them to the man with the muckrake in John Bunyan's "Pilgrim's Progress," who, Roosevelt said, could "look no way but downward, with the muckrake in his hand; who was offered a celestial crown for his muckrake, but who would neither look up nor regard the crown he was offered, but continue to rake to himself the filth of the floor."

The Gridiron speech was off the record. But on April 14, 1906, while dedicating the cornerstone of the House of Representatives office building, the President gave the same speech on the record, publicly labeling the writers as muckrakers—a pejorative as used by Roosevelt—accusing them of being so busy stirring up the mud at their feet that they could not see the good things in America.

THE ROBBER BARONS
WERE MUCKRAKERS

It appears that Roosevelt misinterpreted the "Interpreter" of Bunyan's allegorical narrative. Bunyan's "Interpreter" was actually extolling the virtues of simple poverty. He described how the wealthy were obsessed with looking downward to rake more riches in when they should have been looking upward at the celestial beauty above them. The term "muckraker" would more accurately describe the Robber Barons of Roosevelt's time, not the journalists. Only Ida Tarbell challenged the accuracy of Roosevelt's tirade, in her autobiography.

There was a mixed reaction to Roosevelt's malicious terminology wielded at the journalists he attacked. Some, like Ida Tarbell, were appalled at his satirical criticism of their scholarly research. Others like Upton Sinclair, responded to the challenge by accepting the label with pride. Despite its misinterpretation, "muckraker" became a widely used vituperative term. Most modern day journalists dislike the title and prefer to be called "investigative journalists." Yet, there are a few who have embraced the title, like Jessica Mitford, who proudly wore the crown as "Queen of the Muckrakers."

In reaction to the muckrakers' criticism of corporate America, the fields of advertising and public relations rapidly grew in size and import. The powerful propagandistic vehicles gave corporate America the manipulative tools it needed to refute the exposés. A corporate conspiracy ensued, one designed to discredit journalists, and along with the threat of World War I, and other factors, the curtain came down on the Golden Age of Muckraking.

But there were journalists and other individuals who continued to dedicate themselves to exposing corporate crimes, political corruption, and social injustice, and they did not disappear with the end of that sparkling era. Given its common usage, the term "muckraker" is used herein to describe individuals, journalists and other social reformers, whose words helped to change the course of history and improve life for others.

The stories selected for this book had to have a major, positive impact on society, and be published during the twentieth century (which eliminated some famed pre-1900 muckrakers like Nellie Bly). The stories span a broad spectrum of critical issues, from corporate and political corruption, the environment, to population growth, and civil rights. They are an eclectic collection bound together by a common theme—they all helped make America a better place.

There are a number of common characteristics to be found among the twenty-one authors of the twenty stories featured in this book (one story had two authors). Most of them attended college, were political liberals, came from a middle-class background, and envisioned idealistic goals at an early age.

Education appeared to be one of the strongest variables in the making of a muckraker, and many shared a passion for reading good books and periodicals at an early age. Eighteen of the twenty-one authors attended college and eleven of them attended graduate school. Only one author had no formal schooling: Jessica Mitford. In her customary manner, she would delightedly respond "nil" when asked about her education.

Right-wing media critics who accuse journalists of being liberals will delight in knowing their charges are valid when it comes to these muckrakers. While a few of the authors were apolitical, seventeen of them could be classified as liberals, while some, including Lincoln Steffens, Upton Sinclair, George Seldes, Jessica Mitford, and Michael Harrington, overtly espoused socialist or communist philosophies. There are only two whose politics and background could be considered more conservative than liberal: Ida Mae Tarbell and Bob Woodward.

Fourteen of the authors came from a middle-class economic background, four were upper class, and three lower class.

Seven dedicated themselves explicitly to exposing political and corporate corruption, while eleven had the more general goal of saving or changing the world. Some of them focused their efforts in areas such as women's rights and racial equality, while others simply wanted to be the best possible professional journalists they could be: George Seldes, Edward R. Murrow, and Bob Woodward.

Not surprisingly, more than half were career journalists or authors, while the remaining nine were reformers from the fields of science, welfare, teaching, nursing, politics, religion, and law.

Books were the predominant vehicle used by muckrakers to tell their stories, and all but two of these were works of nonfiction. Four issues were exposed through newspaper or magazine articles, three originated in newsletters, one story was aired on television, and another was drawn from the pulpit.

There are six general categories covered in the twenty stories included here. Six focus on corporate corruption, four discuss civil rights, three are about military issues, the environment, and politics, and one concerns poverty.

To do justice to each of the authors and provide a representative example of their work, I have only included twenty pieces. Due to space restrictions we had to leave out a number of deserving authors. For example, there were many muckrakers at the turn of the century, but I felt that Ida Tarbell, Lincoln Steffens, and Upton Sinclair represent that productive period best. The stories are listed chronologically, by birth date of the author.

MUCKRAKING IN THE
NEW MILLENNIUM

The current outlook for muckraking in America in the new millennium is bleak at best. Four of the twenty stories were from the first two decades of the twentieth century. In the four decades from the twenties to the fifties I have selected just three stories. By far, the 1960s and early '70s were the most productive years in contemporary muckraking. Thirteen of the stories that changed America occurred during these turbulent years, a time of individual introspection, idealism, and social activism. Unfortunately, the last quarter of the twentieth century did not produce any comparable earth-shattering exposés.

One factor that may discourage muckraking in the future is the trend from individual investigative reporting toward a corporate group approach. Nineteen stories cited in this book resulted from dedicated individual efforts often at the cost of personal sacrifice. One story, Watergate, emerged from a group effort. This trend, from individual to group journalism, was confirmed when the Pulitzer Prizes were announced in 1999. In the eighty-two-year history of the prize, the Pulitzer Board has overwhelmingly recognized the achievements of individuals. But in 1999 for the first time, seven awards—the majority— went to groups such as newspaper and wire service staffs. Muckraking, however, is most effective when done by individuals with social consciences who won't be deterred from their goals by corporate group-think or allegiance to some corporate entity.

There also is the factor of corporate reaction to muckraking. All of the individuals in this book were attacked in one way or another for their efforts to make a difference. In most cases, the attacks were personal in nature and generally were either published or spoken.

Conversely, litigation against the media became an important variable in journalism in the late twentieth century. When ABC television used undercover journalists to explore meat hazards at the Food Lion grocery chain in North Carolina in 1992, they were sued and found guilty of misrepresenting themselves to get the story. A jury initially awarded Food Lion $5.5 million in punitive damages, and it wasn't until October 1999 that an appeals court overturned the verdict, exonerating ABC. Upton Sinclair got his remarkable story by similarly misrepresenting himself in the meatpacking yards of Chicago in pre-litigious 1906.

Another area of concern that does not bode well for the future of muckraking is the growing censorship resulting from the monopolization of the media. As the publishing and broadcast industries are increasingly owned and controlled by conglomerates, there will be fewer and fewer vehicles available to reformers. There were fifty major media corporations in 1983 and now there are only about half a dozen. While the Internet, a new medium, provides a soapbox for all critics, it must prove its reliability before it can be taken seriously as a dependable news medium.

Finally, despite the appearance of prosperity during the final days of the twentieth century, America is not the secure and prosperous nation it appears to be. Looking behind the skyrocketing stock market and near–record low rates of inflation and unemployment, one can see the other America with its social and economic problems.

If you judge a society by the number of millionaires it has, the United States ranks at the very top. We entered the twenty-first century with more than 3.5 million millionaires and about 150 billionaires, far more than any other nation. Quite a significant increase since 1901 when there were 3,800 millionaires.

If you judge a society by the way it treats its children, the United States ranks near the very bottom. As we enter the twenty-first century, 21 percent of our children, 14.7 million of them, live in poverty—the highest rate in the developed world. Nine out of every ten young people killed in the industrialized world are killed in the United States. In 1995, 3.1 million American children were abused or neglected.

If we treat our own children this way can we be expected to treat one another any better?

The real question is how many people are fully aware of these problems and how many voters have all the information they need to deal with them? When one is not well informed about the social issues of the day, it is far easier to be an apathetic citizen than a responsible one. As Abraham Lincoln said, "I am a firm believer in the people. If given the truth, they can be depended upon to meet any national crisis. The great point is to bring them the real facts."

We need skeptical journalists giving us the real facts, courageous publishers providing the necessary soapbox, an outraged public demanding change, and responsible politicians to pass the legislation necessary to solve the problems.

KEEP THE PUBLIC INFORMED

It all starts with the need for a free, open, and aggressive press. Joseph Pulitzer, the famed publisher, once said, "We are a democracy, and there is only one way to get a democracy on its feet in the matter of its individual, its social, its municipal, its state, its national conduct, and that is by keeping the public informed about what is going on. There is not a crime, there is not a dodge, there is not a trick, there is not a swindle, there is not a vice that does not live by secrecy. Get these things out in the open, describe them, attack them, ridicule them in the press, and sooner or later public opinion will sweep them away."

As we will see from the stories in this book, despite the obstacles, there will always be some crusading individuals willing to undergo great sacrifices, both personal and financial, to expose the crimes, the tricks, and the swindles. If they are given the proper soapbox, pulpit, or stage, they can inspire in us the strength to launch an era in which we can clean up the environment, diminish poverty, provide quality health care for all people, reduce drug abuse and crime, and eventually create the equitable, fair, and just society the United States should be.

The year I spent working on *Stories That Changed America* was one of the most rewarding of my life. I had the opportunity to read and re-read some of my favorite authors. As I searched for stories that had made a difference, an age-old message emerged: if we don't learn from the past, we are destined to repeat it.

I was raised on Horatio Alger and Tom Swift. I saw the nation survive the worst economic depression in history and the greatest war. These experiences provided me with a modicum of optimism with which to observe life. I believe it *is* possible to overcome seemingly insurmountable obstacles, and that there exist solutions to the problems that plague us. If there is a single thesis that unites the authors presented in this book, it is their belief that inequities can be corrected and that one person can make a difference.

From Ida Mae Tarbell, who defeated the most powerful man in America, to Margaret Sanger who went to jail for women's rights, to Woodward and Bernstein who wouldn't take no for an answer and brought down a corrupt president, these writers believed in the power of their words to change America. Together, they proved that old adage: "The pen is mightier than the sword." Weapons may have won the Revolutionary War but it is words that have created the longest lasting democracy in history.

SOURCES: Bagdikian, Ben, *The Media Monopoly*, Fourth Edition, Beacon Press, Boston, 1992; Blanchard, Margaret, editor, *History of Mass Media in the United States: An Encyclopedia*, Garland Publishing, New York, 1997; Bunyan, John, *The Pilgrim's Progress*, Oxford University Press, London, 1967; Chalmers, David Mark, *The Social and Political Ideas of the Muckrakers*, The Citadel Press, New York, 1964; Downie, Jr., Leonard, *The New Muckrakers*, New American Library, New York, 1976; Downs, Robert B., *Books That Changed America*, The Macmillan Company, New York, 1970; Filler, Louis, *The Muckrakers*, Pennsylvania State University Press, 1976; Harrison, John M., and Harry H. Stein, *Muckraking:*

Past, Present, and Future, Pennsylvania State University Press, 1973; Holbrooke, Stewart H., *Lost Men of American History,* The Macmillan Company, New York, 1946; Newey, Vincent, editor, *The Pilgrim's Progress: Critical and Historical Views,* Barnes & Noble Books, Totowa, NJ, 1980; Sinclair, Upton, *The Jungle,* The Jungle Publishing Co., New York, 1906; Swados, Harvey, *Years of Conscience: The Muckrakers,* Meridian Books, The World Publishing Company, Cleveland, 1962; Tarbell, Ida Mae, *The History of the Standard Oil Company,* McClure, Phillips & Co., New York, 1904; Tebbel, John, *The Media in America,* New American Library, New York, 1974; Weinberg, Arthur and Lila, *The Muckrakers,* Simon and Schuster, New York, 1961.

IDA MAE TARBELL

The number of mergers and monopolies among giant corporations at the end of the twentieth century was equaled only by the number of trusts or monopolies created at the start of the twentieth century. In nearly every industry, including oil, steel, and transportation, big corporations were buying out or driving out the competition. But the practice was nowhere greater than within the oil industry, led by John D. Rockefeller and his Standard Oil Company—until a young woman came along to stop the practice and to avenge her father's oil business failure. She was a reluctant muckraker who disdained the label, but went on to become a leader of the muckraking movement in journalism.

Ida Mae Tarbell was born in 1857 in Erie County, Pennsylvania, on the noisy, dirty, and rough oil frontier. Her father, Franklin Tarbell, got in at the start of the oil boom in western Pennsylvania by building wooden tanks to store oil for producers in the region. He later became an independent oil producer himself, buying into an oil farm in the region.

Her mother, Esther McCullough, was an early feminist and suffragette. She bore the major responsibility of raising Ida Mae since her father was often traveling for business. Esther disclosed her strong feminist feelings by naming her first born Ida Minerva. "Ida" came from a character in Tennyson's *The Princess* who fought for the higher education of women and "Minerva" came from the name of the Greek goddess of wisdom. Minerva later evolved into "Mae." Esther often entertained women's suffrage leaders and passed along her belief in women's equality to her daughter. In 1870, Esther, Ida, her younger sister and brother (another brother had died from scarlet fever) moved to a new home in Titusville, Pennsylvania.

Ida showed a strong interest in literature and her early reading materials included *Harper's Weekly, Harper's,* and the *New York Tribune.* While an honor student at Titusville High School, Tarbell began to develop an interest in biology, and the microscope became her constant companion. Her early, and lasting, love of science would later help bring the objectivity of scientific inquiry and a corresponding penchant for accuracy to her journalism.

Tarbell got her first insight into the negative aspects of business monopolies while a teenager in Titusville. From her observations, she came to believe that man had two choices in life: either to choose the fair, open path which sound ethics, sound democracy, and the common law prescribe, or to choose the secretive way by which he can get the better of his fellow man. To Tarbell, the latter was the obvious choice of the powerful oil men, led by John D. Rockefeller: Rockefeller had taken over the oil business in Western Pennsylvania in its earliest days. She would not write about these early observations until more than three decades later.

One of the few career choices open to women at the time was teaching. After high school, Tarbell attended nearby Allegheny College and was offered a job as "preceptress" at $500 a year at the Poland Union Seminar, Poland, Ohio, in August 1880. Her responsibilities included teaching Greek, Latin, French, German, English grammar, geology, botany, geometry, arithmetic, and trigonometry. Overwhelmed by the diverse course load and low pay, she quit two years later, in June 1882.

Returning to Pennsylvania to live with her parents, Tarbell was offered a job as "annotator" for a magazine called the *Chautauquan,* published in Meadville. She later became a writer for the Chautauquan Assembly's *Daily Herald.* She also earned a Master's degree from Allegheny College in 1883. After six years, she began to feel frustrated over the limited possibilities at the *Chautauquan* and decided to once again change her career.

It was also during this period that she started taking lengthy notes in hopes of writing a novel about the impact of the oil monopoly on the people and their lives in the Western Pennsylvania oil region. After several chapters, she decided she was not a novelist and turned her attention to studying women who succeeded in public life. She was particularly fascinated with Madame Roland, the independent-minded French Revolutionary figure, who was beheaded in 1793. Not finding all the material she needed for a biography, she decided to leave the *Chautauquan* to continue her research in Paris—a bold adventure for a single woman in 1890.

While she was abroad, she supported herself with freelance writing about French life for American readers. When her work caught the eye of S. S. McClure, founder of *McClure's*, he offered her a position with his fledgling magazine. She persuaded him to wait until she completed her book on Madame Roland. In 1893, while she was preparing to write the book, she came to realize that Madame Roland was not the independent woman she expected to find. Though Tarbell was disappointed, she resolved to complete the biography. In June 1894, she returned to America to prepare the manuscript for its final revision.

She was diverted from the Roland biography by a request from S. S. McClure to come to New York to write about Napoleon Bonaparte, a popular media subject of the time. She was hired as a staff writer at *McClure's* for forty dollars a week, and her Napoleon series contributed significantly to the financial success of *McClure's*. The publication of her book, *A Short Life of Napoleon Bonaparte*, helped Tarbell get her biography of Madame Roland published.

Her next assignment at *McClure's* was a series about Abraham Lincoln. These articles were also a great success and brought her national recognition; they were published as *The Life of Abraham Lincoln* in 1897. While she didn't realize it at the time, Lincoln, who was assassinated just three decades earlier, was to become a subject that would dominate Tarbell's life until she died.

McClure decided the next major subject for his magazine would be trusts and the Standard Oil Company, and Tarbell was the obvious choice to write the series. She was born, after all, just before the discovery of oil, about thirty miles away from the first well and there was a big, black, ugly oil derrick by her childhood home. Her father was a small independent oil operator who was being driven to bankruptcy by Standard Oil's monopolistic practices. Tarbell didn't need much encouragement to take on the job.

The series was contentious even before it was written. After being lauded for her articles about Lincoln and Napoleon, she suddenly found herself being urged not to take on Rockefeller and the giant Standard Oil trust: friends, family, and colleagues warned her it was a dangerous undertaking. Others praised her and the magazine for having the courage to confront the corporate bully.

There was a long paper trail to help Tarbell with her research. Standard Oil had been under scrutiny by federal and state governments since it was formed in 1870. The company was allegedly receiving rebates from the railroads and engaging in the restraint of trade.

In addition to Standard Oil court records, there were pamphlets, newspapers and monthly magazine articles criticizing them, as well as a number of civil suits which had generated more court files. Tarbell also had the notes she had taken earlier when she was planning to write a novel about the oil region.

Tarbell benefited from a series of discussions over a two-year period with a Standard Oil executive—an introduction arranged by Samuel Clemens, a.k.a. Mark Twain. The executive, a corporate public relations man ahead of his time, thought he'd be able to manipulate Tarbell with stories about the benefits of monopolies along with reams of statistics to support his perspective. Tarbell was not misled.

When she started her research, the series was to consist of three articles. McClure then expanded it to six, and then twelve. By the time they were through, it amounted to nineteen articles. *The History of the Standard Oil Company* was published as a two-volume set with countless appendices of essential documents in the fall of 1904. A latter-day oil historian would call it "the most important business book ever written."

While Tarbell hoped to lure Rockefeller into responding to her work, his only personal response was to counsel his staff not to mention her name, "Not a word. Not a word about that misguided woman." Standard Oil then launched a national campaign to discredit the book with negative reviews. They distributed five million copies of an essay extolling the benefits of monopolies, and published a book supporting Rockefeller which they distributed free to librarians, ministers, teachers, and prominent citizens throughout the country. Rockefeller also made a number of well-publicized and substantial contributions to charities in his blatant pursuit to gain public support. The campaign failed. In 1906, Congress passed the Hepburn Act, bringing an end to oil company rebates. Another immediate result of Tarbell's work was the formation of the Bureau of Corporations, which would conduct an investigation of the petroleum industry. In 1906, the Bureau reported that Standard Oil was getting preferential treatment from railroads and had been for some time. In the suit that followed, Standard Oil was found guilty and fined twenty-nine million dollars. Attorney General Charles Bonaparte (ironically, the grandnephew of Napoleon) had filed suit under the Sherman Act, charging Standard Oil with conspiring to restrain and monopolize interstate commerce in petroleum. The size of the fine impressed the nation but in 1908, a circuit court of appeals judge upset the ruling.

It was a hollow victory for Standard Oil. The judge found for the plaintiff, Standard Oil appealed, and finally in May of 1911, the Supreme Court upheld the original decision.

The Standard Oil Company was broken up into thirty-eight pieces. Today some of them are operating as Exxon, Mobil, Boron, Chevron, and Amoco.

While Tarbell spent more than five years on the Standard Oil story, she felt her work was incomplete until she documented what happened after the break-up. She wrote twenty thousand words as part of a third volume on Standard Oil, but they never were published.

Meanwhile Tarbell and several other writers, along with her editor, John S. Phillips, had split with S. S. McClure over the editorial direction of the magazine, and left in 1906. Six months later, they published the first issue of a new publication, the *American Magazine*. Tarbell also bought forty acres and a little house in Connecticut where she became an occasional hobbyist farmer.

She remained with the *American Magazine* until 1915 when it was sold to Crowell Publishing Company. Before that time she wrote a number of articles about Abraham Lincoln, tariffs, influential American women, and one (favorable) biography of a corporate executive. Some of her friends accused her of "going over to the enemy," but she was developing a thesis about the Golden Rule in industry, not widely accepted by her colleagues. She perceived progress being made in the conflict between labor and business and felt that muckrakers should be raking up the good as well as the bad.

Tarbell would not return to muckraking. Instead, she spent the rest of her life lecturing on the Chautauqua Circuit, traveling back to France to work on *Red Cross Magazine* and to Italy to write about Benito Mussolini. Tarbell's flawed fascination with powerful men and women is seen in her description of the end of her interview with Mussolini: "Altogether it was an illuminating half-hour, and when Mussolini accompanied me to the door and kissed my hand in the gallant Italian fashion I understood for the first time an unexpected phase of the man which makes him such a power in Italy. He might be—was, I believed—a fearful despot, but he had a dimple."

After the First World War, where she served as a member of the Woman's Committee of the Council of National Defense, her foremost work focused on Abraham Lincoln. She wrote some nine books about him altogether, as well as dozens of articles and essays.

While she was considered an idol to untold numbers of young female journalists for her work on the Standard Oil story, her other work left a different impression. The favorable biographies of corporate leaders and her obsession with Lincoln has led some critics to wonder about Tarbell's dedication to investigative journalism.

There was also a contradiction between the way Tarbell lived and what she believed. While she personally opposed drinking alcohol, she was an anti-prohibitionist, and was accused of selling out to the liquor interests. While she was a role model in many ways for the independent career women of her time, she was an anti-suffragist: She felt that women did not understand the problems and complexities of the man's world and therefore should not be granted the right to vote. While she was never a wife or mother, she felt that these were a woman's most important roles in life. Her book, *The Business of Being a Woman* alienated the suffragette and women's rights movements by expressing these sentiments. She appeared to be anti-birth control as well: Despite at least two personal requests from Margaret Sanger, she refused to lend her name to the budding birth control movement Sanger was developing.

Regardless of her mixed perceptions and her rejection of the muckraker label, Tarbell's efforts as an investigative journalist led to the classic *History of the Standard Oil Company* which in turn led to the dissolution of a giant monopoly. It was an extraordinary achievement for a woman of her time to single-handedly defeat John D. Rockefeller, the most powerful corporate leader of the time. She waited until she was eighty before writing her autobiography, *All in a Day's Work*, a title that speaks to her dedication to the work ethic. Given her accomplishments and being one of the most influential women of her time, it was a modest review of a most remarkable life. In 1999, a national panel of journalists and historians cited the breakup of Standard Oil as one of the top one hundred historic events that changed America during the twentieth century.

Ida Mae Tarbell died in a hospital from pneumonia in Bridgeport, Connecticut, on January 6, 1944. She was buried in Titusville, the original heart of the oil region.

In the following excerpts from *The History of the Standard Oil Company*, Tarbell describes the influences in young Rockefeller's life and how he came to create his first monopoly.

SOURCES. Brady, Kathleen, *Ida Tarbell: Portrait of a Muckraker*, Seaview/Putnam, New York, 1984; Camhi, June Jerome, *Women Against Women: American Anti-Suffragism*, 1880–1920, Carlson Publishing Inc., Brooklyn, New York,

1994; Fleming, Alice, *Ida Tarbell: First of the Muckrakers*, Thomas Y. Crowell Company, New York, 1971; Lowrie, Arthur L., "Ida M. Tarbell: Investigative Journalist Par Excellence," *Ida Tarbell Home Page*, World Web, Pelletier Library of Allegheny College, 1997; Rochersberger, Jr., Robert C., editor, *More Than a Muckraker: Ida Tarbell's Lifetime in Journalism*, University of Tennessee Press, Knoxville, 1994; Tarbell, Ida Mae, *All in the Day's Work: An Autobiography by Ida M. Tarbell*, The Macmillan Company, New York, 1939; Tarbell, Ida Mae, *The History of Standard Oil Company*, McClure, Phillips & Co., New York, 1904; Tarbell, Ida Mae, *The Nationalizing of Business 1878–1898*, The Macmillan Company, New York, 1936; Tomkins, Mary E., *Ida M. Tarbell*, Twayne Publishers, New York, 1974; Treckel, Paula, "Ida Tarbell and 'The Business of Being a Woman,'" *Ida Tarbell Home Page*, World Wide Web, Pelletier Library of Allegheny College, 1997.

The History of the Standard Oil Company

Ida Mae Tarbell

YOUNG JOHN DAVISON ROCKEFELLER

When young Rockefeller was thirteen years old, his father moved from the farm in Central New York, where the boy had been born (July 8, 1839), to a farm near Cleveland, Ohio. He went to school in Cleveland for three years. In 1855 it became necessary for him to earn his own living. It was a hard year in the West and the boy walked the streets for days looking for work. He was about to give it up and go to the country when, to quote the story as Mr. Rockefeller once told it to his Cleveland Sunday school, "As good fortune would have it I went down to the dock and made one more application, and I was told that if I would come in after dinner—our noon-day meal was dinner in those days—they would see if I could come to work for them. I went down after dinner and I got the position, and I was permitted to remain in the city." The position, that of a clerk and bookkeeper, was not lucrative. According to a small ledger which has figured frequently in Mr. Rockefeller's religious instructions, he earned from September 26, 1855, to January, 1856, fifty dollars. "Out of that," Mr. Rockefeller told the young men of his Sunday school class, "I paid my washerwoman and the lady I boarded with, and I saved a little money to put away."

He proved an admirable accountant—one of the early-and-late sort, who saw everything, forgot nothing and never talked. In 1856 his salary was raised to twenty-five dollars a month, and he went on always "saving a little money to put away." In 1858 came a chance to invest his savings. Among his acquaintants was a young Englishman, M. B. Clark. Older by twelve years

33

than Rockefeller he had left a hard life in England when he was twenty to seek fortune in America. He had landed in Boston in 1847, without a penny or a friend, and it had taken three months for him to earn money to get to Ohio. Here he had taken the first job at hand, as man-of-all-work, wood-chopper, teamster. He had found his way to Cleveland, had become a valuable man in the houses where he was employed, had gone to school at nights, had saved money. They were two of a kind, Clark and Rockefeller, and in 1858 they pooled their earnings and started a produce commission business on the Cleveland docks. Local historians credit Clark and Rockefeller with doing a business of $450,000 the first year. The war came on, and as neither partner went to the front, they had full chance to take advantage of the opportunity for produce business a great army gives. A greater chance than furnishing army supplies, lucrative as most people found that, was in the oil business (so Clark and Rockefeller began to think), and in 1862, when an Englishman of ability and energy, one Samuel Andrews, asked them to back him in starting a refinery, they put in $4,000 and promised to give more if necessary. Now Andrews was a mechanical genius. He devised new processes, made a better and better quality of oil, got larger and larger percentages of refined from his crude. The little refinery grew big, and Clark and Rockefeller soon had $100,000 or more in it. In the meantime Cleveland was growing as a refining center. The business which in 1860 had been a gamble was by 1865 one of the most promising industries of the town. It was but the beginning—so Mr. Rockefeller thought—and in that year he sold out his share of the commission business and put his money into the oil firm of Rockefeller and Andrews.

In the new firm Andrews attended to the manufacturing. The pushing of the business, the buying and the selling, fell to Rockefeller. From the start his effect was tremendous. He had the frugal man's hatred of waste and disorder, of middlemen and unnecessary manipulation, and he began a vigorous elimination of these from his business. The residuum that other refineries let run into the ground, he sold. Old iron found its way to the junk shop. He bought his oil directly from the wells. He made his own barrels. He watched and saved and contrived. The ability with which he made the smallest bargain furnishes topics to Cleveland storytellers today. Low-voiced, soft-footed, humble, knowing every point in every man's business, he never tired until he got his wares at the lowest possible figure. "John always got the best of the bargain," old men tell you in Cleveland today, and they wince though they laugh in telling it. "Smooth," "a *savvy* fellow," is their description of him. To drive a good bargain was the joy of his life. "The only time I ever saw John Rockefeller enthusiastic," a man told the writer once, "was when a report came in from the creek that his buyer had secured a cargo of oil at a figure much below the market price. He bounded from his chair with a shout of joy, danced up and down, hugged me, threw up his hat, acted so like a madman that I have never forgotten it."

He could borrow as well as bargain. The firm's capital was limited; growing as they were, they often needed money, and had none. Borrow they must. Rarely if ever did Mr. Rockefeller fail. There is a story handed down in Cleveland from the days of Clark and Rockefeller, produce merchants, which is illustrative of his methods. One day a well-known and rich business man stepped into the office and asked for Mr. Rockefeller. He was out, and Clark met the visitor. "Mr. Clark," he said, "you may tell Mr. Rockefeller, when he comes in, that I think I can use the $10,000 he wants to invest with me for your firm. I have thought it all over."

"Good God!" cried Clark. "We don't want to invest $10,000. John is out right now trying to borrow $5,000 for us."

It turned out that to prepare him for a proposition to borrow $5,000 Mr. Rockefeller had told the gentleman that he and Clark wanted to invest $10,000!

"And the joke of it is," said Clark, who used to tell the story, "John got the $5,000 even after I had let the cat out of the bag. Oh, he was the greatest borrower you ever saw!"

These qualities told. The firm grew as rapidly as the oil business of the town, and started a second refinery—William A. Rockefeller and Company. They took in a partner, H. M. Flagler, and opened a house in New York for selling oil. Of all these concerns John D. Rockefeller was the head. Finally, in June, 1870, five years after he became an active partner in the refining business, Mr. Rockefeller combined all his companies into one—the Standard Oil Company. The capital of the new concern was $1,000,000....

CREATING A MONOPOLY

It was on the second of January, 1872, that the organization of the South Improvement Company [a holding company created by Rockefeller] was completed. The day before the Standard Oil Company of Cleveland increased its capital from $1,000,000 to $2,500,000, "all the stockholders of the company being present and voting therefor."... Three weeks after this increase of capital Mr. Rockefeller had the charter and contracts of the South Improvement Company in hand, and was ready to see what they would do in helping him carry out his idea of wholesale combination in Cleveland. There were at that time some twenty-six refineries in the town—some of them very large plants. All of them were feeling more or less the discouraging effects of the last three or four years of railroad discriminations in favor of the Standard Oil Company. To the owners of these refineries Mr. Rockefeller now went one by one, and explained the South Improvement Company. "You see," he told them, "this scheme is bound to work. It means an absolute control by us of the oil business. There is no chance for anyone outside. But we are going to give everybody a chance to come in. You are to turn over your refinery to my appraisers, and I will give you Standard Oil Company stock or cash, as you prefer, for the value we put upon it. I advise you to take the stock. It will be for your good." Certain refiners objected. They did not want to sell. They did want to keep and manage their business. Mr. Rockefeller was regretful, but firm. It was useless to resist, he told the hesitating; they would certainly be crushed if they did not accept his offer, and he pointed out in detail, and with gentleness, how beneficent the scheme really was—preventing the creek refiners from destroying Cleveland, ending competition, keeping up the price of refined oil, and eliminating speculation. Really a wonder contrivance for the good of the oil business.

That such was Mr. Rockefeller's argument is proved by abundant testimony from different individuals who succumbed to the pressure. Mr. Rockefeller's own brother, Frank Rockefeller, gave most evidence on this point in 1876 when he and others were trying to interest Congress in a law regulating inter-state commerce.

"We had in Cleveland at one time about thirty establishments, but the South Improvement Company was formed and the Cleveland companies were told that if they didn't sell their property to them it would be valueless, that there was a combination of railroad and oil men, that they would buy all they could, and that all they didn't buy would be totally valueless, because they would be unable to compete with the South Improvement Company, and the result was that out of thirty there were only four of five that didn't sell."

"From whom was that information received?" asked the examiner.

"From the officers of the Standard Oil Company. They made no bones about it at all. They said: 'If you don't sell your property to us it will be valueless, because we have got advantages with the railroads.'"

"Have you heard those gentleman say what you have stated?" Frank Rockefeller was asked.

"I have heard Rockefeller and Flagler say so," he answered.

W. H. Doane... told the Congressional committee, which a few months after Mr. Rockefeller's great coup tried to find out what had happened in Cleveland: "The refineries are all bought up by the Standard Oil works; they were forced to sell; the railroads had put up the rates and it scared them. Men came to me and told me they could not continue their business; they became frightened and disposed of their property." Mr. Doane's own business, that of a crude oil shipper, was entirely ruined, all of his customers but one having sold.

A few of the refiners contested before surrendering. Among these was Robert Hanna, an uncle of Mark Hanna, of the firm of Hanna, Baslington and Company. Mr. Hanna had been refining since July, 1869. According to his own sworn statement he had made money, fully sixty percent on his investment the first year, and after that thirty percent. Some time in February, 1872, The Standard Oil Company asked an interview with him and his associates. They wanted to buy his works, they said. "But we don't want to sell," objected Mr. Hanna. "You can never make any more money, in my judgment," said Mr. Rockefeller. "You can't compete with the Standard. We have all the large refineries now. If you refuse to sell, it will end in your being crushed." Hanna and Baslington were not satisfied. They went to see Mr. Watson, president of the South Improvement Company and an officer of the Lake Shore, and General Devereux, manager of the Lake Shore Road. They were told that the Standard had special rates; that it was useless to try to compete with them. General Devereux explained to the gentlemen that the privileges granted the Standard were the legitimate and necessary advantage of the larger shipper over the smaller, and that if Hanna, Baslington and Company could give the road as large a quantity of oil as the Standard did, with the same regularity, they could have the same rate. General Devereux says they "recognized the propriety" of his excuse. They certainly recognized its authority. They say that they were satisfied they could no longer get rates to and from Cleveland which would enable them to live, and "reluctantly" sold out. It must have been reluctantly, for they had paid $75,000 for their works, and had made thirty percent a year on an average on their investment, and the Standard appraiser allowed them $45,000. "Truly and really less than one-half of what they were absolutely worth, with a fair and honest competition in the lines of transportation," said Mr. Hanna, eight years later, in an affidavit.

Under the combined threat and persuasion of the Standard, armed with the South Improvement Company scheme, almost the entire independent oil interest of Cleveland collapsed in three months' time. Of the twenty-six refineries, at least twenty-one sold out. From a capacity of probably not over 1,500 barrels of crude a day, the Standard Oil Company rose in three months time to one of 10,000 barrels. By this maneuver it became mast of over one-fifth of the reining capacity of the United States. Its next individual competitor was Sone and Fleming, of New York, whose capacity was 1,700 barrels. The Standard had a greater capacity than the entire Oil Creek Regions, greater than the combined New York refiners. The transaction by which it acquired this power was so stealthy that not even the best informed newspaper men of Cleveland knew what went on. It had all been accomplished in accordance with one of Mr. Rockefeller's chief business principles—"Silence is golden."

LINCOLN STEFFENS

L incoln Steffens was a reluctant muckraker who didn't even think of himself as such until President Roosevelt demonized the term in 1906. Despite his oft-expressed rejection of the label, he went on to become known as the "King of the Muckrakers."

Lincoln Steffens was well born in the San Francisco's Mission District in 1866. His father, Joseph Steffens, was a conservative businessman who had built a successful career in the importing and exporting of paints, oils, and glass. Lincoln's mother, Elisabeth Louisa Symes, was an ambitious English girl who had traveled by ship from New York to San Francisco with hopes of marriage. The family moved to Sacramento in 1870 when Joseph was given a quarter interest in a branch store his firm opened there.

It was as a child in Sacramento that Steffens learned that all was not what it appeared to be and discovered the political corruption that would eventually provoke him into his career as a muckraker. His lifelong sense of independence developed when he was eight to fifteen, as he explored the state capital's outskirts on a pony. While watching a friend work as a page in the California legislature, Steffens had his first insights into the "old boys' school" and learned how bribery was used to gain political control.

His difficulty understanding and accepting the reality of political corruption weighed upon him and contributed to his poor performances in school. When he began experimenting with alcohol, his father, disgusted with his behavior, sent him off to military school. There, another experience with drinking led to twenty-one days in solitary confinement—and to his decision never to drink to excess again.

When Steffens was rejected by the University of California at Berkeley (UCB) in 1884, his father sent him to a private school with a tutor and he finally entered UCB in 1885. He was a difficult student, more interested in asking his professors questions than in answering theirs. He developed a passion for learning and a particular interest in finding a scientific basis for ethics. After graduating from UCB in 1889 at the age of 23, Steffens persuaded his father to fund his continued education in Europe where he could develop his own curriculum, free from the rigid requirements of traditional universities.

From 1889 to 1892, Steffens traveled through Germany, France, and England, studying art, music, history, economics, and philosophy, but always searching for a scientific explanation of ethics. While studying in Leipzig, he met Josephine Bontecou, an American woman ten years older than he. They were married on November 4, 1891, in England, without his parents' knowledge.

In 1892, after three years of studying in Europe, Steffens returned with Josephine to the United States with vague plans about continuing his education with his father's financial help. Instead, he arrived in New York to discover that his father, finally fed up with his son's fruitless search for truth, had cut off his support. In a letter that was awaiting Steffens at the New York port, his father wrote that Lincoln must know all there was about the theory of life by now—and the time had come to learn the practical side. After suggesting that Lincoln stay in New York and "hustle," his father closed by saying, "Enclosed please find one hundred dollars, which should keep you until you can find a job and support yourself."

Steffens was shocked that he was expected to support both himself and his wife at age twenty-six. He first tried unsuccessfully to sell short stories. Finally, using a contact provided by his father, he landed a job as a reporter with the *New York Evening Post*, a position that would permit him to ask questions and get paid for it.

While covering Wall Street during the panic of 1893, he learned about financial crime. Then, as a reporter covering police headquarters, he learned about political corruption. He was continuing his education in a new way: Police reporting was like a college education, with a variety of courses in police policies and politics, police news, the ghetto, the conflict between labor and management, and Wall Street.

This real-world journalistic education was what would lead Steffens to systematically study political corruption in cities, then states, and finally the federal government. It gave him the impetus to write *The Shame of the Cities*, which launched his career as a muckraker.

In 1897, with his reputation as a journalist growing rapidly, he left the *Post* to become city editor at the *Commercial Advertiser*. While there, Steffens developed a theory of journalism that if reporters wrote about what interested them, it would also interest their readers. (The prevalent theory of the time was that it was up to the editors and reporters to guess what readers wanted and then give it to them. The media employ a modified version of the same theory today.)

Steffens was given the opportunity to test his theory when he left the constricting daily deadline requirements of newspaper reporting to become a writer for *McClure's*. What interested Steffens was political and corporate corruption and he persuaded his editor to let him pursue his interest.

In 1902, Steffens went to St. Louis where he had heard about a political problem involving bribery and the Board of Aldermen. St. Louis had recently grown to become the fourth largest city in the U.S. Its rapid, unplanned growth made it a magnet for political and financial con men. Working with a knowledgeable local attorney, Steffens soon uncovered the widespread political, financial, commercial, and social corruption that was plaguing St. Louis. His investigation led to "Tweed Days in St. Louis," published in *McClure's* in October 1902, the first of his muckraking articles on corruption in the nation's leading cities.

Leaving embarrassed and sometimes imprisoned politicians and corporate executives in his wake, Steffens moved on to publish "The Shame of Minneapolis: The Rescue and Redemption of a City That Was Sold Out"; "The Shamelessness of St. Louis," a sequel to "Tweed Days"; "Pittsburg: A City Ashamed"; "Philadelphia: Corrupt and Content"; "Chicago: Half Free and Fighting On"; and "New York: Good Government to the Test"—all published in *McClure's* in 1903.

After completing the New York series, and possibly burning out, Steffens retreated to his home in Connecticut where he edited his seven articles into *The Shame of the Cities*. It was published by McClure, Phillips & Co. in 1904.

The book was a national sensation and it helped America take a long, hard look at itself. Corruption in the community was not a local problem, but a national problem. *Shame* was a relentless exposé of the nefarious dealings of politicians, corporations, and petty crooks, and it didn't start at the bottom, as many thought it might, but at the top. The corporations were corrupted, the politicians were corruptible, and the crooks prospered.

Steffens demonstrated that it was not just the pot-bellied, cigar-puffing politicians, typified by Boss Tweed, causing the problem, nor was it the gangsters who moved in and out of the backroom deals taking their cut and providing protection. The real villians were the supposedly upstanding corporate executives who believed they should do anything to make business succeed and thus bribery was all right. Equally important, Steffens pointed out that the rest of the city—the victims—knew what was going on and didn't do anything to stop it, and that's what kept the cycle of corruption going.

The articles had an enormous impact, resulting in reform for the individual cities he reported on. They also had a cumulative effect. Political and corporate crime was no longer a local issue—it was a national problem. Steffens raised America's social consciousness and his exposés paved the way for reform programs at all levels, from the cities to the federal government.

The publication of *The Shame of the Cities* marked a milestone in Steffens' career. He followed it up by muckraking the states, including Missouri, Illinois, Wisconsin, Rhode Island, Ohio, and New Jersey.

Having exposed corruption on both the city and state levels, Steffens next moved up to the federal level. With the help of a letter from his friend President Theodore Roosevelt, Steffens was able to penetrate the inner circles of Congress, and there he found the same corrupt state of affairs. The Senate was a chamber of bosses with one senator from each state representing the political machine in his state, and the other senator representing the leading businessmen. Together, they victimized the ordinary citizens.

When he had collected enough hard evidence of corruption in the Senate, Steffens asked Roosevelt, also a reformer, what he was going to do about it. Roosevelt acknowledged the corruption but said he would continue to work with the senators as long as they would support his efforts in turn.

Disappointed by the self-serving response from his one-time idol, Steffens started to question his own motives and ethics. Despite his righteous protests that he could never be bought, he recognized that he would go easy on a story to keep his job, hold his readers, and do what he could to "get by" with his editors.

With his own disturbing introspection and growing staff problems at *McClure's*, Steffens decided to join a group of writers, among them Ida Mae

Tarbell, to purchase the *American Magazine*. After doing a somewhat soft exposé of William Randolph Hearst, he returned to his original love, researching and writing about corruption in the state of Oregon, and the cities of San Francisco and Los Angeles. But he felt he was "going easy" on some of the subjects because of pressure from his colleagues. Steffens finally resolved the issue for himself by resigning from the *American*. It was to be his last full-time job as a journalist.

Nineteen hundred and eleven proved to be a difficult year for Steffens in both his personal and professional lives. His wife Josephine died on January 7, 1911. The deaths of his mother and father followed shortly thereafter. It was also the year of the McNamara brothers' case in the bombing of the *Los Angeles Times*. His involvement in that case as an unofficial negotiator between the prosecution and the defense led to his alienating both the labor movement and the corporate community. His support of the McNamaras earned him a reputation as a "left-wing communist."

Following the debacle in Los Angeles, Steffens once again returned to his home in Connecticut to rest and recover from what he felt was the low point of his life. "I felt defeated, disgraced, somehow, and helpless. No editors would give me work and my manuscripts were regularly returned, often unread."

Depressed by his failure with the McNamara case and still tormented by his inability to find a scientific explanation to social engineering, Steffens finally decided that it was not enough to turn the other cheek but that the ultimate solution was revolution. He spent several years studying the revolutions in Mexico and Russia. Following the World War I Armistice, Steffens went to Russia as a sort of representative of President Wilson to try to negotiate an agreement between the Russian revolutionaries and the leaders of the West. This attempt at peacemaking also failed.

Nonetheless, Steffens was impressed by what he had seen in Russia and on his return he said, "I have seen the future, and it works," a statement that would haunt him for years. Disappointed by the failure of his peace agreement and ostracized at home as a communist sympathizer, Steffens remained in Europe, an expatriate, for nearly eight years after the Armistice.

In 1919, during the Armistice negotiations, Steffens met the woman with whom he would spend the rest of his life, Ella Winter. She was twenty-one and he was fifty-three, but they overcame the age difference and were married in August 1924. They had a son, Pete, and Steffens would consider the years after Pete's birth as the happiest of his life. It was during this time that he decided to write his autobiography. He would later refer to his son and his autobiography as twins: "It is no mere coincidence—if you care to know— that my autobiography and my young son Pete are of about the same age and the same smiling disposition. They were both begun very happily some seven years ago in a villa in a garden on a hill looking down over Mussolini, the Mediterranean and a world of peace at San Remo, Italy."

They returned to the United States in 1927 and bought a house in Carmel, where he would finish his autobiography. It was published in April 1931, and it prompted Steffens' revival as a lion among authors. He concluded his auto- biography observing that the world he had tried so hard to change had changed him instead.

Steffens suffered a stroke in 1933. He was confined to his home where he played host to the famous and not-so-famous who came to pay tribute to the "King of the Muckrakers." In 1936, at the age of seventy, he was still enter- taining visitors and relishing his role of guru of the left. He died on August 9, 1936, just four months after his birthday. The nation's press that had once reviled and rejected him, hailed him as the last, most fearlessly independent of great journalists.

The following excerpt from *The Shame of the Cities* ("Tweed Days in St. Louis") describes one case that Joseph W. Folk, District Attorney of St. Louis, prosecuted. Folk had agreed to run on the Democratic ticket only after he received an assurance from the party leaders that they would not attempt to influence any of his actions in punishing lawbreakers. Assuming that this was just another conventional platitude, the politicians agreed heartily to his demand. It was not long after that they regretted their decision.

SOURCES. Beecroft, John, editor, *Wings*, Literary Guild of America, New York, October 1931; Horton, Russell M., *Lincoln Steffens*, Twayne Publishers, Inc., New York, 1974; Kaplan, Justin, *Lincoln Steffens: A Biography*, Simon & Schus- ter, Inc., New York, 1974; Palermo, Patrick F., *Lincoln Steffens*, Twayne Pub- lishers, Inc., Boston, 1978; Steffens, Lincoln, *The Autobiography of Lincoln Steffens*, Volumes One and Two, Harcourt, Brace & World, Inc., New York, 1931; Steffens, Lincoln, *The Shame of the Cities*, McClure, Phillips & Co., New York, 1904; Stinson, Robert, *Lincoln Steffens*, Frederick Ungar Publishing Co., New York, 1979; Winter, Ella and Herbert Shapiro, editors, *The World of Lincoln Stef- fens*, Hill and Wang, New York, 1962.

The Shame
of the Cities
Lincoln Steffens

TWEED DAYS IN ST. LOUIS

Mr. Folk at once felt the pressure, and it was of a character to startle one. Statesmen, lawyers, merchants, clubmen, churchmen—in fact, men prominent in all walks of life—visited him at his office and at his home, and urged that he cease such activity against his fellow-townspeople. Political preferment was promised if he would yield; a political grave if he persisted. Threatening letters came, warning him of plots to murder, to disfigure, and to blackguard. Word came from Tennessee that detectives were investigating every act of his life. Mr. Folk told the politicians that he was not seeking political favors, and not looking forward to another office; the others he defied. Meantime he probed the deeper into the municipal sore. With his first successes for prestige and aided by the panic among the boodlers, he soon had them suspicious of one another, exchanging charges of betrayal, and ready to "squeal" or run at the slightest sign of danger. One member of the House of Delegates became so frightened while under the inquisitorial crossfire that he was seized with a nervous chill; his false teeth fell to the floor, and the rattle so increased his alarm that he rushed from the room without stopping to pick up his teeth, and boarded the next train.

It was not long before Mr. Folk had dug up the intimate history of ten years of corruption, especially of the business of the North and South and the Central Traction franchise grants, the last-named being even more iniquitous than the Suburban.

Early in 1898, a "promoter" rented a bridal suite at the Planters' Hotel, and having stocked the rooms with wines, liquors, and cigars until they resembled a candidate's headquarters during a convention, sought introduction to members of the Assembly and to such political bosses as had influence with the city fathers. Two weeks after his arrival the Central Traction bill was introduced "by request" in the Council. The measure was a blanket franchise, granting rights of way which had not been given to old-established companies, and permitting the beneficiaries to parallel any track in the city. It passed both Houses despite the protests of every newspaper in the city, save one, and was vetoed by the mayor. The cost to the promoter was $145,000.

Preparations were made to pass the bill over the executive's veto. The bridal suite was restocked, larger sums of money were placed on deposit in the banks, and the services of three legislative agents were engaged. Evidence now in the possession of the St. Louis courts tells in detail the disposition of $250,000 of bribe money. Sworn statements prove that $75,000 was spent in the House of Delegates. The remainder of the $250,000 was distributed in the Council, whose members, though few in number, appraised their honor at a higher figure on account of their higher positions in the business and social world. Finally, but one vote was needed to complete the necessary two-thirds in the upper Chamber. To secure this a councilman of reputed integrity was paid $50,000 in consideration that he vote aye when the ordinance should come up for final passage. But the promoter did not dare risk all upon the vote of one man, and he made this novel proposition to another honored member, who accepted it:

"You will vote on roll call after Mr. ————. I will place $45,000 in the hands of your son, which amount will become yours, if you have to vote for the measure because of Mr. ————'s not keeping his promise. But if he stands out for it you can vote against it, and the money shall revert to me."

On the evening when the bill was read for final passage the City Hall was crowded with ward heelers and lesser politicians. These men had been engaged by the promoter, at five and ten dollars a head, to cheer on the boodling Assemblymen. The bill passed the House with a rush, and all crowded into the Council Chamber. While the roll was being called the silence was profound, for all knew that some men in the Chamber whose reputations had been free from blemish, were under promise and pay to part with honor that night. When the clerk was two-thirds down the list those who had kept count knew that but one vote was needed. One more name was called. The man addressed turned red, then white, and after a moment's hesitation he whispered "Aye!" The silence was so death-like that his vote was heard throughout the room, and those near enough heard also a sigh of relief that escaped from the member who could now vote "no" and save his reputation.

The Central Franchise bill was a law, passed over the mayor's veto. The promoter had expended nearly $300,000 in securing the legislation, but within a week he sold his rights of way to "eastern capitalists" for $1,250,000. The United Railways Company was formed, and without owning an inch of steel rails, or a plank in a car, was able to compel every street railroad in St. Louis, with the exception of the Suburban, to part with stock and right of way and agree to a merger. Out of this grew the St. Louis Transit Company of today.

Several incidents followed this legislative session. After the Assembly had adjourned, a promoter entertained the $50,000 councilman at a downtown restaurant. During the supper the host remarked to his guest, "I wish you would lend me that $50,000 until tomorrow. There are some of the boys outside whom I haven't paid." The money changed hands. The next day, having waited in vain for the promoter, Mr. Councilman armed himself with a revolver and began a search of the hotels. The hunt in St. Louis proved fruitless, but the irate legislator kept on the trail until he came face to face with the lobbyist in the corridor of the Waldorf-Astoria. The New Yorker, seeing the danger, seized the St. Louisan by the arm and said soothingly, "There, there; don't take on so. I was called away suddenly. Come to supper with me; I will give you the money."

The invitation was accepted, and champagne soon was flowing. When the man from the West had become sufficiently maudlin the promoter passed over to him a letter, which he had dictated to a typewriter while away from the table for a few minutes. The statement denied all knowledge of bribery.

"You sign that and I will pay you $5,000. Refuse, and you don't get a cent," said the promoter. The St. Louisan returned home carrying the $5,000, and that was all.

Meanwhile the promoter had not fared so well with other spoilsmen. By the terms of the ante-legislation agreement referred to above, the son of one councilman was pledged to return $45,000 if his father was saved the necessity of voting for the bill. The next day the New Yorker sought out this young man and asked for the money.

"I am not going to give it to you," was the cool rejoinder. "My mamma says that it is bribe money and that it would be wrong to give it to either you or father, so I shall keep it myself." And he did. When summoned before the grand jury this young man asked to be relieved from answering questions. "I am afraid I might commit perjury," he said. He was advised to "Tell the truth and there will be no risk."

"It would be all right," said the son, "if Mr. Folk would tell me what the other fellows have testified to. Please have him do that."

Two indictments were found as a result of this Central Traction bill, and bench warrants were served on Robert M. Snyder and George J. Kobusch. The State charged the former with being one of the promoters of the bill, the definite allegation being bribery. Mr. Kobusch, who is president of a streetcar manufacturing company, was charged with perjury.

The first case tried was that of Emil Meysenburg, the millionaire who compelled the Suburban people to purchase his worthless stock. He was defended by three attorneys of high repute in criminal jurisprudence, but the young Circuit Attorney proved equal to the emergency, and a conviction was secured. Three years in the penitentiary was the sentence. Charles Kratz, the Congressional candidate, forfeited $40,000 by flight, and John K. Murrell also disappeared. Mr. Folk traced Murrell to Mexico, caused his arrest in Guadalajara, negotiated with the authorities for his surrender, and when this failed, arranged for his return home to confess, and his evidence brought about the indictment, on September 8, of eighteen members of the municipal legislature. The second case was that of Julius Lehmann. Two years at hard labor was the sentence, and the man who had led the jokers in the grand jury anteroom would have fallen when he heard it, had not a friend been standing near.

Besides the convictions of these and other men of good standing in the community, and the flight of many more, partnerships were dissolved, companies had to be reorganized, business houses were closed because their proprietors were absent, but Mr. Folk, deterred as little by success as by failure, moved right on; he was not elated; he was not sorrowful. The man proceeded with his work quickly, surely, smilingly, without fear or pity. The terror spread, and the rout was complete.

When another grand jury was sworn and proceeded to take testimony there were scores of men who threw up their hands and crying "*Mea culpa!*" begged to be permitted to tell all they knew and not be prosecuted. The inquiry broadened. The son of a former mayor was indicted for misconduct in office while serving as his father's private secretary, and the grand jury recommended that the ex-mayor be sued in the civil courts, to recover interests on public money he had placed in his own pocket. A true bill fell on a former City Register, and more Assemblymen were arrested, charged with making illegal contracts with the city. At last the ax struck upon the trunk of the greatest oak of the forest. Colonel Butler, the boss who has controlled elections in St.

Louis for many years, the millionaire who had risen from bellowsboy in a blacksmith's shop to be the maker and guide of the Governors of Missouri, one of the men who helped nominate and elect Folk—he also was indicted on two counts charging attempted bribery. That Butler has controlled legislation in St. Louis had long been known. It was generally understood that he owned Assemblymen before they ever took the oath of office, and that he did not have to pay for votes. And yet open bribery was the allegation now. Two members of the Board of Health stood ready to swear that he offered them $2,500 for their approval of a garbage contract.

Pitiful? Yes, but typical. Other cities are today in the same condition as St. Louis before Mr. Folk was invited in to see its rottenness. Chicago is cleaning itself up just now, so is Minneapolis, and Pittsburg recently had a bribery scandal; Boston is at peace, Cincinnati and St. Paul are satisfied, while Philadelphia is happy with the worst government in the world. As for the small towns and the villages, many of these are busy as bees at the loot.

St. Louis, indeed, in its disgrace, has a great advantage. It was exposed late; it has not been reformed and caught again and again, until its citizens are reconciled to corruption. But, best of all, the man who has turned St. Louis inside out, turned it, as it were, upside down, too. In all cities, the better classes—the businessmen—are the sources of corruption; but they are so rarely pursued and caught that we do not fully realize whence the trouble comes. Thus most cities blame the politicians and the ignorant and vicious poor.

Mr. Folk has shown St. Louis that its bankers, brokers, corporation officers—its businessmen—are the sources of evil, so that from the start it will know the municipal problem in its true light. With a tradition for public spirit, it may drop Butler and its runaway bankers, brokers, and brewers, and pushing aside the scruples of the hundreds of men down in blue book, and red book, and church register, who are lying hidden behind the statutes of limitations, the city may restore good government. Otherwise the exposures by Mr. Folk will result only in the perfection of the corrupt system. For the corrupt can learn a lesson when the good citizens cannot. The Tweed regime in New York taught Tammany to organize its boodle business; the police exposure taught it to improve its method of collecting blackmail. And both now are almost perfect and safe. The rascals of St. Louis will learn in like manner; they will concentrate the control of their bribery system, excluding from the profit-sharing the great mass of weak rascals, and carrying on the business as a business in the interest of a trustworthy few. District Attorney Jerome cannot catch the Tammany men, and Circuit Attorney Folk will not be able another time to break the St. Louis ring. This is St. Louis's one great chance.

But, for the rest of us, it does not matter about St. Louis any more than it matters about Colonel Butler *et al*. The point is, that what went on in St. Louis is going on in most of our cities, towns, and villages. The problem of municipal government in America has not been solved. The people may be tired of it, but they cannot give it up—not yet.

UPTON SINCLAIR

He was a romantic dreamer who wanted to change the way people saw the world through his poetry. Fortunately for America, he failed as a poet and instead became a muckraker and social reformer.

Upton Sinclair was born in a lower-class boardinghouse in Baltimore. One of his earliest memories there was waking in the middle of the night when the gaslight was turned on to join his parents in the chase for bedbugs.

His father was a pot-bellied drunkard who slowly killed himself with alcohol; watching him led Upton to become a prohibitionist. His mother was a stern-faced southern aristocrat and suffragette who wouldn't drink coffee or tea because they were stimulants; watching her led Sinclair to become a health-food faddist.

He spent his youth alternating between poverty, living with his parents, and wealth, living with his mother's father in Baltimore. "One night I would be sleeping on a vermin-ridden sofa in a lodginghouse," he wrote, "and the next night under silken coverlets in a fashionable home."

Sinclair later attributed his outrage over the differences between the social classes to his early days when he experienced those differences personally. It was while observing the trappings of wealth at his grandparents' house that he came to hate the "atmosphere of pride and scorn, of values based upon material." In his youth, he resolved never to sell out to the upper class.

Sinclair was educated at home until he was ten when he started public school in New York. He was a voracious reader and much of his early education came from the books he read in his grandfather's library and at public libraries.

Sinclair graduated without distinction from College of the City of New York (CCNY) in June 1897. While at CCNY, he met another student who had sold an article to a magazine and he wondered why he couldn't do that too. Eventually he did, writing children's stories, jokes, serials, and later, poetry.

Fascinated by the classics, he went on to graduate school at Columbia University to study literature and philosophy. Then, at the age of twenty-two, he decided to write the Great American Novel. He rented a small cabin and wrote *Springtime and Harvest*, a lackluster romantic novel of the period. It brought Sinclair his first rejection from publishers and initiated him into self-publishing, the alternative method of bringing his books to the public that he would use often during his career.

He then wrote another novel, *Prince Hagen*, which was also quickly rejected by publishers. Losing hope in both poetry and romance fiction, Sinclair wrote *The Journal of Arthur Stirling*, a semi-autobiographical story of a young poet who commits suicide. In killing the character of the young poet, Sinclair symbolically killed his own aspirations to become a poet and began to prepare himself for a life as a political activist.

In 1902, a friend gave Sinclair a few books on socialism, which reinforced the insights he first had when reading Thorsten Veblen's *The Theory of the Leisure Class*. Suddenly he felt liberated with "the amazing discovery, after all those years, that I did not have to carry the whole burden of humanity's future upon my two frail shoulders!"

He then wrote *Manassas*, a novel of the Civil War, which also received a lukewarm reception from publishers. But it inspired the editor of *The Appeal to Reason*, America's leading socialist newspaper at the time, to offer Sinclair $500 to write a novel about the plight of the wage slaves of the day—America's working class.

A Chicago meatpackers' strike had just been brutally broken by the stockyard owners and Sinclair decided to go to the stockyards there to gather information about the plight of the workers for his novel. He went undercover as a stockyard employee wearing his own shabby clothes and carrying a dinner pail. In the daytime, he wandered about the yards observing the oppressive working conditions, and at night, he visited the workers in their dismal quarters where they would tell him their distressing stories. He also went about the district talking with lawyers, doctors, dentists, nurses, policemen, politicians, real estate agents, and anyone who had a story of the stockyards to tell.

At the end of seven weeks Sinclair had gathered all the images and notes he needed, and "knew the story I meant to tell."

Like his earlier works, *The Jungle* did not receive a welcoming response from the publishers immediately. One publisher, Macmillan, said they would be willing to publish it if Sinclair would simply cut out some of the objectionable passages. Sinclair discussed this with his friend Lincoln Steffens who advised, "It is useless to tell things that are incredible, even though they may be true." Sinclair decided against self-censorship: "I had to tell the truth and let people make of it what they could."

After five publishers rejected *The Jungle*, Sinclair decided to publish it himself. He offered a "Sustainer's Edition" of *The Jungle*, priced at $1.20. Within a month or two he took in four thousand dollars, more money than he had earned for all his writing in the previous five years.

Bolstered by the public interest in the book, Sinclair offered it to Doubleday, Page & Co. To protect Doubleday, the publisher sent proofs of *The Jungle* to James Keeley, managing editor of the *Chicago Tribune* for his comments. Keeley sent back a scathing thirty-two–page report, allegedly prepared by one of his professional journalists, contradicting Sinclair's allegations. Sinclair persuaded Doubleday to send an investigator of its own to assess the situation first hand. The first person the investigator met in the stockyards was a publicity agent for the meatpackers who admitted that he had read *The Jungle* and had "prepared a thirty-two page report for James Keeley of the *Tribune*."

With their own investigator supporting Sinclair's charges, Doubleday published *The Jungle* in February 1906. The controversy started at once. The meat industry's attack began with a series of articles by meatpacking giant J. Ogden Armour published in the *Saturday Evening Post*. Armour rejected the "unscrupulous attacks" on his great business, which was "noble in all its motives," and "turned out products free from every blemish." This response sounds like the denials of the modern-day beef trust in Texas that sued television's Oprah Winfrey in 1997 for "disparaging" remarks about hamburgers.

The meatpacking industry resorted to every possible tactic to censor Sinclair's book. They tried to discourage editors from reviewing it and librarians from carrying it. Outraged by their efforts, Sinclair protested in a letter to the *New York Times*, published May 18, 1906, and charging that the librarians in Chicago and St. Louis who had found the book unfit for circulation and removed it from their shelves had been intimidated.

As it turned out, Sinclair got welcome support from an unlikely source. President Roosevelt said he was receiving a hundred letters a day about the charges in *The Jungle* and invited Sinclair to the White House to give a briefing on the conditions in Chicago preparatory to Roosevelt's launching of his own investigation.

Thrust into the spotlight by Roosevelt's interest, *The Jungle* and its author became an international cause célèbre overnight.

Winston Churchill, then a member of Parliament, wrote a five-thousand-word article urging English readers to buy *The Jungle*. In his preface to *Major Barbara*, George Bernard Shaw writes how Sinclair stripped the veneer from the huge meatpacking industry in Chicago and revealed it "as a sample of what is going on all over the world underneath the top layer of prosperous plutocracy."

As a result of the subsequent national outcry demanding food protection laws, Roosevelt undertook an official investigation of the Chicago stockyards. The commissioners he sent found "evidence of practically everything charged in *The Jungle*." The nation's first Pure Food and Drug Act, establishing food inspection regulations, was passed consequently with Roosevelt's strong support. This was the origin of today's Food and Drug Administration.

With *The Jungle*, Sinclair had arrived. The *New York Evening World* reported, "Not since Byron awoke one morning to find himself famous has there been such an example of world-wide celebrity won in a day by a book as has come to Upton Sinclair." *The Jungle* was translated into seventeen languages and was a bestseller in America and Great Britain for six months. In 1914, it was made into a movie.

In 1962, Sinclair optimistically summarized his experience with *The Jungle*: "I aimed at the public's heart, and by accident I hit it in the stomach... I helped to clean up the yards and improved the country's meat supply. Now the workers have strong unions and, I hope, are able to look out for themselves."

The Jungle was the defining moment of Sinclair's life, the achievement of his greatest dream—to help make the world a better place. Sinclair tried to follow it up with extra-literary efforts such as his short-lived utopian colony in Helicon Hall, the Inter-Collegiate Socialist Society, and his colorful but doomed campaign for governor of California called End Poverty In California (EPIC). Historians say his opponent conducted the dirtiest political campaign in California history until Richard Nixon's campaign, which defeated Helen Gahagan Douglas in 1950.

But Sinclair was a prolific author and soon returned to writing reality-based novels for which he would earn the title "Muckrake Man" by examining a number of other social institutions. Among the more than ninety books he wrote were exposés of Wall Street, *The Moneychangers* (1908); the coal mining industry, *King Coal* (1917); organized religion, *The Profits of Religion* (1918); the press, *The Brass Check* (1919); educational institutions, *The Goose-step* (1923) and *The Goslings* (1924); world literature, *Mammonart: An Essay in Economic Interpretation* (1925); the oil industry, *OIL!* (1927); American publishing, *Money Writes!* (1927); and the judicial process, *Boston* (1928).

While no single book brought Sinclair the success and renown he received with *The Jungle*, a series of books did.

In 1939, Sinclair embarked on what he was to call the most important part of his literary career—the writing of the eleven books in the Lanny Budd series. The series was born out of Sinclair's despair and anger over the tragedy of World War I and the abortive peace settlement that followed it. His immediate concern was World War II, which was rapidly approaching.

When he first started creating the adventures of Lanny Budd, he expected it to be a single novel covering six years of World War I. Instead, it turned into eleven volumes, 7,364 pages, more than four million words, covering a forty-year period. The first book in the series, *World's End*, was published in 1940, and the last, *The Return of Lanny Budd* was published in 1953.

With his easy-going style, Sinclair took readers into the smoke-filled backrooms where U.S. and world leaders plotted to achieve their own goals with little regard for people's lives. Through his lightly fictionalized picture of reality, Sinclair introduced the public to the duplicitous actions and sinister motives of the world's elite that led to millions of casualties in both wars.

All the books in the series were bestsellers, and *World's End* was singled out by the Literary Guild, with subsequent books selected by other book clubs. The third in the series, *Dragon's Teeth*, won Sinclair the Pulitzer Prize for fiction in 1942. He was elected to the National Institute of Arts and Letters the same year.

With all the honors and acclaim Sinclair received for the Lanny Budd series, the books did not have the impact on American society of *The Jungle*. *The Jungle* led to significant improvements in the nation's food supply and the miserable conditions of working people. With its publication, Sinclair had fulfilled the deep commitment to social justice he first made when he vowed never to sell out to the elite class in America. In his autobiography, published in 1962, Sinclair cautioned us all: "Nature has been and can be so cruel to us that surely we should busy ourselves not to commit cruelties against one another."

On the occasion of Sinclair's eightieth birthday, President Truman wrote, "He has been a burr under the saddle of people who cannot appreciate what working men have to contend with." In 1967, President Lyndon Johnson invited Sinclair to the White House to witness the signing of the Wholesome Meat Act, which was designed to close some loopholes in the original 1906 Pure Food and Drug Act. When he died a year later at the age of 89, Sinclair was still witnessing the impact of a novel he had written more than sixty years earlier.

The following are three excerpts from *The Jungle*. The first describes a guided tour of the stockyards taken by Jurgis Rudkus on his first day of work. The second describes Bubbly Creek, an arm of the Chicago River polluted by drainage from the stockyards and the source of the lard sold in grocery stores. The third describes what meatpacking plants do with spoiled meat.

SOURCES. Harris, Leon, *Upton Sinclair: American Rebel*, Thomas Y. Crowell Co., New York, 1975; Sinclair, Upton, *American Outpost: A Book of Reminiscences*, Farrar & Rinehart, Inc., New York, 1932; Sinclair, Upton, *The Autobiography of Upton Sinclair*, Harcourt Brace & World, Inc., New York, 1962; Sinclair, Upton, editor, *The Cry for Justice: An Anthology of the Literature of Social Protest*, The John C. Winston Company, Philadelphia, 1915; Sinclair, Upton, *The Journal of Arthur Stirling*, Upton Sinclair, Pasadena, California, 1903; Sinclair, Upton, *The Jungle*, The Jungle Publishing Co., New York, 1906; Sinclair, Upton, *My Lifetime in Lettters*, University of Missouri Press, Columbia, Missouri, 1960.

The Jungle
Upton Sinclair

TOUR OF THE STOCKYARDS
(From Chapter Three)[1]

Then Jokubas pointed out the place where the cattle were driven to be weighed, upon a great scale that would weigh a hundred thousand pounds at once and record it automatically. It was near to the east entrance that they stood, and all along this east side of the yards ran the railroad tracks, into which the cars were run, loaded with cattle. All night long this had been going on, and now the pens were full; by tonight they would all be empty and the same thing would be done again.

"And what will become of all these creatures?" cried Teta Elzbieta.

"By tonight," Jokubas answered, "they will all be killed and cut up; and over there on the other side of the packing houses are more railroad tracks, where the cars come to take them away."

There were two hundred and fifty miles of track within the yards, their guide went on to tell them. They brought about ten thousand head of cattle every day, and as many hogs, and half as many sheep—which meant some eight or ten million live creatures turned into food every year. One stood and watched, and little by little caught the drift of the tide, as it set in the direction of the packing houses. There were groups of cattle being driven to the chutes, which were roadways about fifteen feet wide, raised high above the pens. In these chutes the stream of animals was continuous; it was quite uncanny to watch them, pressing on to their fate, all unsuspicious—a very river of death. Our friends were not poetical, and the sight suggested to them no metaphors of human destiny; they thought only of the wonderful efficiency of it all. The chutes into which the hogs went climbed high up—to the very top of the distant buildings; and Jokubas explained that the hogs went up by the power of their own legs, and then their weight carried them back through all the processes necessary to make them into pork.

"They don't waste anything here," said the guide, and then he laughed and added a witticism, which he was pleased that his unsophisticated friends should take to be his own: "They use everything about the hog except the squeal."...

They climbed a long series of stairways outside of the building, to the top of its five or six stories. Here were the chute, with its river of hogs, all patiently toiling upward; there was a place for them to rest to cool off, and then through another passageway they went into a room from which there is no returning for hogs.

It was a long, narrow room with a gallery along it for visitors. At the head there was a great iron wheel, about twenty feet in circumference, with rings here and there along its edge. Upon both sides of this wheel there was a narrow space, into which came the hogs at the end of their journey; in the midst of them stood a great burly negro, bare-armed and bare-chested. He was resting for the moment, for the wheel had stopped while men were cleaning up. In a minute or two, however, it began slowly to revolve, and then the men upon each side of it sprang to work. They had chains which they fastened about the leg of the nearest hog, and the other end of the chain they hooked into one of the rings upon the wheel. So, as the wheel turned, a hog was suddenly jerked off his feet and borne aloft.

At the same instant the ear was assailed by a most terrifying shriek; the visitors started in alarm, the women turned pale and shrank back. The shriek was followed by another, louder and yet more agonizing—for once started upon that journey, the hog never came back; at the top of the wheel he was shunted off upon a trolley, and went sailing down the room. And meantime another was swung up, and then another, and another, until there was a double line of them, each dangling by a foot and kicking in frenzy—and squealing. The uproar was appalling, perilous to the eardrums; one feared there was too much sound for the room to hold—that the walls must give way or the ceiling crack. There were high squeals and low squeals, grunts, and wails of agony; there would come a momentary lull, and then a fresh outburst, louder than ever, surging up to a deafening climax. It was too much for some of the visitors—the men would look at each other, laughing nervously, and the women would stand with hands clenched, and the blood rushing to their faces, and the tears starting in their eyes.

Meantime, heedless of all these things, the men upon the floor were going about their work. Neither squeals of hogs nor tears of visitors made any difference to them; one by one they hooked up the hogs, and one by one with a swift stroke they slit their throats. There was a long line of hogs, with squeals and lifeblood ebbing away together; until at last each started again, and vanished with a splash into a huge vat of boiling water.

It was all so very businesslike that one watched it fascinated. It was porkmaking by machinery, porkmaking by applied mathematics. And yet somehow the most matter-of-fact person could not help thinking of the hogs; they were so innocent, they came so very trustingly; and they were so very human in their protests—and so perfectly within their rights! They had done nothing to deserve it; and it was adding insult to injury, as the thing was done here, swinging them up in this cold-blooded, impersonal way, without a pretense at apology, without the homage of a tear. Now and then a visitor wept, to be sure; but this slaughtering-machine ran on, visitors or no visitors. It was like some horrible crime committed in a dungeon, all unseen and unheeded, buried out of sight and of memory....

Then the party went across the street to where they did the killing of beef— where every hour they turned four or five hundred cattle into meat. Unlike the place they had left, all this work was done on one floor; and instead of there being one line of carcasses which moved to the workmen, there were fifteen or twenty lines, and the men moved from one to another of these. This made a scene of intense activity, a picture of human power wonderful to watch. It was all in one great room, like a circus amphitheater, with a gallery for visitors running over the center.

Along one side of the room ran a narrow gallery, a few feet from the floor; into which gallery the cattle were driven by men with goads which gave them electric shocks. Once crowded in here, the creatures were prisoned, each in a separate pen, by gates that shut, leaving them no room to turn around; and while they stood bellowing and plunging, over the top of the pen there leaned one of the "knockers," armed with a sledgehammer, and watching for a chance to deal a blow. The room echoed with the thuds in quick succession, and the stamping and kicking of the steers. The instant the animal had fallen, the "knocker" passed on to another; while a second man raised a lever, and the side of the pen was raised, and the animal, still kicking and struggling, slid out to the "killing bed." Here a man put shackles about one leg, and pressed another lever, and the body was jerked up into the air. There were fifteen or twenty such pens, and it was a matter of only a couple of minutes to knock fifteen or twenty cattle and roll them out. Then once more the gates were opened, and another lot rushed in; and so out of each pen there rolled a steady stream of carcasses, which the men upon the killing beds had to get out of the way.

The manner in which they did this was something to be seen and never forgotten. They worked with furious intensity, literally upon the run—at a pace with which there is nothing to be compared except a football game. It was all highly specialized labor, each man having his task to do; generally this would consist of only two or three specific cuts, and he would pass down the line of fifteen or twenty carcasses, making these cuts upon each. First there came the "butcher," to bleed them; this meant one swift stroke, so swift that you could not see it—only the flash of the knife; and before you could realize it, the man had darted on the next line, and a stream of bright red was pouring out upon the floor. This floor was half an inch deep with blood, in spite of the best efforts of men who kept shoveling it through holes; it must have made the floor slippery, but no one could have guessed this by watching the men at work.

The carcass hung for a few minutes to bleed; there was no time lost, however, for there were several hanging in each line, and one was always ready. It was let down to the ground, and there came the "headsman," whose task it was to sever the head, with two or three swift strokes. Then came the "floorsman," to make the first cut in the skin; and then another to finish ripping the skin down the center; and then half a dozen more in swift succession, to finish the skinning. After they were through, the carcass was again swung up; and while a man with a stick examined the skin, to make sure that it had not been cut, and another rolled it up and tumbled it through one of the inevitable holes in the floor, the beef proceeded on its journey. There were men to cut it, and men to split it, and men to gut it and scrape it clean inside. There were some with hose which threw jets of boiling water upon it, and others who removed the feet and added the final touches. In the end, as with the hogs, the finished beef was run into the chilling room to hang its appointed time.

The visitors were taken there and shown them, all neatly hung in rows, labeled conspicuously with the tags of the government inspectors—and some, which had been killed by a special process, marked with the sign of the kosher rabbi, certifying that it was fit for sale to the orthodox. And then the visitors were taken to the other parts of the building, to see what became of each particle of the waste material that had vanished through the floor; and to the pickling rooms, and the salting rooms, the canning rooms, and the packing rooms, where choice meat was prepared for shipping in refrigerator cars, destined to be eaten in all the four corners of civilization.

BUBBLY CREEK LARD
(From Chapter Nine)[2]

"Bubbly Creek" is an arm of the Chicago River, and forms the southern boundary of the yards; all the drainage of the square mile of packing houses empties into it, so that it is really a great open sewer a hundred or two feet wide. One long arm of it is blind, and the filth stays there forever and a day. The grease and chemicals that are poured into it undergo all sorts of strange transformations, which are the cause of its name; it is constantly in motion, as if huge fish were feeding in it, or great leviathans disporting themselves in its depths. Bubbles of carbonic acid gas will rise to the surface and burst, and make rings two or three feet wide. Here and there the grease and filth have caked solid, and the creek looks like a bed of lava; chickens walk about on it, feeding, and many times an unwary stranger has started to stroll across, and vanished temporarily. The packers used to leave the creek that way, till every now and then the surface would catch on fire and burn furiously, and the fire department would have to come and put it out. Once, however, an ingenious stranger came and started to gather this filth in scows, to make lard out of; then the packers took the cue, and got out an injunction to stop him, and afterwards gathered it themselves. The banks of "Bubbly Creek" are plastered thick with hairs, and this also the packers gather and clean.

SPOILED MEAT
(From Chapter Fourteen)[3]

With one member trimming beef in a cannery, and another working in a sausage factory, the family had a first-hand knowledge of the great majority of Packingtown swindles. For it was the custom, as they found, whenever meat was so spoiled that it could not be used for anything else, either to can it or else to chop it up into sausage. With what had been told them by Jonas, who had worked in the pickle rooms, they could now study the whole of the spoiled-meat industry on the inside, and read a new and grim meaning into that old Packingtown jest—that they use everything of the pig except the squeal.

Jonas had told them how the meat that was taken out of pickle would often be found sour, and how they would rub it with soda to take away the smell, and sell it to be eaten on free-lunch counters; also of all the miracles of chemistry which they performed, giving to any sort of meat, fresh or salted, whole or chopped, any color and any flavor and any odor they chose. In the pickling of hams they had an ingenious apparatus, by which they saved time and increased the capacity of the plant—a machine consisting of a hollow needle attached to a pump; by plunging this needle into the meat and working with his foot, a man could fill a ham with pickle in a few seconds. And yet, in spite of this, there would be hams found spoiled, some of them with an odor so bad that a man could hardly bear to be in the room with them. To pump into these the packers had a second and much stronger pickle which destroyed the odor—a process known to the workers as "giving them thirty per cent." Also, after the hams had been smoked, there would be found some that had gone to the bad. Formerly these had been sold as "Number Three Grade," but later on some ingenious person had hit upon a new device, and now they would extract the bone, about which the bad part generally lay, and insert in the hole a white-hot iron. After this invention there was no longer Number One, Two, and Three Grade—there was only Number One Grade. The packers were always originating such schemes—they had what they called "boneless hams," which were all the odds and ends of pork stuffed into casings; and "California hams," which were the shoulders, with big knuckle joints, and nearly all the meat cut out; and fancy "skinned hams," which were made of the oldest hogs, whose skins were so heavy and coarse that no one would buy them—that is, until they had been cooked and chopped fine and labeled "head cheese!"

It was only when the whole ham was spoiled that it came into the department of Elzbieta. Cut up by the two-thousand-revolutions-a-minute flyers, and mixed with half a ton of other meat, no odor that ever was in a ham could make any difference. There was never the least attention paid to what was cut up for sausage; there would come all the way back from Europe old sausage that had been rejected, and that was mouldy and white—it would be dosed with borax and glycerine, and dumped into the hoppers, and made over again for home consumption. There would be meat that had tumbled out on the floor, in the dirt and sawdust, where the workers had tramped and spit uncounted billions of consumption germs. There would be meat stored in great piles in rooms; and the water from leaky roofs would drip over it, and thousands of rats would race about on it. It was too dark in these storage places to see well, but a man could run his hand over these piles of meat and sweep off handfuls of the dried dung of rats. These rats were nuisances, and the packers would put poisoned bread out for them; they would die, and then rats, bread, and meat would go into the hoppers together. This is no fairy story and no joke; the meat would be shoveled into carts, and the man who did the shoveling would not trouble to lift out a rat even when he saw one—there were things that went into the sausage in comparison with which a poisoned rat was a tidbit. There was no place for the men to wash their hands before they ate their dinner, and so they made a practice of washing them in the water that was to be ladled into the sausage. There were the butt-ends of smoked meat, and the scraps of corned beef, and all the odds and ends of the waste of the plants, that would be dumped into old barrels in the cellar and left there. Under the system of rigid economy which the packers enforced, there were some jobs that it only paid to do once in a long time, and among these was the cleaning out of the waste barrels. Every spring they did it; and in the barrels would be dirt and rust and old nails and stale water—and cart load after cart load of it would be taken up and dumped into the hoppers with fresh meat, and sent out to the public's breakfast. Some of it they would make into "smoked" sausage—but as the smoking took time, and was therefore expensive, they would call upon their chemistry department, and preserve it with borax and color it with gelatine to make it brown. All of their sausage came out of the same bowl, but when they came to wrap it they would stamp some of it "special," and for this they would charge two cents more a pound.

1. Upton Sinclair, *The Jungle*, The Jungle Publishing Co., New York, 1906, pages 37-38, 39-41, 44-46.
2. Upton Sinclair, *The Jungle*, page 112.
3. Upton Sinclair, *The Jungle*, pages 160-162.

MARGARET SANGER

I n the beginning of the twentieth century, there was no legal birth control in the United States. The term didn't even exist. Contraceptives were illegal for married couples to use except in the case of medical emergency. Contraceptive information was so suppressed that it was a criminal offense to send it through the mail, or lecture about it. Only well-educated and wealthy men and women had access to such information and products.

Thousands of women were plagued by continual pregnancies. Many would stand in long lines outside the dingy offices of five-dollar abortionists. Suggested ways to end a pregnancy for less fortunate women included drinking herbal teas, drinking turpentine, rolling down stairs, or inserting slippery elm, knitting needles, shoe-hooks, or coat hangers. The alternative to these extreme (and often fruitless) measures was a string of pregnancies that often led to the early death of the mother or the baby or both.

It wasn't until 1971, nearly three quarters of a century later, that Connecticut finally passed legislation approving the use of birth control by unmarried couples; it was the last state in the nation to do so. If it hadn't been for a dedicated young nurse in the early 1900s, no one knows how long it would have taken for American women to wrest control over their bodies away from the state. Even now, at the beginning of the twenty-first century, the issue is still inflammatory.

Margaret Louisa Higgins was born September 14, 1879, in Corning, New York, to Anne Purcell and Michael Hennessy Higgins. Her mother was a devout

Catholic and loyal wife who would die at an early age. Her father was a free-thinking socialist who taught her to help others and to think for herself. He would often say to her, "Leave the world better because you, my child, have dwelt in it."

Margaret was the sixth of eleven children and remembered her mother as either being pregnant or nursing. Her father, a Civil War veteran, was a sculptor who made a living chiseling headstones for local cemeteries.

Margaret attended Corning public schools through the eighth grade and then, with the financial support of two older sisters, attended Claverick College and the Hudson River Institute. While she originally flirted with the idea of becoming an actress, she decided instead to teach, but after a year of teaching, she returned home to nurse her mother who was then dying from tuberculosis. After eighteen pregnancies, of which there were only eleven live births, and those all weighing at least ten pounds, Anne Higgins was in a weakened condition. She died on March 31, 1899, just a few months after Margaret returned home.

Her experience nursing her mother persuaded Margaret she could do more to help people through nursing than through teaching and she undertook a yearlong program at White Plains Hospital. She finished her training at the Manhattan Eye and Ear Clinic in New York City in 1900 at the age of twenty-one. In 1902, she met and married William Sanger—an architect with an artist's temperament and a rebellious attitude like her father's. Sanger quit nursing and they moved to the suburbs of Westchester County where they had three children, Stuart, Grant, and Peggy. Their bucolic life gave no indication of the turbulent times ahead. By the time Peggy was born they were bored with country living, and moved back to Manhattan where William gave up his work as a draftsman and started painting. Sanger returned to nursing to help support the family and they both became involved in the bohemian culture of Greenwich Village. There they mixed with many of the other rebels of the period, including Emma Goldman, Eugene Debs, Jack London, Upton Sinclair, and Bill Haywood.

Working as a visiting obstetrical nurse in the slums of the Lower East Side, Sanger was appalled by the health conditions and the tragedies surrounding births in families where there were too many children already. She recalled how her own mother might have died because of so many pregnancies. Many women pleaded with her for information about pregnancy prevention, but there was little she could do for them.

One day in 1912, a young mother who had begged just a few months earlier for some means of birth control, died from a failed self-induced abortion. It was then that an outraged Sanger decided women had a right to the knowledge that she felt they needed to save themselves. Sanger resolved to "seek out the root of evil, to do something to change the destiny of mothers whose miseries were vast as the sky."

Having made this vow, Sanger quit nursing to learn more about birth control both in the United States and Europe, where family-planning clinics were already in place. She returned to New York in 1914 with a three-pronged approach to promoting birth control. It called for education, organization, and legislation. She had conceived the genesis of a movement but had no name for it. After trying several terms she decided "birth control" was the most descriptive. She spent the rest of her life spreading the word about birth control.

Her immediate challenge was to educate the public with the information on birth control she had gathered in Europe. She launched a magazine entitled the *Woman Rebel*, in March 1914. It was printed on eight pages of cheap paper and bore the slogan, "No Gods, No Masters," on the masthead. On page one of the premiere issue Sanger exhorted women to think for themselves and promised to give them the information they needed to prevent unwanted pregnancies.

The magazine's stated goal brought Sanger into immediate conflict with the Comstock Act of 1873, named for America's chief censor of the time, Anthony Comstock. The act outlawed "obscene, lewd and lascivious" publications and barred birth-control material specifically from the mail. In short order, the U.S. Post Office, which was authorized to enforce the Comstock Act, refused to deliver the publication, but Sanger was not to be deterred and she continued to distribute her magazine.

When it recognized that the post office could not stop Sanger's campaign, the federal government indicted her on nine counts of breaking obscenity laws; the indictment carried a maximum penalty of forty-five years in prison. Rather than take such a chance, Sanger fled the country with forged documents, using the alias Bertha Watson. She spent two years in Europe (where contraceptive supplies were easily available in shops) furthering her knowledge of European methods of birth control. While in Europe she decided to separate from her husband.

After her attorneys managed to get the obscenity charges against her dropped, Sanger returned to the United States in 1915. She resumed her fight where she left off, opening the nation's first family-planning clinic on October 16, 1916. The clinic was located at 46 Amboy Street, in Brownsville, a slum area of Brooklyn where she felt poor women most needed information on contraception. When the clinic opened, one hundred fifty women—some shawled, some hatless—lined up to visit.

On October 24, 1916, the clinic was raided and Sanger and her staff were arrested. She was convicted and sent to prison for thirty days. The widespread publicity resulting from the raid and her imprisonment brought Sanger and her crusade a number of wealthy supporters, which gave her the resources to build an organized movement for birth control reform for the first time.

After her release from prison, she started another clinic, this time in her home. Recognizing the need to educate people beyond New York, Sanger launched a national publication, the *Birth Control Review*, in 1917. Over the years, she received more than one million letters from distraught women across the country. She subsequently selected five hundred of the best letters to be published in the book, *Motherhood in Bondage* (1928).

Sanger lectured throughout the United States for several years before returning to Europe in 1920. In London, she started a relationship with H. G. Wells. Returning to America in 1921, she founded the American Birth Control League and held the First National Birth Control Conference at the Plaza Hotel in New York. Two years later, she created the Clinical Research Bureau in New York to develop inexpensive and more effective methods of contraception. Sanger favored women-controlled contraceptives and felt that a flexible diaphragm, carefully fitted by medically trained staff, was the most effective device.

In 1923, she divorced William Sanger and married a wealthy oilman many years older than she, Noah Slee, who became a major funder for the birth control movement. Her daughter Peggy died of tuberculosis in 1915, and with her two sons now in college, Sanger was able to devote herself to promoting information about birth control. She lectured throughout the United States and abroad and lobbied Washington legislators, and the American Medical Association (AMA) which had opposed her efforts from the start.

One of Sanger's most personally gratifying victories occurred some years later. In early 1936, the Supreme Court ruled to allow the mailing of birth control information, striking down the infamous Comstock Act. Following this, the AMA reversed its position and agreed that doctors had the right to distribute birth control devices to their patients.

After 1936, although she was plagued by bouts of consumption, Sanger continued to work to promote sex education and for the availability of more effective and cheaper birth control methods such as condoms and spermicidal jellies. In 1939, the American Birth Control League and the Clinical Research Bureau merged into the Birth Control Federation of America, later renamed Planned Parenthood.

Sanger moved to Tucson, Arizona, in 1942. She continued her worldwide campaign for family planning and helped found the International Planned Parenthood Federation in 1952. On September 6, 1966, at the age of eighty-seven, she died of arteriosclerosis in a nursing home in Tucson.

While there were many extraordinary victories in her lifelong fight for birth control, they did not come without opposition. She fought the Catholic Church (opposed to any form of birth control), politicians who feared being associated with such a sensitive issue, women's groups who thought she should focus her attention on women's suffrage instead, and censors like Anthony Comstock who felt contraception and abortion were obscene subjects. She was imprisoned eight times for her actions.

Despite all the obstacles, Sanger left a heritage of achievements not equaled by many since. She wrote thirteen books, edited several others, and published countless articles and pamphlets about women's issues and birth control. But even with all her successes, she recognized the hostility the subject of birth control raised. When once she was asked if she was happy that the struggle was over, Sanger replied that it wasn't over and cautioned its advocates never to relax into thinking that victory is forever: "There is always the threat of its being snatched from you." Renewed violent attacks on family-planning clinics in the present day prove the validity of Sanger's warning.

Finally, while there is no lifetime guarantee to Sanger's birth control victories, her work has already saved the lives of countless women and surely improved the lives of all women everywhere.

The late H. G. Wells, who may have been biased by the love affair he had with Sanger, described her as "the greatest woman in the world; the movement she started will grow to be, a hundred years from now, the most influential of all time in controlling man's destiny on earth." As her father had advised her, Sanger left the world a better place because she had dwelt in it.

The following are four articles from early issues of her groundbreaking magazine, the *Woman Rebel*.

They reveal her anger about the way women were treated, her contempt for those who would stop her, and, above all, her need to educate the women of her time.

SOURCES. Baskin, Alex, *Margaret Sanger, The Woman Rebel and the Rise of the Birth Control Movement in the United States*, Archives of Social History, New York, 1976; Chesler, Ellen, *Woman of Valor*, Simon & Schuster, New York, 1992; Dash, Joan, *A Life of One's Own: Three Gifted Women and the Men They Married*, Harper & Row, New York, 1973; Katz, Esther, "Margaret Sanger: Biographical Sketch," *Margaret Sanger Papers Project*, World Wide Web, 1997; Sanger, Margaret, *Happiness in Marriage*, Maxwell Reprint Company, Elmsford, New York, 1969 (reprint of the 1926 edition); Sanger, Margaret, *Margaret Sanger: An Autobiography*, Maxwell Reprint Company, Elmsford, New York, 1970 (reprint of the 1938 edition); Sanger, Margaret, *Motherhood in Bondage*, Maxwell Reprint Company, Elmsford, New York, 1956 (reprint of the 1928 edition); Sanger, Margaret, *The New Motherhood*, Maxwell Reprint Company, Elmsford, New York, 1970 (reprint of the 1922 edition); Sanger, Margaret, *The Pivot of Civilization*, Maxwell Reprint Company, Elmsford, New York, 1969 (reprint of the 1922 edition); Sanger, Margaret, *What Every Boy and Girl Should Know*, Maxwell Reprint Company, Elmsford, New York, 1969 (reprint of the 1927 edtion); Steinem, Gloria, "Leaders and Revolutionaries—Margaret Sanger," *Time 100*, World Wide Web, 1998.

The Woman Rebel
Margaret Sanger

THE AIM
(March 1914)

This paper will not be the champion of any "ism."

All rebel women are invited to contribute to its columns.

The majority of papers usually adjust themselves to the ideas of their readers but the WOMAN REBEL will obstinately refuse to be adjusted.

The aim of this paper will be to stimulate working women to think for themselves and to build up a conscious fighting character.

An early feature will be a series of articles written by the editor for girls from fourteen to eighteen years of age. In this present chaos of sex atmosphere it is difficult for the girl of this uncertain age to know just what to do or really what constitutes clean living without prudishness. All this slushy talk about white slavery, the man painted and described as a hideous vulture pouncing down upon the young, pure and innocent girl, drugging her through the medium of grape juice and lemonade and then dragging her off to his foul den for other men equally as vicious to feed and fatten on her enforced slavery—surely this picture is enough to sicken and disgust every thinking woman and man who has lived even a few years past the adolescent age. Could any more repulsive and foul conception of sex be given to adolescent girls as a preparation for life than this picture that is being perpetuated by the stupidly ignorant in the name of "sex education"?...

It is these and kindred facts upon which the WOMAN REBEL will dwell from time to time and from which it is hoped the young girl will derive some knowledge of her nature, and conduct her life upon such knowledge.

It will also be the aim of the WOMAN REBEL to advocate the prevention of conception and to impart such knowledge in the columns of this paper.

Other subjects, including the slavery through motherhood; through things, the home, public opinion and so forth, will be dealt with.

It is also the aim of this paper to circulate among those women who work in prostitution; to voice their wrongs; to expose the police persecution which hovers over them and to give free expression to their thoughts, hopes and opinions.

And at all times the WOMAN REBEL will strenuously advocate economic emancipation.

ABORTION IN THE
UNITED STATES
(May 1914)

It is a well-recognized fact that "criminal" abortion prevails today to such an extent that it is estimated that one-third of all pregnancies result in "criminal" abortion.

It is said a hundred thousand "criminal" abortions occur each year in the United States, and six thousand at the lowest estimate die yearly from the direct result of this. "Criminal" abortions arise from a perverted sex relationship under the stress of economic necessity, and their greatest frequency is among married women.

Prominent authorities claim that "criminal" abortions are fifty percent of all abortions that occur, and this is considered a conservative estimate.

Just why there is such danger in abortions can be readily understood when we realize the process of growth of the embryo. During the first six weeks after conception the ovum becomes implanted in the uterus. The second six weeks is occupied with the formation of the placenta (afterbirth). This is the period when abortion most easily occurs, because of the firmly adhering covering of the embryo to the walls or lining of the uterus.

When instruments are used they often rupture the membrane and the entire placenta may be left, though the fetus comes away. The covering or envelope of the ovum may come away in a shredlike discharge after an abortion, all of which necessitates a careful curettage (or scraping) to avoid resulting conditions of blood poisoning and disease. Most of the deaths are the result of sepsis (or decay) of some kind. Often the fetus is found macerated (or softened) and the whole region of the reproductive organs is in a highly inflamed condition. Rarely if ever is an abortion complete, and only in a very small percentage, authorities claim, is there reason to believe the ovum is expelled unbroken. Consequently the uterus needs careful investigation after each case of abortion.

When an abortion is properly done by one specialized to do so, the cost is usually tremendous. What a wholesale lot of misery, expense, unhappiness and worry will be avoided when woman shall posses the knowledge of prevention of conception!

In Paris up to a few years ago the instruments to produce abortion were sold openly in the marketplace, while all the mechanical preventatives were, and are, openly displayed in the windows of the drugstores. Abortions, with their horrible consequences, are quite needless and unnecessary when the subject of preventative means shall be open to all to discuss and use. How soon this shall be, depends on you.

SUPPRESSION
(June 1914)

To suppress is an act of weakness. To suppress an idea is an admission that you are afraid of it, that its life is a threat upon yours. The persistent efforts of the Post Office to suppress this paper emphasize its fear of the propaganda for birth control. Suppression of the idea by the Church also indicates that our parasitic institutions thrive upon the exploitation of Poverty—that Stupidity and Ignorance and Slavery are the foundations of Church, State, and Business.

Our fight is for the personal liberty of the women who work. A woman's body belongs to herself alone. It is her body. It does not belong to the Church. It does not belong to the United States of America or to any other government on the face of the earth. The first step toward getting life, liberty and the pursuit of happiness for any woman is her decision whether or not she shall become a mother. Enforced motherhood is the most complete denial of a woman's right to life and liberty. The Church and the government deny personal liberty to the women of the United States. They deny this liberty in the most complete and vital manner that it can be denied. And the federal government arbitrarily suppresses any woman who dares to assert this right of personal freedom.

THE WOMAN REBEL has been calling upon women who work to fight against all things which enslave them, and has been trying to teach these women how to free themselves. The Post Office has inaugurated a campaign to stamp THE WOMAN REBEL out of existence. In a certain sense, the Post Office is to be congratulated upon its insight into the importance of our fight for birth control. Perhaps more than certain revolutionists, almost as much as the Catholic Church, the government realizes that once the women of the United States are awakened to the value of birth control, these institutions—Church, State, Big Business—will be struck such a blow that they will be able only to beg for mercy from the workers. Consequently, the government officials are keenly awake to the necessity of nipping the idea of birth control in the bud. So free speech vanishes, liberty of the press becomes a thing of the past, a joke, personal liberty a mockery. If THE WOMAN REBEL were allowed to pass, the fight for free bodies would sweep the country like a conflagration. The revolutionary movement would be doubled in strength. This our benign government realizes. Therefore its attempts—futile attempts—to crush out this idea.

But it is too late. The attempts at the suppression of a feeble effort like THE WOMAN REBEL only add fuel to the fire, only strengthen our cause, create new interest, and rejuvenate the revolutionary spirit in women. It is altogether too late to attempt a suppression of this idea of free bodies among working women.

If THE WOMAN REBEL were allowed to publish with impunity elementary and fundamental truths concerning personal liberty and how to obtain it, the birth control movement would become a movement of tremendous power in the emancipation of the working class. The attempted suppression is thus primarily a blow at the entire working class of America, intended for no other purpose than to retard the economic and spiritual emancipation of working men, women and children.

If you working women of the United States support THE WOMAN REBEL in this fight for the freedom of your own bodies, you will recreate the revolutionary spirit of your class, the ardor of which you yourselves have enchained in thousands of cases.

Nothing will cause the downfall of parasitic institutions like the Church, the State, and Big Business more than these attempts at suppression.

A LITTLE LESSON FOR THOSE
WHO OUGHT TO KNOW BETTER
(September–October 1914)

QUERY: What is Birth Control?

ANSWER: A Science which teaches that poverty and social evils can be greatly reduced by encouraging people to have small families.

Q: Why should people only have small families?

A: (1) In order to be able to feed, clothe, house and educate their children properly;

(2) In order to preserve the mother's health, strength and happiness;

(3) In order to avoid overcrowding the labor market and keeping down wages by competition.

Q: How can people limit their families?

A: In two ways. One is by ceasing to live a natural mated life. The other is to employ the means which have been discovered for avoiding having children without giving up the sex life.

Q: Is it not wrong to use artificial means for avoiding having children?

A: It is not wrong provided that no means are employed which would injure the parents or any child which is once on the way.

Q: Are not artificial methods of restricting families bad for the health?

A: It used to be thought so. But within the last few years it has become clear that there is no justification for this belief. Here are some facts:

(a) Doctors nearly all have small families nowadays.

(b) The presidents of the British Association and of the American Medical Association have both spoken in favor of family limitation.

(c) In 1911 the Hungarian Medical Senate gave a judgment in favor of permitting the use of preventive means.

(d) Wherever small families have become the rule the health of the nation has improved; and it is not improved when families have remained large.

Q: Does not family limitation mean race suicide?

A: No, it does not. Large families mean race slaughter, because so many mouths cannot be fed, and large numbers perish.

Q: Would not a knowledge of preventive means encourage young people in immorality?

A: Perhaps it might if it were taught to very young people without warning them properly in other ways and warning them of the terrible risk of disease. But if young people are told that they can marry because there is no need of having children before they can support them, and if they are given the knowledge when they marry, it will improve morality by taking them away from temptation.

GEORGE SELDES

George Seldes was an eighteen-year-old high school student when he took his first job as a cub reporter. He went on to become the living link between the Golden Age of Muckraking, launched by Lincoln Steffens, and the post-Watergate investigative journalism era of Woodward and Bernstein. Along the way, he interviewed nearly every important personality in the world. He was the most censored journalist in American history.

George Seldes was born to George Sergius Seldes and Anna Saphro on November 16, 1890, in a utopian colony started by his father in Alliance, New Jersey. His mother, manager of the local fourth-class post office, died when he was six. George was raised to be "a nonconformist, a libertarian, and a freethinker" by his father, a pharmacist. Perhaps the most important advice for the future muckraker came from his father who cautioned him to "question everything; take nothing for granted." His father also passed on his love of words to George and to George's younger brother, Gilbert. While George shunned formal education and became a journalist, Gilbert won a scholarship to Harvard and became one of the country's leading drama critics.

Seldes attended public schools until his junior year of high school. When he failed his classes and was asked to repeat a year, he dropped out instead. Later Seldes would make a brief effort to continue his education at Harvard, but left to devote himself full-time to pursuing a career in journalism.

Seldes's early education came from reading "books of value" recommended by his father; these included works by Ida Mae Tarbell and Lincoln Steffens. At fifteen, George had his first lesson in questionable news judgment when he saw a story about the start of the Russian revolution relegated to page three, while a small local fire was featured on the front page.

On February 9, 1909, Seldes was hired as a cub reporter for the *Pittsburgh Leader* at the princely sum of $3.50 a week. Still a teenager, he soon found himself interviewing famous figures like William Jennings Bryan and Theodore Roosevelt. It was the start of a writing career that would span more than three-quarters of a century. It was also the time of his first awareness of censorship, as he observed the advertising department manipulating the *Leader*'s editorial content. In 1910, he changed papers, joining the larger *Pittsburgh Post*, where he served as night editor.

In 1918, he went to Europe as a correspondent with the American Expeditionary Forces to cover World War I. He sold his stories to a syndicate that sent its reports to the *St. Louis Globe-Democrat* and other newspapers.

Seldes got the biggest story of his career, and experienced the most serious case of censorship at the end of World War I. On Armistice Day, he and three other journalists drove into Germany—in violation of the armistice regulations. They got an exclusive interview with Field Marshal Paul von Hindenburg, who had directed the German war effort and military strategies. In tears, Hindenburg confessed that the Germans had lost the war to the American infantry on the battlefield. This extraordinary story was censored by the U.S. Army under pressure from a group of journalists, including Edwin L. James of the *New York Times*, who didn't want their papers to know they had been scooped.

Seldes always felt that if Hindenburg's statement had been more widely publicized, Hitler would not have been able to appeal to the masses and World War II would have been prevented. The story would have undermined Hitler's false claim that Germany lost World War I because of a "stab in the back" from Socialists, Communists, and Jews. Years later, Seldes wrote that James, who had since become managing editor of the *New York Times*, ordered his staff "never to mention my newsletter or my books or my name." Seldes was not mentioned by the *Times* until the early 1980s when he started receiving national awards for his contributions to the field of journalism.

After the war, Seldes stayed in Europe working for the *Chicago Tribune*. He served as head of the *Tribune*'s Berlin bureau from 1920–25 and directed the

Roman bureau from 1924 to 1925, when Mussolini expelled him "because he refused to write his news to suit the fascist regime." He filed dispatches as a war correspondent during the French campaign in 1926-1927.

Seldes returned to the United States. In 1927, he was sent to Mexico by his boss at the Tribune, Colonel Robert Rutherford McCormick, to cover "the coming Communist revolution." Instead of finding the revolution, Seldes learned that the real news was at the U.S. Embassy, where representatives of American oil interests were conspiring to topple the government in order to appropriate Mexico's oil reserves.

After winning a promise from the *Tribune*'s managing editor to publish both sides of the issue, Seldes wrote a series of ten columns about what he found in Mexico: five reporting the official State Department line, the other five revealing the other side of the issue based on what he had observed or verified himself. The *Tribune* ran only the first five, supporting American business interests. Seldes quit the *Tribune* in disgust and became a freelance journalist and a pioneering press critic. He launched his twenty-one–book career in 1929 with the aptly titled *You Can't Print That*.

In 1937, Seldes and his wife, Helen Larkin, an American woman he met in Paris in 1929, went to Spain to cover the Spanish Civil War for the *New York Post*. Seldes felt that if the world's free press printed the truth about what was happening in Europe, and particularly in Spain, the civilized nations of the world would have rallied to support the Spanish Republic instead of abandoning it to be destroyed by the fascist forces of Germany and Italy. The *Post* caved in to pressure from Franco supporters and dropped Seldes's reports. With that, Seldes quit newspaper reporting for good, and in 1940 launched his own publication, *In fact*.

In fact was a weekly newsletter "For the Millions Who Want a Free Press" (later "An Antidote for Falsehood In the Daily Press"). It was the nation's first successful periodical of press criticism and had 176,000 subscribers at its peak in 1947. Week after week, *In fact* would castigate the mainstream media for failing to cover the important issues. In his guide to propaganda in the media, *The Facts Are...*, published during World War II, the section "How To Read the Editorial Page" consisted of one word: "Don't." By 1950, the newsletter was "red-baited to death by the McCarthyites."

Seldes's *In fact* inspired I. F. Stone to publish *I. F. Stone's Weekly* in 1953. Stone originally wanted to restart *In fact*, but Seldes warned him about the pressure and red-baiting it would be subject to from the government and the media. He urged Stone to start his own newspaper and gave him his subscription list to help get started.

Seldes was one of the first media watchdogs to criticize the press for censoring information connecting tobacco with cancer. In 1938, he tried, without success, to get the press to report the results of a five-year study, conducted by Dr. Raymond Pearl of the Department of Biology at Johns Hopkins University. The seven-thousand–person study revealed that smoking decreases life expectancy. In 1940, the same year Seldes started his newsletter, he began a ten-year crusade against tobacco, publishing some one hundred items on the subject in the five hundred published issues of *In fact*. Few of his exposés were ever published in the mainstream media.

Ironically, despite his many years of outstanding journalism and media criticism, Seldes's most popular acclaim came from a brief appearance in a Hollywood movie and from a book that was not about the media. The movie was the 1981 Academy Award winner *Reds*, in which Seldes was one of the witnesses. His appearance brought him immediate national recognition. His best-known book, *The Great Quotations*, was rejected by twenty publishers before it was accepted by Lyle Stuart, Inc., in 1961. It sold more than a million copies worldwide.

Seldes wrote more than twenty books about major historic events and the media including *You Can't Print That* (1929); *Freedom of the Press* (1935); *Sawdust Caesar* (1935); *Lords of the Press* (1938); *You Can't Do That* (1938); *Facts and Fascism* (1943); *Tell the Truth and Run* (1953); *Never Tire of Protesting* (1968); and *Even the Gods Can't Change History* (1976). His autobiography, *Witness to a Century: Encounters with the Noted, the Notorious, and the Three SOBs* was published in 1987 when he was 96 years old. The "three SOBs" were Gabriele D'Annunzio, poet, novelist, and early Fascist; Errol Flynn, Hollywood star and Nazi sympathizer; and any one of three of America's most powerful columnists and radio commentators—Fulton Lewis, Jr., Westbrook Pegler, or George E. Sokolsky—all of whom were rabid supporters of Senator Joseph McCarthy.

Seldes popularized access journalism. He never depended on tips, rumors, or anonymous "reliable" sources. Seldes always went to the original source for the story. In his career, he met and interviewed more than eight hundred prominent historical figures like General John Pershing, General Douglas MacArthur, Albert Einstein, Woodrow Wilson, Calvin Coolidge, Sigmund Freud,

General George Patton, Jr., Lenin, Mussolini, Trotsky, Pablo Picasso, Eleanor Roosevelt, J. Edgar Hoover, Harry S Truman, and Marshal Joseph Broz Tito.

Although the *New York Times* and much of the other major media in the United States censored Seldes for more than half a century, his place in journalism's hall of fame is secure. He published America's first successful journalism review. He was the first journalist to castigate the media for failing to reveal the link between cigarettes and cancer. He called for a journalist's ethics code and lived long enough to see a national code adopted and journalism schools offering ethics courses.

Seldes acknowledged it was sometimes best to "tell the truth and run," which became the title of a feature-length documentary film commemorating his life and contribution to journalism. The film received numerous national awards and was a 1996 Academy Award Oscar nominee.

Following the death of his wife, Helen, in 1979, Seldes lived alone with his cat, Peepers, in a brick house in the rural community of Hartland-Four-Corners, Vermont.

Shortly after he received a pacemaker for his heart at the age of 94, he proclaimed, "I want to continue work until the last day. If you have a pacemaker, that's good for seven years. Let's see, 101. Well, I'll settle for 100." He continued to be active until about a year before his death in 1995 at the age of 104.

The following are three brief excerpts from Seldes's many writings focusing on two of his favorite and most controversial subjects: cigarettes and the press. The first two items, from *In fact*, criticize the media for witholding information about cancer. The third, about the corrupt press, is from his self-published book, *The Facts Are....*

SOURCES. Holhut, Randolph T., *The George Seldes Reader: An Anthology of the Writings of America's Foremost Journalistic Gadfly*, Barricade Books, Inc., New York, 1994; Seldes, George, editor, *In fact* (all issues, 1940–1950); Seldes, George, *Even the Gods Can't Change History: The Facts Speak for Themselves*, Lyle Stuart, Inc., Secaucus, New Jersey, 1976; Seldes, George, *Freedom of the Press*, The Bobbs-Merrill Co., New York, 1935; Seldes, George, *The Facts are... : A Guide to Falsehood and Propaganda in the Press and Radio*, In fact, Inc., New York, 1942; Seldes, George, *Lords of the Press*, Blue Ribbon Books, New York,

1941; Seldes, George, *Never Tire of Protesting*, Lyle Stuart, Inc., New York, 1968; Seldes, George, *Tell the Truth and Run*, Greenberg, New York, 1953; Seldes, George, *Witness to a Century: Encounters with the Noted, the Notorious, and the Three SOBs*, Ballantine Books, New York, 1987; Seldes, George, *You Can't Print That! The Truth Behind the News 1918–1928,* Garden City Publishing Co., Inc., Garden City, New York, 1929.

In fact
George Seldes

CIGARETS SHORTEN LIFE
(December 2, 1940)

Fact is, Johns Hopkins University investigation revealed one of the most shocking and sensational stories in American history, dealing with heavy smoking as contributory cause of death. Almost all big papers taking cigaret advertising suppressed story or buried couple of paragraphs. Next to automobiles, tobacco is largest US advertiser.

IN FACT:
TOBACCO SHORTENS LIFE
(January 13, 1941)

Smoking shortens life. Between the ages of thirty and sixty, 61 percent more heavy smokers die than nonsmokers. A human being's span of life is impaired in direct proportion to the amount of tobacco he uses, but the impairment among even light smokers is "measurable and significant."

The facts for the foregoing statements come from Johns Hopkins University, department of biology. They constitute one of the most important and incidentally one of the most sensational stories in recent American history, but there is not a newspaper or magazine in America (outside scientific journals) which has published all the facts....

MAKE USERS' FLESH CREEP

For generations there have been arguments about tobacco. Moralists preached against cigarets. Scientists differed. But in February 1938, Dr. Raymond Pearl, head biologist, Johns Hopkins, gave the New York Academy of Medicine the scientific result of a study of the life histories of some seven thousand Johns Hopkins cases which, for newspapers, should have constituted a story "to scare the life out of tobacco manufacturers and make the tobacco users' flesh creep," as *Time* commented (March 7, 1938).

The Associated Press, United Press and special correspondents of New York papers heard Dr. Pearl tell the story. But a paragraph or two buried under less important matter, in one or two papers was all the great free press of America cared to make known to its readers, the consumers of two hundred billion cigarets a year...

SIXTY-ONE PERCENT EXCESS DEATHS

Writing in La Follette's *Progressive* (no advertising taken) Francis A. Porter popularized Dr. Pearl's tables as follows:

DEATHS FROM AGE 30 TO 60 (PER 100,000) AMONG

Nonsmokers	33,436
Moderate smokers	38,089
Heavy smokers	53,774

PERCENTAGE OF EXCESS DEATHS AMONG

Moderate smokers	14%
Heavy smokers	61%

JOURNALISTIC BOMBSHELL

When the Town Meeting of the Air announced a debate, "Do We Have a Free Press?" January 16, 1939, the present editor of IN FACT sent to Secretary of the Interior Ickes documentary evidence proving that we do *not* have a free press. In the debate Mr. Ickes easily bested Frank Gannett, chain newspaper owner. During the question period someone asked for examples of news suppression and Mr. Ickes mentioned some casually, adding, "I understand that at Johns Hopkins University there is a very sensational finding resulting from the study of the effect of cigaret smoking that has not appeared, so far as I know, in any newspaper in the United States. I wonder if that is because the tobacco companies are such large advertisers."...

DOCUMENTATION

The tobacco story, to be exact, appeared in some country papers, and one or two big city papers. Here is what happened in the great free press metropolis of New York:

Herald Tribune	totally suppressed
Sun	totally suppressed
News	totally suppressed
Mirror	totally suppressed
Post	totally suppressed
Journal-American	totally suppressed
World-Telegram	carried few lines
Times	carried few lines

The tables had been seen by the press. The leading authority in America, if not in the world, had made a great discovery and presented the first scientific study in a controversial matter in which some fifty million Americans consuming two hundred billion cigarets were interested, and 75% of the New York press suppressed the story, 25% half-suppressed it, and 100% of the press manhandled it.

The Facts Are...
George Seldes

Chapter One:
THE GREATEST POWER
IN WAR AND PEACE[1]

It is more than likely that in the time intervening between the writing of this book and the day it is read the World War now being fought far away will have become a reality, a matter of life and death, to millions of Americans. There may be long casualty lists, there may be bombardments of great coastal cities, and the facts of the greatest struggle for the welfare of humanity against its greatest enemy (Fascism) will be felt as well as known.

The conduct of this war, the making of the unity necessary to win it, or the spreading of disunity which for the first time in the history of the Republic may endanger its existence, will depend considerably on the press, and the kind of peace which will follow will depend even more than did the Versailles peace, on the conduct of the press of all nations. Today we are fighting for our lives. We have been attacked. The enemy is Fascism. There can therefore be no room in the anti-Fascist world at this time for doubt about the justness of the war, or its causes, as there were in the last war, but when peace nears all of us will have to be on the alert to prevent the present movement against world Fascism from being diverted into many strange channels by public opinion created by a press which is still in Fascist or semi-Fascist control even in democratic nations.

I believe that the press will be the instrument for uniting America for war and that it will be still more powerful in making a peace which may benefit all peoples or certain interests. I also believe that most of the world press is controlled by special interests and as a result is corrupt. Therefore it is necessary to explain and expose this corruption of the press and to question its handling of the news of the war, so that we may judge its role in creating a better world—for which this war is being fought.

What is the most powerful force in America today?

Answer: public opinion.

What makes public opinion?

Answer: the main force is the press.

Can you trust the press?

Answer: the baseball scores are always correct (except for a typographical error now and then). The stock market tables are correct (within the same limitation). But when it comes to news which will affect you, your daily life, your job, your relation to other peoples, your thinking on economic and social problems, and, more important today, your going to war and risking your life for a great ideal, then you cannot trust about 98 percent (or perhaps 99 1/2 percent) of the big newspaper and big magazine press of America.

But why can't you trust the press?

Answer: because it has become Big Business. The big city press and the big magazines have become commercialized, or big business organizations, run with no other motive than profit for owner or stockholder (although hypocritically still maintaining the old American tradition of guiding and enlightening the people). The big press cannot exist a day without advertising. Advertising means money from Big Business. The truth about Big Business is told in the three or four hundred volumes of government reports... Besides naming thousands of newspapers, scores of magazines, many writers and college professors as being corrupted by the special interests, and receiving the price paid, which ranges all the way from a five-dollar bill and a few drinks at a bar to a million-dollar mortgage, the reports come to these documented conclusions:

1. America is in the hands of two hundred industrial and fifty financial families.

2. These families run this country.

3. They supply the funds which elect the officials of the United States, from state legislatures to the presidency.

4. They control billions in stocks and bonds, they control the economic life of the nation.

5. They control legislation; they control Congress; they maintain the most powerful lobby in Washington, and usually get what they want.

6. They use the American Newspaper Publishers Association (the big newspaper owners) as an instrument to maintain their control of America.

7. They use advertising (in newspapers and magazines) to make this stranglehold on public opinion possible.

In other words, they control you.

Very few people will accept these seven statements as facts, yet they are facts known to everyone in the newspaper business, in big business, in politics; they are known to all who read the small free liberal magazines and to everyone who is part of the ruling group. The facts appear in government documents. But these are also the facts which have been suppressed in the popular newspapers and magazines, and that of course is the reason America is kept in ignorance of the most vital matters affecting the life, happiness and welfare of the majority of its citizens.

I have written several books on the press and I am publishing a weekly newsletter devoted largely to criticizing the big city newspapers (the public opinion-making newspapers) and exposing their corruption, because I still believe that the press is the greatest force in the world and can be used for good or evil. And I believe that the American press by its control of public opinion can either fool all the people into restoring a world in which forty-three million people (one-third of the nation) will again live in economic slavery without sufficient food, clothing and shelter, or it can, if it wants to, bring out of this united effort against native as well as foreign Fascism a world approaching the Jeffersonian ideal.

In 1787 Jefferson declared that "the basis of our government is the opinion of the people"; given the choice of "a government without newspapers, or newspapers without government," he would prefer the latter. Think of it! Jefferson was willing to let the press itself rule the country instead of merely creating the public opinion that rules.

But Jefferson did not foresee that the American press which creates opinion and which rules indirectly would become almost exclusively a millionaire's press, or a corporation-influenced press, or the medium of big business via its advertising, and therefore the corrupt press which serves private interests rather than the public interest.... If America is to be bossed by the public opinion created by its press, if it is to fight and win this war, if it is to make a great peace, then it should know the power of the most powerful force which is abroad in the land.

---

1. George Seldes, *The Facts Are...: A Guide to Falsehood and Propoganda in the Press and Radio*, In Fact, Inc., New York, 1942, pages 1–4.

JOHN
STEINBECK

He was ambitious, hardworking, successful, ruggedly handsome, wealthy, world traveled, shy, and private, yet he spent his time working and living with some of the poorest, most oppressed people in America. The words he chose to describe them helped change their lives. The words also brought him a Pulitzer Prize and made him one of only a handful of American authors to receive the Nobel Prize for Literature.

John Steinbeck was born in a large Victorian house on the right side of the tracks in Salinas, a small town south of San Francisco near Monterey Bay. He was a second generation American: His paternal grandparents had emigrated from Germany, and his maternal grandparents came from Ireland. His father, John Ernst Steinbeck, managed the Sperry Flour Mill in Salinas, owned his own feed store, was bookkeeper for Spreckles Sugar, and served eleven years as treasurer of Monterey County. His mother, Olive Hamilton, a strong, outgoing woman, was a schoolteacher.

The Steinbeck's upper-middle-class family life has been described as secure and happy. John was an only son with three sisters, Esther, Elizabeth, and Mary. His father, a quiet family man, recognized his son's aptitude and encouraged him to become a writer. His mother, energetic and active in club work, first wanted John to become a banker but later supported his interest in writing. She hoped he would become as successful as Booth Tarkington, a novelist popular at the time. Books were a big part of the family life and the parents would often take turns reading *Treasure Island*, *Paradise Lost*, and the

Bible to the children in the sitting room after dinner. When John was ten years old, his Aunt Molly gave him a copy of *Morte d'Arthur* which, along with the Bible, would prove to be the most influential book in his life.

Steinbeck started high school in 1915 in a small, two-story brick school-house in Salinas. He was a good B student, a better-than-average athlete in track and basketball, a member of the student cadet company, and, though he was somewhat of a loner, he was elected president of his senior class. He also served as the associate editor of *El Cabilan*, the school yearbook. During his teens, he started writing short stories under a pseudonym, and developed his literary aspirations. The summer before college, Steinbeck worked as a laborer, side-by-side with men upon whom he would later model characters in his novels.

In 1919, he started a rather checkered academic career at Stanford University. Registered in the liberal arts program, he immediately started to argue with his professors about taking required courses. He remained an average student, failed to make the freshman football team, and continued to be a recluse. In the second year, he skipped classes to spend more time writing short stories, and became a voracious reader of European and American writers. Late in the fall semester of 1920, the dean warned him about his failing academic record, and Steinbeck withdrew from the university leaving a note saying he had "gone to China."

He spent two years away from Stanford working at various jobs, first on a sugar beet ranch south of Salinas, and then at his father's flour mill. He also spent much of his free time writing at the family's vacation cottage in Pacific Grove, and developed self-confidence as a writer. He returned to Stanford in January 1923, determined to make a success of himself. He majored in journalism, took courses that interested him, and managed to earn As and Bs in the next three years. With the encouragement of a writing teacher, he rededicated himself to becoming an author. He had two short stories published in the *Stanford Spectator*, and three poems in the *Stanford Lit*. In June 1925, at the age of twenty-three, he left Stanford with passable grades but no degree. He did have an incomplete manuscript for *A Lady in Infra-Red,* which later became his first published novel, renamed *Cup of Gold.*

Staying at the family cottage in Pacific Grove, he spent six months attempting to revise and complete *Lady*. Finally, frustrated by his lack of progress, and tortured with the restlessness that would dominate his life, he left for New York. He went by freighter and arrived with only three dollars in his pocket. There he worked as a laborer again, as one of the men who built (the original) Madison Square Garden. He was hired then fired from a job as reporter for the *New York American* because, as he later admitted, he was "a lousy reporter." Meanwhile, he kept writing short stories.

When his stories would not sell, he traveled back to California in July 1926 working as a deckhand on a freighter. He returned to his novel while working odd jobs around Lake Tahoe. It was at this time that he made his first professional sale with a short story, "The Gifts of Tiban." Written under the pseudonym John Stern, it was published in the March 1927 issue of the *Smokers Companion*.

In his mid- and late twenties, Steinbeck grew into a big, ruggedly handsome man. From among the many women whose company he enjoyed, one particular woman stood out, twenty-two-year-old Carol Henning, whom he met in 1928. They were married in 1930. During the early years of the Depression, Carol worked as a typist, secretary, library cataloguer, and copyreader to support the family while Steinbeck concentrated on his writing. His family also helped out with a twenty-five–dollar monthly stipend and the use of the rent-free cottage in Pacific Grove. *Cup of Gold*, which he said was "no good," was published in 1929, bringing him an advance of $400.

John and Carol Steinbeck became members of the West Coast intellectual bohemia that found refuge in the Monterey-Carmel area. One member of the group who drew Steinbeck's attention was Edward Ricketts, a marine biologist and operator of the Pacific Biological Laboratories in Monterey. Ricketts taught Steinbeck about the activities and habitats of the fish and other animals that lived along the coast. He became Steinbeck's best friend and they later collaborated on *Sea of Cortez*, a technical study of marine life in the Gulf of California. Ricketts also inspired the character of the original Doc in *Cannery Row*, a marine biologist who lives in the bohemian section of Monterey near the fish canneries, and for several other Steinbeck characters.

Steinbeck's stay in Monterey during the Depression was productive and profitable. He was disturbed, however, by the ethnic and racial prejudice he observed around him. He gradually discovered his own talent as a humanistic writer of social protest. His subsequent novels reflect his social conscience. In the following years he wrote *The Pastures of Heaven* (1932); *To a God Unknown* (1933); *Tortilla Flat* (1935); *In Dubious Battle* (1936); *Of Mice and Men* (1937); *The Long Valley* (1938); and *The Grapes of Wrath* (1939). *Tortilla Flat* was Steinbeck's first popular book, an immediate bestseller, and a Book-of-the-Month Club selection. It made him a national literary celebrity, and it also made him financially independent.

With all of his writing, Steinbeck also found time to indulge his wander-lust. In 1936, he and Carol bought a used car and took an extended trip to Mexico. After returning to Monterey, Steinbeck soon left on another trip that would lead to his most celebrated novel, *The Grapes of Wrath*. He traveled three hundred miles down the San Joaquin Valley, living and working with migrants in fields along the way.

In 1937, after *Of Mice and Men* was published, the Steinbecks traveled by freighter through the Panama Canal to Philadelphia and New York, and then to England, Ireland, Sweden, and Russia. Back in the United States, Steinbeck worked with playwright George Kaufman on a dramatization of *Of Mice and Men*. The play opened on Broadway in November 1937 and won the highly esteemed Drama Critics' Circle Award.

In 1940, Steinbeck and his friend Ricketts sailed the Gulf of California, studying and collecting marine invertebrates along the shoreline. *Sea of Cortez* was published in December.

It was then that the United States entered World War II. Too old to volunteer, Steinbeck spent the war years as an advisor to the military, writing propaganda films such as *The Moon is Down*, *Lifeboat*, and *Bombs Away: The Story of a Bomber Team*. He was a war correspondent in Europe for the *New York Herald Tribune*.

The war years and travel took a toll on Steinbeck's marriage to Carol and they divorced in 1942. In March 1943, he married Gwyndolen Conger (Gwen Verdon), an actress/singer he had met earlier in California. They had two sons, Thom and John, born in 1944 and 1946. Restless as always, Steinbeck moved with his family from New York to Mexico to California, back to New York, back to Monterey, and finally back to New York.

While significant, his post-war writing did not meet the quality or renown of his Depression-era writing, with the possible exceptions of *Cannery Row* (1945), which he dedicated to Ricketts, and *Travels with Charley* (1962), a warm reminiscence of his three-month tour of America with his French poodle in a small trailer truck.

In 1948, Steinbeck suffered two major losses: His marriage to Gwen fell apart, and Ricketts died from injuries sustained in a car-train wreck. Despondent over his losses, Steinbeck threw himself into his writing, working on a film script, *Viva Zapata!*, and a long book about the Salinas Valley that was to be entitled *East of Eden* (1952). In 1949, he met Elaine Scott who, along with his renewed interest in writing, helped him recover from his despair and they were married in December 1950.

Steinbeck disliked the attention fame brought him, and was comfortable with the anonymity of living in New York. Following a trip to Europe in 1952, he and Elaine settled back down in New York. Suddenly, he started to take an interest in American politics, invigorated by the intensity and success of the political activism he had witnessed in Europe. He supported the Democrats' presidential candidate, Adlai Stevenson, in his (unsuccessful) campaigns of 1952 and 1956, loudly criticized Senator McCarthy, the rabid anti-communist senator from Wisconsin, and became friends with Lyndon Johnson, the Texas senator, campaigning for him in his 1964 presidential campaign. He was later an advisor to President Johnson.

To his subsequent regret, Steinbeck initially supported Johnson's Vietnam policies. After visiting Vietnam at the age of sixty-four, however, he grew disillusioned and advised Johnson to pull the American troops out. Both of Steinbeck's sons, Thom and John, fought in Vietnam.

Steinbeck wrote twenty-eight books of fiction and nonfiction altogether, along with numerous short stories, articles, plays and screenplays. His lifelong passion for the tales of King Arthur was fulfilled with his translation of Mallory's *Morte d'Arthur*, the book his aunt had once given him. His translation was published posthumously as *The Acts of King Arthur and His Noble Knights* in 1976.

Steinbeck suffered several strokes, the first in 1961. He died peacefully in his New York apartment on December 20, 1968.

Of all of Steinbeck's books, *The Grapes of Wrath* was the greatest literary and political success, a runaway bestseller that had the most impact on American society. Like Sinclair's *The Jungle*, it struck a raw nerve in American society, and like Sinclair he was able to raise the issue with President Roosevelt, this time Franklin Delano Roosevelt. Twentieth-Century Fox made the book into a critically acclaimed film, and the attention that it brought to the poorest workers forced migrant camps in California to improve their living conditions.

The Grapes of Wrath also brought Steinbeck a Pulitzer Prize in 1940. And in 1962, Steinbeck became the sixth American to receive the prestigious Nobel Prize for Literature, for his pre-war Depression-era work.

Through the depiction of one family—the Joads—*The Grapes of Wrath* chronicles the lives of the hundreds of thousands of homeless migrants who traveled to California in the 1930s. They came from the drought-ravaged dust bowls of Kansas, Oklahoma, Texas, New Mexico, Nevada, and Arkansas after being dispossessed, seeking work and "the good life" in California. Most of them found neither. Instead of a land of milk, honey, and oranges for the taking, they were met with hostility, anger, and slave wages—when they were lucky enough to get jobs. The derogatory term "Okies" describes these migratory agricultural workers forced to leave their homes because of drought and farm foreclosures. It became a national slur and found its place in the American lexicon. Nearly sixty years later, Steinbeck's protagonist, Tom Joad, was memorialized with an album by Bruce Springsteen, *The Ghost of Tom Joad*.

The depth of Steinbeck's feeling for the migrant workers, his outrage over the way they were treated, and the simplicity of his stories made him an effective voice of American social protest.

The following excerpt from *The Grapes of Wrath* is one of the expository chapters used by Steinbeck to evoke the miserable experiences of the migrants. It vividly describes how the Joads and thousands of other families like them were driven off their tenant farm houses and forced to head west to California.

SOURCES. Benson, Jackson J., *The True Adventures of John Steinbeck, Writer: A Biography*, The Viking Press, New York, 1984; Fensch, Thomas, editor, *Conversations with John Steinbeck*, University Press of Mississippi, Jackson, 1988; Fontenrose, Joseph, *John Steinbeck: An Introduction and Interpretation*, Barnes & Noble, Inc., New York, 1963; Kiernan, Thomas, *The Intricate Music: A Biography of John Steinbeck*, Little, Brown & Co., Boston, 1979; McCarthy, Paul, *John Steinbeck*, Ungar Publishing Co., New York, 1980; Parini, Jay, *John Steinbeck: A Biography*, Henry Holt & Co., New York, 1995; Steinbeck, John, *Cannery Row*, The Viking Press, New York, 1945; Steinbeck, John, *Of Mice and Men*, Random House, New York, 1937; Steinbeck, John, *The Grapes of Wrath*, The Viking Press, New York, 1939; Valjean, Nelson, *John Steinbeck: The Errant Knight*, Chronicle Books, San Francisco, 1975.

The Grapes of Wrath
John Steinbeck

WHO CAN WE SHOOT?
(From Chapter Five)[1]

The owners of the land came onto the land, or more often a spokesman for the owners came. They came in closed cars, and they felt the dry earth with their fingers, and sometimes they drove big earth augers into the ground for soil tests. The tenants, from their sun-beaten dooryards watched uneasily when the closed cars drove along the fields. And at last the owner men drove into the dooryards and sat in their cars to talk out of the windows. The tenant men stood beside the cars for a while, and then squatted on their hams and found sticks with which to mark the dust.

In the open doors the women stood looking out, and behind them the children—corn-headed children, with wide eyes, one bare foot on top of the other bare foot, and the toes working. The women and the children watched their men talking to the owner men. They were silent.

Some of the owner men were kind because they hated what they had to do, and some of them were angry because they hated to be cruel, and some of them were cold because they had long ago found that one could not be an owner unless one were cold. And all of them were caught in something larger than themselves. Some of them hated the mathematics that drove them, and some were afraid, and some worshiped the mathematics because it provided a refuge from thought and from feeling. If a bank or a finance company owned the land, the owner man said, The Bank—or the company—needs—wants—insists—must have—as though the Bank or the company were a monster, with thought and feeling which had ensnared them. These last would take no responsibility for the banks or the companies because they were men and slaves, while the banks were machines and masters all at the same time. Some of the owner men were a little proud to be slaves to such cold and powerful

95

masters. The owner men sat in the cars and explained. You know the land is poor. You've scrabbled at it long enough, God knows.

The squatting tenant men nodded and wondered and drew figures in the dust, and yes, they knew, God knows. If the dust only wouldn't fly. If the top would only stay on the soil, it might not be so bad.

The owner men went on leading to their point: You know the land's getting poorer. You know what cotton does to the land; robs it, sucks all the blood out of it.

The squatters nodded—they knew, God knew. If they could only rotate the crops they might pump blood back into the land.

Well, it's too late. And the owner men explained the workings and the thinkings of the monster that was stronger than they were. A man can hold land if he can just eat and pay taxes; he can do that.

Yes, he can do that until his crops fail one day and he has to borrow money from the bank.

But—you see, a bank or a company can't do that, because those creatures don't breathe air, don't eat side-meat. They breathe profits, they eat the interest on money. If they don't get it, they die the way you die without air, without side-meat. It is a sad thing, but it is so. It is just so.

The squatting men raised their eyes to understand. Can't we just hang on? Maybe the next year will be a good year. God knows how much cotton next year. And with all the wars—God knows what price cotton will bring. Don't they make explosives out of cotton? And uniforms? Get enough wars and cotton'll hit the ceiling. Next year, maybe. They looked up questioningly.

We can't depend on it. The bank—the monster has to have profits all the time. It can't wait. It'll die. No, taxes go on. When the monster stops growing, it dies. It can't stay one size.

Soft fingers began to tap the sill of the car window, and hard fingers tightened on the restless drawing sticks. In the doorways of the sun-beaten tenant houses, women sighed and then shifted feet so that the one that had been down was now on top, and the toes working. Dogs came sniffing near the owner cars and wetted on all four tires one after another. And chickens lay in the sunny dust and fluffed their feathers to get the cleansing dust down to the skin. In the little sties the pigs grunted inquiringly over the muddy remnants of the slops.

The squatting men looked down again. What do you want us to do? We can't take less share of the crop—we're half starved now. The kids are hungry all the time. We got no clothes, torn, an' ragged. If all the neighbors weren't the same, we'd be ashamed to go to meeting.

And at last the owner men came to the point. The tenant system won't work any more. One man on a tractor can take the place of twelve or fourteen families. Pay him a wage and take all the crop. We have to do it. We don't like to do it. But the monster's sick. Something's happened to the monster.

But you'll kill the land with cotton.

We know. We've got to take cotton quick before the land dies. Then we'll sell the land. Lots of families in the East would like to own a piece of land.

The tenant men looked up alarmed. But what'll happen to us? How'll we eat?

You'll have to get off the land. The plows'll go through the dooryard.

And now the squatting men stood up angrily. Grampa took up the land, and he had to kill the Indians and drive them away. And Pa was born here, and he killed weeds and snakes. Then a bad year came and he had to borrow a little money. An' we was born here. There in the door—our children born here. And Pa had to borrow money. The bank owned the land then, but we stayed and we got a little bit of what we raised.

We know that—all that. It's not us, it's the bank. A bank isn't like a man. Or an owner with fifty thousand acres, he isn't like a man either. That's the monster.

Sure, cried the tenant men, but it's our land. We measured it and broke it up. We were born on it, and we got killed on it, died on it. Even if it's no good, it's still ours. That's what makes it ours—being born on it, working on it, dying on it. That makes ownership, not a paper with numbers on it.

We're sorry. It's not us. It's the monster. The bank isn't like a man.

Yes, but the bank is only made of men.

No, you're wrong there—quite wrong there. The bank is something else than men. It happens that every man in a bank hates what the bank does, and yet the bank does it. The bank is something more than men, I tell you. It's the monster. Men made it, but they can't control it.

The tenants cried, Grampa killed Indians, Pa killed snakes for the land. Maybe we can kill banks—they're worse than Indians and snakes. Maybe we got to fight to keep our land, like Pa and Grampa did.

And now the owner men grew angry. You'll have to go.

But it's ours, the tenant men cried. We—

No. The bank, the monster owns it. You'll have to go.

We'll get our guns, like Grampa when the Indians came. What then?

Well—first the sheriff, and then the troops. You'll be stealing if you try to stay, you'll be murderers if you kill to stay. The monster isn't men, but it can make men do what it wants.

But if we go, where'll we go? How'll we go? We got no money.

We're sorry, said the owner men. The bank, the fifty-thousand-acre owner can't be responsible. You're on land that isn't yours. Once over the line maybe you can pick cotton in the fall. Maybe you can go on relief. Why don't you go on west to California? There's work there, and it never gets cold. Why, you can reach out anywhere and pick an orange. Why, there's always some kind of crop to work in. Why don't you go there? And the owner men started the cars and rolled away....

The tractors came over the roads and into the fields, great crawlers moving like insects, having the incredible strength of insects. They crawled over the ground, laying the track and rolling on it and picking it up. Diesel tractors, puttering while they stood idle; they thundered when they moved, and then settled down to a droning roar. Snub-nosed monsters, raising the dust and sticking their snouts into it, straight down the country, across the country, through fences, through dooryards, in and out of gullies in straight lines. They did not run on the ground, but on their own roadbeds. They ignored hills and gulches, water courses, fences, houses.

The man sitting in the iron seat did not look like a man; gloved, goggled, rubber dust mask over nose and mouth, he was a part of the monster, a robot in the seat. The thunder of the cylinders sounded through the country, became one with the air and the earth, so that earth and air muttered in sympathetic vibration. The driver could not control it—straight across country it went, cutting through a dozen farms and straight back. A twitch at the controls could swerve the cat', but the driver's hands could not twitch because the monster that built the tractor, the monster that sent the tractor out, had somehow got into the driver's hands, into his brain and muscle, had goggled him and muzzled him—goggled his mind, muzzled his speech, goggled his perception, muzzled his protest. He could not see the land as it was, he could not smell the land as it smelled; his feet did not stamp the clods or feel the warmth and power of the earth. He sat in an iron seat and stepped on iron pedals. He could not cheer or beat or curse or encourage the extension of his power, and because of this he could not cheer or whip or curse or encourage himself. He did not know or own or trust or beseech the land. If a seed dropped did not germinate, it was nothing. If the young thrusting plant withered in drought or drowned in a flood of rain, it was no more to the driver than to the tractor.

He loved the land no more than the bank loved the land. He could admire the tractor—its machined surfaces, its surge of power, the roar of its detonating cylinders; but it was not his tractor. Behind the tractor rolled the shining disks, cutting the earth with blades—not plowing but surgery, pushing the cut earth to the right where the second row of disks cut it and pushed it to the left; slicing blades shining, polished by the cut earth. And pulled behind the disks, the harrows combing with iron teeth so that the little clods broke up and the earth lay smooth. Behind the harrows, the long seeders—twelve curved iron penes erected in the foundry, orgasms set by gears, raping methodically, raping without passion. The driver sat in his iron seat and he was proud of the straight lines he did not will, proud of the tractor he did not own or love, proud of the power he could not control. And when that crop grew, and was harvested, no man had crumbled a hot clod in his fingers and let the earth sift past his fingertips. No man had touched the seed, or lusted for the growth. Men ate what they had not raised, had no connection with the bread. The land bore under iron, and under iron gradually died; for it was not loved or hated, it had no prayers or curses.

At noon the tractor driver stopped sometimes near a tenant house and opened his lunch: sandwiches wrapped in waxed paper, white bread, pickle, cheese, Spam, a piece of pie branded like an engine part. He ate without relish. And tenants not yet moved away came out to see him, looked curiously while the goggles were taken off, and the rubber dust mask, leaving white circles around the eyes and a large white circle around nose and mouth. The exhaust of the tractor puttered on, for fuel is so cheap it is more efficient to leave the engine running than to heat the Diesel nose for a new start. Curious children crowded close, ragged children who ate their fried dough as they watched. They watched hungrily the unwrapping of the sandwiches, and their hunger-sharpened noses smelled the pickle, cheese, and Spam. They didn't speak to the driver. They watched his hand as it carried food to his mouth. They did not watch him chewing; the eyes followed the hand that held the sandwich. After a while the tenant who could not leave the place came out and squatted in the shade beside the tractor.

"Why, you're Joe Davis's boy!"

"Sure," the driver said.

"Well, what you doing this kind of work for—against your own people?"

"Three dollars a day. I got damn sick of creeping for my dinner—and not getting it. I got a wife and kids. We got to eat. Three dollars a day, and it comes every day."

"That's right," the tenant said. "But for your three dollars a day fifteen or twenty families can't eat at all. Nearly a hundred people have to go out and wander on the roads for your three dollars a day. Is that right?"

And the driver said, "Can't think of that. Got to think of my own kids. Three dollars a day, and it comes every day. Times are changing, mister, don't you know? Can't make a living on the land unless you've got two, five, ten thousand acres and a tractor. Crop land isn't for little guys like us any more. You don't kick up a howl because you can't make Fords, or because you're not the telephone company. Well, crops are like that now. Nothing to do about it. You try to get three dollars a day someplace. That's the only way."

The tenant pondered. "Funny thing how it is. If a man owns a little property, that property is him, it's part of him, and it's like him. If he owns property only so he can walk on it and handle it and be sad when it isn't doing well, and feel fine when the rain falls on it, that property is him, and someway he's bigger because he owns it. Even if he isn't successful he's big with his property. That is so."

And the tenant pondered more. "But let a man get property he doesn't see, or can't take time to get his fingers in, or can't be there to walk on it—why, then the property is the man. He can't do what he wants, he can't think what he wants. The property is the man, stronger than he is. And he is small, not big. Only his possessions are big—and he's the servant of his property. That is so, too."

The driver munched the branded pie and threw the crust away. "Times are changed, don't you know? Thinking about stuff like that don't feed the kids. Get your three dollars a day, feed your kids. You got no call to worry about anybody's kids but your own. You get a reputation for talking like that, and you'll never get three dollars a day. Big shots won't give you three dollars a day if you worry about anything but your three dollars a day."

"Nearly a hundred people on the road for your three dollars. Where will we go?"

"And that reminds me," the driver said, "you better get out soon. I'm going through the dooryard after dinner."

"You filled in the well this morning."

"I know. Had to keep the line straight. But I'm going through the dooryard after dinner. Got to keep the lines straight. And—well, you know Joe Davis, my old man, so I'll tell you this. I got orders wherever there's a family not moved out—if I have an accident—you know, get too close and cave the house in a little—well, I might get a couple of dollars. And my youngest kid never had no shoes yet."

"I built it with my hands. Straightened old nails to put the sheathing on. Rafters are wired to the stringers with baling wire. It's mine. I built it. You bump it down—I'll be in the window with a rifle. You even come too close and I'll pot you like a rabbit."

"It's not me. There's nothing I can do. I'll lose my job if I don't do it. And look—suppose you kill me? They'll just hang you, but long before you're hung there'll be another guy on the tractor, and he'll bump the house down. You're not killing the right guy."

"That's so," the tenant said. "Who gave you orders? I'll go after him. He's the one to kill."

"You're wrong. He got his orders from the bank. The bank told him, 'Clear those people out or it's your job.'"

"Well, there's a president of the bank. There's a board of directors. I'll fill up the magazine of the rifle and go into the bank."

The driver said, "Fellow was telling me the bank gets orders from the East. The orders were, 'Make the land show profit or we'll close you up.'"

"But where does it stop? Who can we shoot? I don't aim to starve to death before I kill the man that's starving me."

"I don't know. Maybe there's nobody to shoot. Maybe the thing isn't men at all. Maybe, like you said, the property's doing it. Anyway I told you my orders."

"I got to figure," the tenant said. "We all got to figure. There's some way to stop this. It's not like lightning or earthquakes. We've got a bad thing made by men, and by God that's something we can change." The tenant sat in his doorway, and the driver thundered his engine and started off, tracks falling and curving, harrows combing, and the phalli of the seeder slipping into the ground. Across the dooryard the tractor cut, and the hard, foot-beaten ground was seeded field, and the tractor cut through again; the uncut space was ten feet wide. And back he came. The iron guard bit into the house-corner, crumbled the wall, and wrenched the little house from its foundation so that it fell sideways, crushed like a bug. And the driver was goggled and a rubber mask covered his nose and mouth. The tractor cut a straight line on, and the air and the ground vibrated with its thunder. The tenant man stared after it, his rifle in his hand. His wife was beside him, and the quiet children behind. And all of them stared after the tractor.

---

1. "Chapter 5," from *The Grapes of Wrath* by John Steinbeck (New York: Penguin, 1992, pages 42–46, 47–53). Copyright 1939, renewed © 1967 by John Steinbeck. Used by permission of Viking Penguin, a division of Penguin Putnam Inc.

J. WILLIAM FULBRIGHT

President Harry S Truman called him "an overeducated Oxford S.O.B." Senator Joseph McCarthy called him "Senator Halfbright." President Lyndon Johnson said he was "unable to park his bicycle straight." But following the disastrous Bay of Pigs invasion of Cuba, President John F. Kennedy said, "You're the only one who can say 'I told you so.'"

James William Fulbright was born April 9, 1905, in Sumner, Missouri and raised in Fayetteville in the Arkansas Ozarks. His father, Jay Fulbright was a stern, hardworking, ambitious, and successful farmer. His mother, Roberta, who came from a prominent but not wealthy family, highly regarded the industry, thrift, and hard work that brought wealth. It was Roberta who taught her youngest son that the wealthy have an obligation to help the less fortunate.

Jay Fulbright, a frugal man, saved and invested his money, buying a bank, a retail grocery store, a wholesale grocery store, a chicken-and-egg business, a lumber mill, a retail lumber and cement company, an ice company, a hotel, a Coca-Cola franchise, and the local daily newspaper. He was a local conglomerate and soon became the third richest man in Fayetteville.

James William Fulbright, who preferred to be called Bill, was the fourth of six children. He was raised in a secure, socially active, and family-oriented environment. From an early age, he showed an aptitude for learning and athletics and by the time he entered the University of Arkansas (UA) at the age of 17, he was regarded as an "all-American boy." He maintained a straight B average while starring in tennis and football. He was also elected president of his fraternity, Sigma Chi, and the president of the student body, as well as being active in many other student organizations.

While at UA, his father suddenly died and after a period of uncertainty, his mother Roberta, who could be characterized as an early feminist, took over. She assumed control of all the various businesses her husband had run, including her favorite one, the newspaper, while holding the family together during the crisis. Through her newspaper activities she developed an interest in public life and taught the value of public service to her children.

After graduating from the University of Arkansas in 1925, Fulbright was granted a Rhodes Scholarship to Oxford. One of the goals for the Rhodes program was the training of future public figures, and Fulbright was an apt student. He soon became a popular figure on the Oxford campus, playing tennis, rugby, and lacrosse, as well as taking part in other campus organizations. He also discovered gaps in his own education and started to develop an intellectual curiosity that would stay with him.

He graduated from Oxford with the equivalent of a B-plus average in 1928 and spent the fall and winter on the Continent, where he observed and learned about European culture and political life. He returned to Arkansas in April 1929 to help with the family businesses.

While visiting a friend in Washington, D.C., in 1930, he met and courted Elizabeth Williams. They married in June 1932 and had two daughters, Elizabeth and Roberta. Meanwhile, Fulbright was attending George Washington University Law School from which he graduated second in a class of one hundred thirty-five. Fulbright was soon hired as an attorney in the anti-trust division of the Department of Justice, then taught law at George Washington before returning with his family to Arkansas again to run the family concerns and teach part time at UA. He started teaching law full time at UA in the spring of 1935. Following the unexpected death of the university's president in September 1939, Fulbright was appointed to the position. At thirty-four, he was the youngest university president in the United States, an achievement that brought him national recognition for the first time.

His tenure as university president was tempestuous and short-lived. Two years later in June 1941, he was fired by the UA board of trustees over a political disagreement with the governor of Arkansas. Once again he returned to working in the Fulbright businesses, but his restlessness soon caused him to explore other interests. Upon learning that the congressman from the third congressional district in Arkansas was going to run for Senate, Fulbright decided to become a congressional candidate. After fighting a strong campaign in the spring of 1942, describing himself as "just a boy from the Ozarks," he won the Democratic primary with the largest margin of votes in three decades. He went on to handily win the general election, which was normal for southern Democrats in those days.

The highlight of Fulbright's term as congressman came in September 1943, when the House passed the Fulbright Resolution, which called for the creation of an international organization to prevent future aggression. A similar bill was passed by the Senate, and the two acts are seen to have paved the way for the United Nations. The Fulbright Resolution brought him increased national attention and strongly identified him as a leader for world peace.

As he won recognition as an expert in foreign affairs, Fulbright offered a clue to his future directions in a letter to the *New York Herald-Tribune* where he coined the term "arrogance of power." He also started to plan for a run for the Senate. After the hardest political campaign he ever fought, Fulbright was elected senator of Arkansas in 1944.

Almost from the start of his thirty-year tenure in the Senate, Fulbright was identified as a leader in international affairs and a follower on domestic issues. One of his early victories was the passage of the UN Charter, approved by the Senate in July 1945 and in effect the following October.

Fulbright's abiding interest in furthering good international relations and peace led to the famous scholarly exchange program. Starting in September 1945, Fulbright introduced the original motion for the Fulbright Act and shepherded it carefully through the Senate and House. Finally, on August 1, 1946, he stood beside President Truman as he signed it into law. The law established the Fulbright Scholarship Program supporting the exchange of students and professors between foreign countries. It evolved into the leading international program of its kind. In its first fifty years, it awarded nearly a quarter of a million scholarships to students and faculty in more than one hundred thirty countries. In 1997, the *New York Times* cited the Fulbright Program as one of the innovative ideas that most changed education in the United States.

In June 1950, North Korea invaded the Republic of Korea, and a war was underway. President Truman committed American troops as part of a United Nations force. This led to the first of two serious errors of judgment by Fulbright; the other occurred at the start of the Vietnam War. During the critical early months of the Korean conflict, Fulbright, normally a leader on international affairs, was silent on the issue. It was not until January 1951 that he finally commented on the war, surprising his congressional colleagues with a request that the United States pull its troops out. Unfortunately, the die was cast by then and Fulbright's comments received little attention. His opposition to the war, however, coupled with his attacks on the corrupt Reconstruction Finance Corporation, made Fulbright one of Truman's most outspoken critics during the last two years of Truman's term.

Fulbright was also unpopular with Senator McCarthy, whose anti-communist witch hunt was in full force by the early 1950s. Fulbright was one of the first senators to oppose the powerful McCarthy and in 1954, he was the only senator to oppose funding for McCarthy's Permanent Investigations Subcommittee, the source of McCarthy's power. Fulbright was one of the leaders of the censure movement and had a hand in writing the resolution that finally brought McCarthy down (after he had been crippled by the Army hearings and the scathing Edward R. Murrow CBS television documentary).

Following his triumph in bringing down McCarthy, Fulbright returned his attention to foreign affairs. He was named chairman of the Senate Foreign Relations Committee on January 30, 1959, and was acknowledged to be the Democrats' leading spokesman on international issues.

In late 1960 and early 1961, there were growing rumors that the United States was going to support an invasion of Cuba by Cuban exiles. Concerned with the outcome, Fulbright prepared a memorandum for President Kennedy, saying the invasion would be "a great mistake," and urged Kennedy to stop it. Kennedy was not persuaded and on April 19, 1961, the disastrous Bay of Pigs ensued.

Fulbright was less prescient on the next international incident involving the United States, and it led to a major blemish on his career. On August 6, 1964, Fulbright introduced a resolution that gave President Johnson (who had assumed the presidency following Kennedy's assassination), unprecedented power to retaliate against North Vietnam for reported attacks on U.S. destroyers in the Gulf of Tonkin. Only two senators, Ernest Gruening of Alaska and Wayne Morse of Oregon, voted against the resolution. The reports were later proven erroneous; the resolution became the legal justification for America's entry into the Vietnam War.

Embarrassed by his failure to protest both the Korean and Vietnam Wars in their early days, Fulbright was quick to criticize President Johnson's decision in September 1965 to intervene with U.S. troops in the civil war in the Dominican

Republic. His warnings were ignored, however, and by the time the U.S. withdrew in 1966, some twenty-one thousand U.S. troops, both Army and Marines, had been sent to the tiny country. It was another foreign policy disaster.

In early 1966, Fulbright conducted a series of live televised Senate hearings criticizing the Vietnam War. They helped turn the tide of public opinion against U.S. involvement in Vietnam and also led to President Johnson's decision not to seek reelection in 1968.

Ever-contemptuous of the arrogance of power, Fulbright began criticizing the political machinations in Washington. One of his favorite subjects was the military institution, which he targeted in his book, *The Pentagon Propaganda Machine*, warning of the dangers of militarism to a democratic society. It was the first book by a political leader, to describe explicitly how the military purposely propagandized the unsuspecting American people into lavishly supporting a ravenous military machine.

Fulbright was less progressive on the issue of racial equality in the United States. His failure to support the Civil Rights Act of 1964 and the Voting Rights Act of 1965 (for fear of losing his southern constituency) contributed to his defeat in his 1974 campaign for reelection to the Senate. Despite this, he had achieved world prominence as a candid critic of U.S. involvement in the Vietnam War. He was one of the few American politicians, other than presidents, whose names are known throughout the world. Fulbright characterized himself as a dissenter and proved that a healthy democracy needs dissenters as well as patriots. He continued to write and speak out about his convictions after he left the Senate until his health started to fail in 1988 following the first of three strokes.

In a footnote to history, President Clinton, who had served as an intern in Fulbright's senate office in the 1960s and was also a Rhodes scholar from Arkansas, awarded Fulbright the Presidential Medal of Freedom in 1993. Ironically, like Clinton, Fulbright was an investor in James McDougal's infamous Whitewater land deal.

J. William Fulbright died of complications from a series of strokes on February 9, 1995 at the age of eighty-nine in Washington, D.C. In 1996, the U.S. Post Office issued a stamp crediting Fulbright with a career that "has helped to create a more understanding world."

Fulbright was a prolific author. His books describe his political philosophies and hopes for international understanding. These include *Old Myths and New Realities* (1964); *The Arrogance of Power* (1966); *The Crippled Giant:*

American Foreign Policy and its Domestic Consequences (1972); and *The Price of Empire* (1989).

The following excerpts are taken from *The Pentagon Propaganda Machine*. Published in 1970, the book inspired the award-winning CBS documentary *The Selling of the Pentagon* broadcast on February 23, 1971. Fulbright served as a consultant for the program. The book and the documentary exposed and attacked the use of taxes to propogandize the American people to support a bloated military budget.

SOURCES. Brown, Eugene, *J. William Fulbright: Advice and Dissent*, University of Iowa Press, Iowa City, 1985; Fulbright, J. William with Seth P. Tillman, *The Price of Empire*, Pantheon Books, New York, 1989; Fulbright, J. William, *Old Myths and New Realities*, Random House, New York, 1964; Fulbright, J. William, *Prospects for the West*, Harvard University Press, Cambridge, 1963; Fulbright, J. William, *The Arrogance of Power*, Random House, New York, 1966; Fulbright, J. William, *The Crippled Giant: American Foreign Policy and its Domestic Consequences*, Random House, New York, 1972; Fulbright, J. William, *The Pentagon Propaganda Machine*, Liveright, New York, 1970; "J. William Fulbright," *Newsmakers* 4, Gale Research, Inc., 1995; Johnson, Haynes and Bernard M. Gwertzman, *Fulbright: The Dissenter*, Doubleday & Co., Garden City, New York, 1968; Meyer, Karl E., *Fulbright of Arkansas: The Public Positions of a Private Thinker*, Robert B. Luce, Inc.,Washington, D.C., 1963; Powell, Lee Riley, *J. William Fulbright and His Time*, Guild Bindery Press, Memphis, 1996; Woods, Randall Bennett, *Fulbright: A Biography*, Cambridge University Press, 1995.

The Pentagon Propaganda Machine
J. William Fulbright

Here Fulbright has heard reports of extraordinary efforts by the Department of Defense to sell the American public a controversial anti-ballistic missile (ABM) program and has had his staff investigate the public relations activities of the department. The following excerpts recount his reaction.

From Chapter One:
THE STARBIRD MEMORANDUM[1]

The results of these inquiries amazed me for I had had no idea of the extent to which the Pentagon had been staffed and armed to promote itself and the military services. In use is every device and technique of the commercial public relations man and even some that he cannot afford such as cruises on aircraft carriers and "firepower" demonstrations by battalions of artillery and squadrons of aircraft, all designed to shape public opinion and build an impression that militarism is good for you.

A most unsettling aspect of these various campaigns was the scant attention the disclosure of their existence attracted and the lack of reaction from the American people who were being sold a bill of goods. This complaisant acceptance of things military is one of the most ominous developments in modern America.

It seems to me that we have grown distressingly used to war. For more than fourteen of the past twenty-eight years we have been fighting somewhere, and we have been ready to fight almost anywhere for the other fourteen. War and the military have become a part of our environment, like pollution.

Violence is our most important product. We have been spending nearly eighty billion dollars a year on the military, which is more than the profits of all American business, or, to make another comparison, is almost as much as the total spending of the federal, state, and local governments for health, education, old age and retirement benefits, housing, and agriculture. Until the past session of the Congress, these billions have been provided to the military with virtually no questions asked.

The military has been operating for years in the Elysium of the public relations man, a seller's market. Take the climate into which the Sentinel ABM program was introduced. Many people looked on it, as they now look on Safeguard, not as a weapon but as a means of prosperity. For the industrialist it meant profits; for the worker new jobs and the prospect of higher wages; for the politician a new installation or defense order with which to ingratiate himself with his constituents. Military expenditures today provide the livelihood of some ten percent of our work force. There are 22,000 major corporate defense contractors and another 100,000 subcontractors. Defense plants or installations are located in 363 of the country's 435 congressional districts. Even before it turns its attention to the public-at-large, the military has a large and sympathetic audience for its message.

These millions of Americans who have a vested interest in the expensive weapons systems spawned by our global military involvements are as much a part of the military-industrial complex as the general and the corporation heads. In turn, they have become a powerful force for the perpetuation of these involvements, and have had an indirect influence on a weapons development policy that has driven the United States into a spiraling arms race with the Soviet Union and made us the world's major salesman of armaments.

A Marine war hero and former Commandant of the Corps, General David M. Shoup, has said, "America has become a militaristic and aggressive nation." He could be right. Militarism has been creeping up on us during the past thirty years. Prior to World War II, we never maintained more than a token peacetime army. Even in 1940, with Nazi Germany sweeping over Europe, there were fewer than half a million men in all of the armed services. The Army, which then included the Air Corps, had one general and four lieutenant generals. In October 1941, six weeks before Pearl Harbor, the extension of the draft law was passed by but a single vote. Many of those who voted no did so for partisan political reasons, but antimilitarism certainly was a consideration for some. Today we have more than 3.5 million men in uniform and nearly 28 million veterans of the armed forces in the civilian population. The Air Force alone has twelve four-star generals and forty-two lieutenant generals. The

American public has become so conditioned by crises, by warnings, by words that there are few, other than the young, who protest what is happening.

The situation is such that last year Senator Allen J. Ellender of Louisiana, hardly an apostle of the New Left, felt constrained to say:

"For almost twenty years now, many of us in the Congress have more or less blindly followed our military spokesmen. Some have become captives of the military. We are on the verge of turning into a military nation."

This militarism that has crept up on us is bringing about profound changes in the character of our society and government—changes that are slowly undermining democratic procedure and values.

Confronted in the past generation with a series of challenges from dynamic totalitarian powers, we have felt ourselves compelled to imitate some of the methods of our adversaries. I do not share the view that American fears of Soviet and Chinese aggressiveness have been universally paranoiac, although I think there have been a fair number of neurotic anxieties expressed. The point is that the very objective we pursue—preservation of a free society—prescribes certain kinds of policies even though they might be tactically expedient. We cannot, without doing ourselves the very injury that we seek to secure ourselves against from foreign adversaries, pursue policies which rely primarily on the threat or use of force, because policies of force and the pre-eminence given to the wielders of force—the military—are inevitably disruptive of democratic values. Alexis de Tocqueville, that wisest of observers of American democracy, put it this way:

"War does not always give democratic societies over to military government, but it must invariably and immeasurably increase the powers of civil government; it must almost automatically concentrate the direction of all men and the control of all things in the hands of the government. If that does not lead to despotism by sudden violence, it leads men gently in that direction by their habits."[2]

During the twenty years Senator Ellender cited we have not only been infected by militarism but by another virus as virulent—an ideological obsession about communism. The head of steam built up in the country by the late Joe McCarthy has never really been blown off, and the extremists of the right utilize it to keep the hatreds that have developed over the years as hot as possible. This heat and the ideas espoused by these extremists produce such deceptively quick and simple solutions as "Bomb Hanoi!" Or "Overthrow Castro!" Or "America: Love It or Leave It!" If we would only proclaim and pursue our dedication to total victory over world communism, they say, root out the subversives—real and imaginary—at home, make our allies follow our lead in world affairs, all of our troubles would soon be solved.

This heated climate makes militarism luxuriate, for the military solution is also the simple solution. I am not, of course, implying that the men of our military forces are of the extreme right. They are in the main patriotic, hard-working men, but their parochial talents have been given too much scope in our topsy-turvy world. There is little in the education, training, or experience of most soldiers to equip them with the balance of judgment needed to play the political role they now hold in our society.

The nation needs its military men as brave and dedicated public servants. We can get along without them as mentors and opinion-molders. These roles have never been and, in a time when subtlety of mind and meticulous attention to questions of right over might ought to command us, should not now be their proper business....

From Chapter Two:
INFORMATION TO PROPOGANDA[3]

In November 1969, Vice President Spiro T. Agnew in his speech castigating television commentators gave us his view of a "small group of men" who help shape public opinion by deciding what "forty to fifty million Americans will learn of the day's events in the nation and in the world." There is another group of people much larger than that attacked by the Vice President—numbering approximately twenty-eight hundred—working to shape public opinion. This group is even less known to the public since its members are never seen or heard directly. It is made up of government employees and military men on active duty whose job is selling the public on the Department of Defense, the individual military services, and their appropriations.

This vast apparatus has grown quietly since World War II, obediently serving the aims of successive administrations and its own ends at the same time. Apparently its activities do not disturb the Vice President, whose quest for objectivity is directed at administration critics rather than supporters....

Very few Americans, I am convinced, have much cognizance of the extent of the military sell or its effects on their lives through the molding of their opinions, the opinions (and votes on appropriations) of their representatives in the Congress, and the opinions of their presumed ombudsmen in the American press. Even those few who have given serious thought to this matter have had available to them only sparse information about the military information apparatus.

To my knowledge, although this mind-shaping machine has now and then come under attack when its activities were so glaring and obvious that they could not be hidden, and although scholars in the communications field have written learnedly about it, no one has attempted to describe for the general public its parts and standard operating procedures.

---

1. J. William Fulbright, *The Pentagon Propoganda Machine*, Liveright, New York, 1970, pages 11–16.

2. Alexis de Tocqueville, *Democracy in America*, Vol. 2, Harper & Row, New York, 1965, page 625.

3. Fulbright, *Propoganda*, pages 25–26, 29.

RACHEL CARSON

When Rachel Louise Carson was a young girl, her mother took her for long walks in the woods and along streams, where she learned to marvel at the beauty of nature. She read the poetry of John Masefield, struck by the beauty of his words evoking the nature she observed. She would later combine both of these experiences and build a life and a career around them. She became a writer, scientist, and ecologist. Once dismissed as an "hysterical woman," Carson was an unlikely revolutionist whose words helped launch a worldwide environmental movement in the early 1960s.

The youngest of three children, Rachel Carson was born to Robert Warden Carson and Maria McLean in Springdale, Pennsylvania, on May 27, 1907. Her sister, Marion, was ten years older than she, and brother, Robert, eight years older. Her father was a quiet, reserved man who was a traveling insurance salesman and an electrician. He was frequently ill and unable to provide little more than the basics for his family. Rachel's mother, a former schoolteacher who was raised in a strongly female household, was an avid reader. She passed her love of books and her independent value system on to her children.

Carson grew up in a simple farm house on sixty-four acres outside Springdale, a western Pennsylvania river town. As soon as Rachel was old enough to walk, her mother taught her about the wonders of nature and the creatures of the woods, streams, and ponds near her home.

Masefield's poetry inspired Carson with its descriptions of the sea and world of nature, from the time she began reading. Sensing this was her destiny, Carson started writing stories almost as soon as she learned to write. Her first official publication was in the children's section of *St. Nicholas Magazine* when she was ten. It was a popular medium for aspiring very young authors of the time, and had published William Faulkner, F. Scott Fitzgerald, Edna St. Vincent Millay, and E. B. White. After four stories had been accepted and published in one year, Carson was convinced she could fulfill her dream.

She attended the Springdale Grammar School, earning mostly As. When illness forced her to take protracted absences from school, her mother tutored her until she was well, focusing on reading and natural history. Springdale didn't have a high school, so she later attended tutorial high school classes at the elementary school and then completed her final two years at Parnassus High School where she graduated first in her class.

Carson entered Pennsylvania College for Women, now Chatham College, in 1925, and worked on the school newspaper. She became fascinated by a required course in biology, and switched her major from English composition to biology. She graduated in 1929 magna cum laude and won a scholarship to continue her studies at Johns Hopkins University in Baltimore, Maryland. She supplemented her postgraduate studies with research at the Marine Biological Laboratory in Woods Hole, Massachusetts, where she learned about the ocean first hand. She received her M.A. in zoology from Johns Hopkins in 1932.

Between 1932 and 1936, she taught biology at Johns Hopkins and the University of Maryland. She was also hired by the U.S. Bureau of Fisheries in 1935 to write a radio show, "Romance Under the Waters." This allowed her to explore marine life and describe the beauty of it to radio audiences.

In 1936, after being the first woman to take and pass the civil service test, the Bureau of Fisheries hired her as a full-time junior biologist. Over the next fifteen years, she rose through the ranks to become chief editor of all publications for the U.S. Fish and Wildlife Service. She wrote explanatory pamphlets on conservation and natural resources and edited scientific articles for the service. In her free time, she turned her government research into lyrical prose, blending science and poetry in descriptions of nature. Though she would have liked to concentrate on her creative writing, she kept working for the government through the 1940s to support her family. She was providing for her mother and her sister's two orphaned daughters. Later, in 1957, she adopted her grandnephew, Roger.

In 1937, she wrote an essay entitled "Undersea" for the *Atlantic Monthly*. It was so well received that she was encouraged to write her first book, *Under the*

Sea-Wind, published in 1941. She wrote her first bestseller, *The Sea Around Us*, in 1951, winning the National Book Award for nonfiction that year. It has since been translated into thirty languages. She also received a Guggenheim Foundation Fellowship. The RKO film *The Sea Around Us* won the Oscar for best full-length documentary in 1953. The success of the book and film brought Carson fame and financial success, permitting her to resign from her job and devote herself to creative writing. Her third and final book in the "sea" series was the highly acclaimed *The Edge of the Sea*, published in 1955.

Carson's books about the sea describe a world that was unknown to most people, and further introduced them to the idea that human beings are but one small part of nature distinguished by their power to alter it, in some cases negatively and irreversibly.

Carson changed her focus and became an impassioned activist for nature. She was disturbed by the widespread and indiscriminate commercial use of poisonous chemicals developed during World War II, and she wanted to warn people of the dangers the toxins pose to the environment.

When a New England birdwatcher wrote that sprays designed to kill mosquitoes and gypsy moths were wiping out bird populations in a wildlife sanctuary as well, Carson was moved to begin writing *Silent Spring*, a book documenting the effects of pesticides, which would voice her outrage about them. This quiet, private woman who wrote so lovingly about nature had decided to challenge the beliefs and practices of leading agricultural and academic scientists—and the government. She called for a dramatic change in the way mankind viewed the natural world.

From 1957 until her death in 1964, Carson dedicated her life to researching, writing, and then defending *Silent Spring*. She interviewed scientists and others throughout the world. She sifted through thousands of research papers and articles. This muckraking led to a well-documented exposé of the dire environmental consequences that could result from the overuse of pesticides.

Silent Spring was published in 1962, and among the millions of people worldwide who were touched by it one was particularly suited to do something about it. President Kennedy demanded that the chemicals cited in the book be tested, and ordered his Science Advisory Committee to study the effects of pesticides. Despite a massive propaganda campaign and political pressure from the chemical industry, the president's Science Advisory Committee published a formal report that backed the main points of *Silent Spring*. It supported Carson's findings that pesticides were silencing many life forms. Kennedy described her book as the only popular source of dependable information on the impact of such chemicals. The committee then condemned the indiscriminate use of pesticides, changing the tenor of national debate: The question was not whether there was a problem with pesticides but what must be done to solve the problem.

The book started a worldwide environmental revolution. England's Prince Philip endorsed the book: "I strongly recommend Rachel Carson's *Silent Spring* if you want to see what is going on." The Book-of-the-Month Club predicted the book was "certain to be history-making in its influence upon thought and public policy all over the world." Nearly every country in which *Silent Spring* was published held hearings on environmental legislation.

Chemical manufacturers launched an aggressive public relations campaign and distributed brochures lauding the benefits of pesticides. Major industry associations flooded the press with articles declaring that these chemicals were mankind's only sure defense against starvation and disease. The chemical companies threatened to withdraw their advertisements from magazines and newspapers that reviewed *Silent Spring* favorably and gave doctors information kits to relieve patients' fears about chemical poisoning.

While Carson was attacked as an alarmist, she continued to speak out, reminding the public of the hazards of poisonous chemicals, and calling for new federal policies to protect public health and the environment.

Partially because of publicity from the chemical industry's campaign, *Silent Spring* was an immediate bestseller. More than forty bills were introduced to regulate pesticide use in various states by the end of 1962. The influence of *Silent Spring* has been compared to Tom Paine's *Common Sense* and Sinclair's *The Jungle*. In the longer term, her exposé of unrestricted pesticide spraying led to a ban on DDT and the founding of the Environmental Protection Agency. While Carson herself did not expect *Silent Spring* to bring about a complete change in environmental policy, it did help create the entire environmental movement. One biographer, Linda Lear, said Carson proved the way one person can make an enormous difference. Lear added, "*Silent Spring* is one of those rare books that really does change the world."

In 1999, *Silent Spring* was selected by a national panel of journalists and historians as one of the top one hundred news stories of the twentieth century. The Modern Library cited it as the fifth best nonfiction book of the century.

The controversy caused by her book still resonates and Carson's plea for the future is as relevant now as when she first articulated it in 1958. If some of the catastrophic environmental events envisioned by Carson haven't been realized, it could well be because her warnings created awareness and spurred societal responses in time to avert them.

Carson, who never married, lived in Silver Springs, Maryland, and summered in a cottage on the rock-lined Maine coast. After a long battle with breast cancer, she died on April 14, 1964 at the age of fifty-six in her home in Silver Springs, Maryland.

In 1970, the Rachel Carson National Wildlife Refuge was dedicated in Maine. President Carter posthumously awarded her the Presidential Medal of Freedom, the government's highest civilian award, in 1980. On May 29, 1981, the Rachel Carson stamp was issued by the U.S. Post Office. In March 1999, *Time* honored Carson as one of the twenty-five great minds of the twentieth century, explaining that while the threats from toxic chemicals are more severe now than when she wrote the book, "one shudders to imagine how much more impoverished our habitat would be had *Silent Spring* not sounded the alarm."

An excerpt from *Silent Spring* follows. "A Fable for Tomorrow" describes what could happen if we continue the unregulated spraying of poisonous pesticides. Although it was a fable, it shocked the world into recognizing the gravity of the situation. The remainder of the book documents how pesticides have "already silenced the voices of spring" in America.

SOURCES. Brooks, Paul, *The House of Life: Rachel Carson at Work*, Houghton Mifflin Co., Boston, 1972; Carson, Rachel, *Silent Spring*, Houghton Mifflin Co., Boston, 1962; Gartner, Carol B., *Rachel Carson*, Frederick Ungar Publishing Co., New York, 1983; Graham, Frank, Jr., *Since Silent Spring*, Houghton Mifflin Co., Boston, 1970; Hynes, H. Patricia, *The Recurring Silent Spring*, Pergamon Press, New York, 1989; Lear, Linda, *Rachel Carson: Witness for Nature*, Henry Holt & Co., New York, 1997; McCay, Mary A., *Rachel Carson*, Twayne Publishers, New York, 1993.

Silent Spring
Rachel Carson

Chapter One:
A FABLE FOR TOMORROW[1]

There was once a town in the heart of America where all life seemed to live in harmony with its surroundings. The town lay in the midst of a checkerboard of prosperous farms, with fields of grain and hillsides of orchards where, in spring, white clouds of bloom drifted above the green fields. In autumn, oak and maple and birch set up a blaze of color that flamed and flickered across a backdrop of pines. Then foxes barked in the hills and deer silently crossed the fields, half hidden in the mists of the fall mornings.

Along the roads, laurel, viburnum and alder, great ferns and wildflowers delighted the traveler's eye through much of the year. Even in winter the roadsides were places of beauty, where countless birds came to feed on the berries and on the seed heads of the dried weeds rising above the snow. The countryside was, in fact, famous for the abundance and variety of its bird life, and when the flood of migrants was pouring through in spring and fall people traveled from great distances to observe them. Others came to fish the streams, which flowed clear and cold out of the hills and contained shady pools where trout lay. So it had been from the days many years ago when the first settlers raised their houses, sank their wells, and built their barns.

Then a strange blight crept over the area and everything began to change. Some evil spell had settled on the community: mysterious maladies swept the flocks of chickens; the cattle and sheep sickened and died. Everywhere was a shadow of death. The farmers spoke of much illness among their families. In the town the doctors had become more and more puzzled by new kinds of sickness appearing among their patients. There had been several sudden and unexplained deaths, not only among adults but even among children, who would be stricken suddenly while at play and die within a few hours.

There was a strange stillness. The birds, for example—where had they gone? Many people spoke of them, puzzled and disturbed. The feeding stations in the backyards were deserted. The few birds seen anywhere were moribund; they trembled violently and could not fly. It was a spring without voices. On the mornings that had once throbbed with the dawn chorus of robins, catbirds, doves, jays, wrens, and scores of other bird voices there was now no sound; only silence lay over the fields and woods and marsh.

On the farms the hens brooded, but no chicks hatched. The farmers complained that they were unable to raise any pigs—the litters were small and the young survived only a few days. The apple trees were coming into bloom but no bees droned among the blossoms, so there was no pollination and there would be no fruit.

The roadsides, once so attractive, were now lined with browned and withered vegetation as though swept by fire. These, too, were silent, deserted by all living things. Even the streams were now lifeless. Anglers no longer visited them, for all the fish had died.

In the gutters under the eaves and between the shingles of the roofs, a white granular powder still showed a few patches; some weeks before it had fallen like snow upon the roofs and the lawns, the fields and streams.

No witchcraft, no enemy action had silenced the rebirth of new life in this stricken world. The people had done it themselves.

This town does not actually exist, but it might easily have a thousand counterparts in America or elsewhere in the world. I know of no community that has experienced all the misfortunes I describe. Yet every one of these disasters has actually happened somewhere, and many real communities have already suffered a substantial number of them. A grim specter has crept upon us almost unnoticed, and this imagined tragedy may easily become a stark reality we all shall know.

What has already silenced the voices of spring in countless towns in America? This book is an attempt to explain.

---

1. Excerpts from *Silent Spring* by Rachel Carson (New York: Houghton Mifflin, 1994, pages 1–3). Copyright © 1962 by Rachel L. Carson, renewed 1990 by Roger Christie. Reprinted by permission of Houghton Mifflin Co. All rights reserved.

I. F.
STONE

He was called a radical, liberal, Communist, iconoclast, prophet, independent, scholar, humanist, and a gadfly of American journalism. He was described as a short, curly-haired man with dimples and an unassuming manner; he was always skeptical but never cynical. His colleagues in journalism threw him out of the National Press Club in Washington, D.C., and yet he became one of America's most revered journalists. His reporting helped bring an end to one of the nation's most disastrous wars.

Isidore Feinstein was born on December 14, 1907, in Philadelphia. In 1938, he legally changed his name to Isidor Feinstein Stone, and always wrote under the name I. F. Stone, and was called Izzy.

The son of immigrant Russian Jewish shopkeepers, he had two brothers, Marcus and Louis, and one sister, Judith. His father, Bertrand, started out as a horse-and-buggy peddler selling housewares, acquired a fortune through retail sales and real estate, and lost it all in the Depression. His mother, Katherine Novack, started suffering from a series of nervous breakdowns after Isidor's birth. His parents were described as liberal Democrats.

The Stone home had an upstairs library where the introspective Isidor spent much of his time as a youngster. His introduction to radical thought and socialism came through books. By age twelve, he was reading Jack London's *Martin Eden* and Herbert Spencer's *First Principles,* as well as *The Nation* and *New Republic.*

Stone was destined to be a journalist from an early age. By the time he was fourteen, he was publishing his own underground neighborhood newspaper.

The *Progress* addressed international issues such as the function of the League of Nations, arms control, and colonialism. When his schoolwork started to suffer because of the time spent on the paper, his parents made him give it up after three issues. They did permit him to work as a cub reporter for the Camden, New Jersey, *Post-Courier*, where he covered local affairs after school. At fourteen, I. F. Stone was already interested in freedom of thought and had successfully started his career as a journalist.

Uninspired by his high school teachers and preoccupied with his extracurricular reading and journalism, Stone graduated forty-ninth out of fifty-two in his class. He was fortunate to be accepted at the University of Pennsylvania, where he studied philosophy. At the age of twenty, when he was a junior, with a lackluster academic record, he dropped out to become a full-time journalist with the *Philadelphia Inquirer*.

From 1927 to 1953, Stone worked as a reporter and editorial writer for a number of mostly liberal newspapers including the *Inquirer,* the *Camden Post-Courier*, the *Philadelphia Record*, the *New York Post, PM*, and its successors, the *New York Star* and the *New York Daily Compass*. He also was a regular, respected contributor to *The Nation,* the *New York Review of Books*, and the *New Republic*, and wrote a number of books on both national and international issues. His candid writing style about critical domestic issues and foreign affairs earned him a national reputation as a skilled, informed, and provocative journalist. His politics earned him a reputation as a radical and rabid anti-fascist.

In 1928, he married Esther Roisman, a bright and pretty girl from West Philadelphia whom he had met "on a borrowed dollar and a blind date" two years earlier. She was devoted to Stone and the two were inseparable for the next sixty years. He dedicated his final book, *The Trial of Socrates*, to her, "without whom this, and so much else of me, would not have been possible." They had a daughter, Celia, and two sons, Jeremy and Christopher, all three of whom became successful professionals.

In 1941, the National Press Club banished Stone because he brought a black judge to lunch at the club. When he applied for readmission in 1956, he was again blackballed. It wasn't until June 19, 1981, that the press corps finally allowed him back in.

One of Stone's favorite targets was FBI head J. Edgar Hoover, whom he described variously as "the glorified Dick Tracy" or "the immortalized secret police chief." In response, the FBI closely monitored and harassed Stone and his family for three decades, from the Depression to the Vietnam War. At the height of the McCarthy era, 1950–1954, Stone was investigated for espionage and only later exonerated. When his FBI file was finally released in 1994, it contained more than 2,000 pages. Despite his outspoken radicalism, he was never called before any of the investigative committees in the 1950s.

When *PM*, the legendary progressive New York daily, closed in 1948, Stone moved to its successor, the *New York Star*, which folded in 1949. Stone then moved on to its descendant, the *New York Daily Compass*. In 1952, the *Daily Compass* went out of business and, in the words of biographer Robert C. Cottrell, Stone became "an unemployed, middle-aged journalist and Old Leftist who appeared to be yet another victim of the temper of the times."

The quintessential outsider, Stone found himself considered a pariah at other newspapers. Even *The Nation* didn't have room for him, so he decided to start his own paper. With his $3,500 in severance pay from the *Compass*, a $3,000 interest-free loan, the mailing lists of *PM*, the *Star*, the *Compass*, and *In fact*, along with the support of his wife Esther (who became his secretary and business manager) and his brother Marc, Stone launched *I. F. Stone's Weekly*. It was a four-page, tightly written and controversial newsletter. It had no advertising, and it retained its annual subscription price of $5 from its launch date, January 17, 1953, to its final issue, December 14, 1971. Albert Einstein, Bertrand Russell, and Eleanor Roosevelt were among its charter subscribers.

I. F. Stone's Weekly promoted civil rights, shook up the establishment, stirred up a national public debate over the Vietnam War, exposed bureaucratic waste, spoke out for the First Amendment, and decried "American imperialism" in Southeast Asia and Central America.

Hard of hearing, he had great difficulty following speeches, press conferences, and testimony at congressional hearings. Because of his image as a Communist sympathizer, his traditional sources dried up. For these reasons, he developed the modus operandi that became his trademark. He would painstakingly monitor all of the material published daily in government reports, minutes from committee meetings and hearings, the Congressional Record, and the nation's leading newspapers. He was always searching for discrepancies, trends, and significant facts overlooked by other journalists. Following the paper trail, as popularized by Stone, is now the norm for investigative journalism. One of Stone's most fulfilling achievements was exposing charlatans in public service. He warned his colleagues and others, "All governments are run by liars."

In 1971, Stone shut down the *Weekly*, its circulation having grown from 5,300 to 70,000, citing health problems and increased mailing costs as the reasons. Three years later, Stone achieved a new kind of international fame as the star of the 1974 Cannes Film Festival. The film *I. F. Stone's Weekly* was a critical and commercial success. It documents Stone's painstaking information-gathering process. It is now required viewing in many journalism schools.

After Stone closed the paper, he continued to contribute articles to *The Nation* and the *New York Review of Books*. He also undertook a new challenge—as an investigative *scholar*. After teaching himself to read Ancient Greek, he spent a decade examining the life and trial of Socrates in 399 B.C. His critical analysis of a trial that happened over two thousand years ago was published as the bestselling *The Trial of Socrates*. Stone argued that the Athenians were right in finding Socrates guilty but wrong to sentence him to death. It was to be his twelfth and final book.

While Stone was universally described as the gadfly of American journalism by the mainstream media, his contributions went far beyond irritating naysaying. For fifty years, he was the scourge of the Washington establishment and corporate America, and the mainstream media, forcing them to acknowledge their errors.

Stone traveled the country, and the world, to lecture people about civil rights, peace, and economic justice. He used to tell aspiring journalists that if they expected to make great changes in America, they would be disappointed. "All you can do, if you're lucky," he said, "is change the odds a little." His own life contradicted his thesis: I. F. Stone changed the odds a lot.

Stone's early and persistent criticism of U.S. involvement in Vietnam helped end that tragic war. He pioneered a new form of investigative journalism. He was the link between the investigative journalism of George Seldes and that of Watergate journalists Woodward and Bernstein. He forced the nation to confront its own shortcomings in civil liberties. He exposed the hazards of nuclear testing. And he taught the nation how much a single individual can accomplish.

I. F. Stone died peacefully in a Boston hospital on June 18, 1989, at the age of 81.

The following is his warning about what might happen if the U.S. continued its policies in Vietnam. It is taken from the December 23, 1963, issue of *I. F. Stone's Weekly*. The lead warned, "The war in Vietnam is being lost"—a statement that could only be unpopular at the time. It should be noted that this alert came almost a year before the fictitious Gulf of Tonkin incident dragged the U.S. into the war, and nearly ten years before a peace treaty was signed, ending the longest war in U.S. history. It was also written before more than 50,000 American lives were lost.

SOURCES. Middleton, Neil, editor, *The* I. F. Stone's Weekly *Reader*, Random House, New York, 1973; Patner, Andrew, *I. F. Stone: A Portrait*, Pantheon Books, New York, 1988; Cottrell, Robert C., *Izzy: A Biography of I. F. Stone*, Rutgers University Press, New Brunswick, 1992; Stone, I. F., *The Haunted Fifties*, Vintage Books, New York, 1963; Stone, I. F., *The Trial of Socrates*, Little, Brown & Co., Boston, 1988; Stone, I. F., *The War Years: 1939–1945*, Little, Brown & Co., Boston, 1988.

I. F. Stone's Weekly

A CRISIS AND A TURNING POINT APPROACHES IN VIETNAM
(December 23, 1963)[1]

The war in Vietnam is being lost. Only a few weeks ago, Secretary McNamara and General Taylor reported on their return from Saigon that "the major part" of our military role there could be "completed by the end of 1965." Now Hanson W. Baldwin, our most respected military expert, writes (*New York Times*, 7 December) that "unless public support in the U.S. and among its allies can be maintained *during years of frustration*, there is no possibility of victory." The italics are ours. President Johnson at his first meeting with the press that same day announced that Secretary McNamara is going back to Vietnam on another tour of inspection. It begins to look as if the Secretary of Defense has become a commuter between Washington and Saigon.

It is clear that we are heading for a new crisis in South Vietnam; rebel attacks are mounting in size and frequency; the loss of arms to them is growing. At the same time Cambodia has formally asked Britain and the Soviet Union as co-chairmen of the 1954 Geneva Conference on Indochina to reconvene it. In August of last year, when Cambodia asked the Geneva conferees to reassemble and guarantee its neutrality, President Kennedy shied away from the idea. But this time the attitude of the American government seems to have changed. When the Foreign Minister of Cambodia was here to attend the President's funeral, he spoke with Undersecretary of State Harriman and was assured that we would not place obstacles in the way of reconvening the conference for this purpose. The first Geneva Conference met, it will be recalled, to end the Korean war, and then went on to end the first Indo-Chinese war as well. The new session could become a vehicle for the peaceful ending of the war in South Vietnam too. We are approaching a turning point, either to risk widening the conflict by intervening with our own combat troops, or settling the war at the conference table.

Prince Sihanouk of Cambodia indicated these wider possibilities when he called for an independent South Vietnam linked in a neutral confederation with Cambodia. "The reunification of Vietnam is the end to be attained but it is for the moment premature if not impossible, as responsible leaders of North Vietnam have admitted to me," said Prince Sihanouk (Agence France-Press, *Le Monde*, 4 December), adding that he thought, "the Communist camp would content itself with a South Vietnam completely neutral, as is Cambodia." An article in the *Peking Review* (22 November) confirms this view. China would like new trade ties with the West to replace the broken trade ties with the Soviet Union. Peace in South Vietnam would remove a major obstacle to such relations. In South Vietnam itself the National Liberation Front has made clear in a clandestine interview (*Le Monde*, 24 August), that it did not wish to "exchange one dictatorship for another." A democratic South Vietnam, an honourable and face-saving peace are possible. Unfortunately the U.S. public have been conditioned to such oversimplified and fallacious views on Asian foreign policy as to make negotiation difficult. The Cambodian Foreign Minister had a friendly talk with the new President, but if Mr. Johnson were a combination of Machiavelli and King Solomon we would still have trouble with this one. Three ideas widely held in this country are obstacles to a sensible settlement. One is that problems arising in the areas bordering China can be settled without taking its views into account. We had to negotiate with China to end the Korean War and we will have to sit down at Geneva with China again to end the Vietnamese war. The second is that neutralism is a menace second only to Communism, though the only one of three Indochinese states which is stable today, free from guerrilla war and any internal Communist threat is neutralist Cambodia.

The third obstacle to peace is the public acceptance of the CIA as a proper agency of government. The first thing to be said of the CIA is that in Southeast Asia, at least, it has proven itself politically incompetent. Its favourite Indochinese protégés, Diem in South Vietnam and Phoumi Nosavan in Laos, have been utterly discredited; the latter only opened the door to Communism, the former had to be "removed" when his failure and instability became too notorious. The one Indochinese ruler the CIA has always regarded with disfavour is the only one who has succeeded. Cambodia under Sihanouk's leadership, Majority Leader Mansfield told the Senate the other day (20 November), "has developed within its borders a remarkable degree of progress and political cohesion and stability and a level of human freedom and political participation in the life of the nation which exceeds most if not all of the other nations of Southeast Asia." Yet as the *Washington Post* said in a recent editorial (14 November), the CIA "has for a long time tended to consider the non-aligned Sihanouk as a pernicious fellow."

The second thing to be said of the CIA is that the very existence of a secret agency which boasts of "cloak-and-dagger" activities in countries with which we are at peace creates suspicions which poison our foreign relations. Both President Johnson and Secretary Harriman denied to the Cambodia Foreign Minister that the CIA has been engaged in plots against its government. But no one can be sure that the right hand of our government really knows what this left hand is doing.

Cambodia's first charges of a CIA plot were made in 1959 when it expelled Victor Matsui, an official of the U.S. Embassy, for activities incompatible with diplomacy; Cambodia claimed that rebel groups had been given radio transmitters with which they kept in touch with the U.S. Embassy. The next incident was the capture of an anti-Sihanouk emissary with 270 kilograms of pure gold for the rebels; he confessed that he had been in contact with CIA agents not only in Cambodia but in Washington. Later an elaborate "gift" was presented at the Royal Palace and turned out to be an ingenious bomb intended to kill the King and Queen; three members of the court lost their lives when it exploded. It had come by ship from Vietnam and its intricacy led the Cambodians to suspect skilled CIA hands at work. Then they learned that the secret radio was operating from a house in Saigon under the very nose of the U.S. and Vietnamese authorities, and felt this could not happen without their connivance. Another assassination attempt came last spring, when the President of Communist China visited Cambodia. Conspirators were caught in an attempt to mine the road over which he would pass with Prince Sihanouk on his way from the airport. The latest incident was the confession of a rebel infiltrator from South Vietnam that anti-Sihanouk forces worked out of strategic hamlets near the Cambodian border in close liaison with both Vietnamese and U.S. military authorities. These are the incidents which led Prince Sihanouk to break off American aid, fearing the aid agencies were a means by which hostile American agents penetrated his country.

Again I ask—in the wake of our own president's assassination—how long are we going to maintain what other nations consider an assassination agency of our own?

---

1. From *The* I. F. Stone's Weekly *Reader* by I. F. Stone, edited with intro. by Neil Middleton (New York: Random House, 1973, pages 206–209). Copyright © 1963 by I. F. Stone. Reprinted by permission of Random House, Inc.

EDWARD R. MURROW

In the 1940s and 1950s, the United States was assaulted by forces that severely jeopardized the social fabric of the nation. From 1941 to 1945, the United States was threatened by fascist forces bent on world domination. From 1950 to 1954, the United States was subject to a reign of domestic terror orchestrated by a United States Senator.

During the forties, the stories told by one broadcast journalist helped America understand World War II and the need to enter the conflict. In the fifties, the same journalist helped bring down the powerful and ruthless Senator McCarthy, a rabid anti-communist Republican from Wisconsin.

Egbert Roscoe Murrow was born in a small log cabin in Polecat Creek, North Carolina, near Greensboro, on April 24, 1908. He had two older brothers: Lacey, born in 1904, and Dewey, born in 1906. His parents, Roscoe and Ethel, were Scottish-Irish Quakers who were influenced by the liberal concepts discussed at meetings of the Society of Friends. Endowed with a strong social conscience, they taught their sons a sense of right and wrong, and to respect the property and opinions of others. Years later, Murrow would attribute his success, intelligence, and moral values to the fundamental training he received at home.

His father was a hardworking, good-natured, honest man who loved his family and respected his wife's intelligence. Egbert's mother, a former schoolteacher, was an enterprising, bright woman who taught her sons the value of diligence and setting goals. Her favorite song was, "You Must Hoe to the End of the Row," a virtue she followed and taught her sons.

When Egbert was six, the family moved west to Blanchard, a small farming and sawmill community about seventy miles north of Seattle, Washington. Murrow attended Blanchard Grammar School and later Edison High School, where he graduated in 1925. While in school, he spent his summers working on local farms. His experience laboring in the fields would one day influence his approach to one of his most powerful television documentaries, *Harvest of Shame*. After graduation, he worked as a logger for a year to save money before attending Washington State College (WSC, now Washington State University), and continued to work in the woods in the summers during college.

At WSC he met a dedicated speech teacher, Ida Lou Anderson, who would become his friend and his first mentor. She trained Murrow to become a star debater, and imbued him with the need for integrity in work and life that would complement his parents' training and stay with him forever.

His high school and college extracurricular activities centered around theatre and politics. In his sophomore year, he played the lead in George Kelly's *Craig's Wife*, listing himself in the playbill as Edward R. Murrow, officially replacing "Egbert," a name he hated. He served as junior class president in 1928 and was elected president of the student body in 1929.

In the spring of 1930, Murrow spoke for the first time on radio over KWSC, the Washington State College radio station. He spoke as part of a broadcasting class called "Radio Speaking," the first class of its kind in the nation.

He was elected president of the National Student Federation of America (NSFA) his senior year at Washington State, and after graduation in 1930, he spent two years as an NSFA representative, visiting colleges throughout the U.S. and Europe. At an NSFA convention in New Orleans he met Janet Huntington Brewster whom he would marry in 1933. While with NSFA, Murrow worked with CBS to develop a radio show entitled, *University on the Air*, which featured famous personalities. One of the first people Murrow arranged to have interviewed was Albert Einstein.

In the fall of 1932, he left NSFA and joined the Institute of International Education (IIE) where he worked as an assistant director until 1935. He also helped the Emergency Committee in Aid of Displaced German Scholars place two hundred eighty-eight refugee academics and scientists in U.S. universities. Murrow said later that the only good education he ever got was from the German professors who were thrown out of German universities by Hitler.

In September 1935, Murrow joined CBS as Director of Talks, assigned to locate speakers for broadcasting. He remained with CBS for most of his career.

He was promoted to European Director in February 1937, and sent to the London headquarters. His radio career began here with his coverage of the war few Americans had yet to hear about. It was during his broadcasts from London that he initiated his trademark opening salutation, "This," pausing a moment for effect, "is London," and his closing thought, "Good night and good luck."

His broadcasts from London rooftops, the sounds of bombs in the background, brought the war in Europe home and helped prepare America for its own entry into the war. "I think probably in a minute we shall have the sound of guns in the immediate vicinity.... You'll hear the explosions. There they are!" In London Murrow mentored a number of CBS correspondents including Charles Collingwood, Bill Downs, Richard C. Hottelet, David Schoenbrun, Eric Sevareid, William Shirer, Howard K. Smith, and Bob Trout. They later became known as members of an exclusive club called "Murrow's Boys."

He returned to America in 1945 where he was offered the position of Vice President for Public Affairs at CBS. He was no longer in a position to broadcast but he was able to develop several significant new programs including *As Others See Us*, *You Are There*, *CBS Reviews the Press*, and *Hear It Now*. He also created the first documentary unit at CBS.

In spring 1946, he quit the vice presidency and became a full-time broadcaster again. In the fall of 1947, he took over the CBS evening news program, renamed *Edward R. Murrow with the News*. He briefly recreated his role as World War II correspondent in 1950 when he spent six weeks covering the Korean War.

With Fred Friendly, a CBS producer, Murrow developed the half-hour weekly television documentary program, *See It Now*, in June 1951, a successor to *Hear It Now*, with Murrow as the narrator. The opening episode aired November 18, 1951, and it was the first coast-to-coast live network program. The documentary series proved both successful and controversial.

In nearly seven years, *See It Now* took on some of the most contentious issues of the day including communism, McCarthyism, nuclear testing, political corruption, and apartheid in South Africa. It established standards of excellence for television reporting rarely seen since.

One of the most explosive and forceful broadcasts made by Murrow was his series on McCarthy. The eleven McCarthy programs started in 1950 with Murrow's broadcast response to a *New York Times* editorial and ended on May 2, 1957, with his cryptic report on McCarthy's death. In taking on McCarthy, Murrow faced one of America's most powerful and feared figures of the time. McCarthy's anti-communist crusade, fueled by false accusations of disloyalty, ruined the reputations and careers of many people, driving some to suicide. Few others had the courage to confront McCarthy before Murrow. While Murrow did not lack the courage to challenge McCarthy, he thought it was the better part of valor not to tell CBS Chairman of the Board Bill Paley and President Frank Stanton about the McCarthy television program until shortly before it went on the air.

On March 9, 1954, Murrow educated tens of millions of Americans about the nation's most despicable demagogue. Through skillful editing and narration, he gave McCarthy the rope with which to hang himself. And that is what McCarthy did. The same words that had destroyed so many lives finally destroyed his own.

Television had never seen such an extraordinary public reaction. The CBS switchboard was jammed for more than nineteen hours after the program aired. There were tens of thousands of comments, by phone and mail, to CBS, its sponsors—and Congress. One report estimated the program generated in excess of a hundred thousand communications, overwhelmingly supporting Murrow. It was, at that time, the largest positive response a television program had ever had.

CBS gave McCarthy airtime for a rebuttal, which he used only to damage his public image further by seeming almost as a caricature of himself. He struggled to regain his power with an investigation of the U.S. Army but the hearings, which were broadcast live, only sealed McCarthy's fate.

In December, 1954, McCarthy was censured by the U.S. Senate for "contemptuous, contumacious, denunciatory, unworthy, inexcusable and reprehensible" conduct. It ended his political career. On May 2, 1957, he died, an alcoholic and broken man, from hepatitis at age forty-nine. But his legacy, a reign of terror and fear that plagued America for nearly five years, would continue in one guise or another throughout the Cold War.

Murrow's March 9, 1954, broadcast has come to be known as "television's finest hour." It revealed the power of the medium to fight evil by telling the people what was really happening. It marked the peak of Murrow's career and his postwar influence at CBS.

Continually bombarded with attacks by conservative columnists, right-wing politicians, cautious affiliates, and timid advertisers, Paley canceled *See It Now* in May 1958; the last program aired on July 7. When Murrow asked why, Paley said, "I don't want this constant stomachache every time you do a controversial subject." The lesson of what happened to America's leading television broadcaster for taking on sensitive subjects was not lost on other journalists.

While he did many outstanding documentaries after the McCarthy series, none was as powerful. However his 1960 documentary, *Harvest of Shame*, forced America to recognize the tragic plight of migrant farm workers. The documentary also nearly destroyed Murrow's reputation. When, in 1961, he was sworn in as director of the United States Information Agency (USIA) by President Kennedy, he asked the BBC not to broadcast the program. In his new role, he was concerned about besmirching America's image internationally. Murrow was widely attacked for trying to suppress his own program—and the BBC refused anyway.

Murrow was also criticized for a series he developed called *Person To Person*, a celebrity interview show that ran from 1953 to 1959. His resignation in 1959 was a sign of his increasing disillusionment with television. In 1958, Murrow had spelled out his dissatisfaction with the media in a memorable talk before the Radio and Television News Directors' Association Convention in Chicago. It was a scathing indictment of television's penchant for profit-making entertainment programming at the expense of news and educational programs. Murrow lashed out at those in broadcasting and their corporate sponsors for failing to be responsible to the public trust.

Murrow's health, impaired by years of drinking, smoking, and depression, started to deteriorate. In 1959, for the first time, he had to cancel a broadcast because of illness. However, he and Fred Friendly planned the creation of yet another news documentary program, *CBS Reports*. The new series debuted in the fall of 1960 with "The Year of the Polaris," a report on the submarine-launched missile. The best in the series, *Harvest of Shame* was originally aired as part of this series, and purposely on November 25, the day after Thanksgiving—while most Americans were still digesting their huge Thanksgiving dinners.

On January 28, 1961, just a week after his inauguration, President Kennedy asked Murrow to be director of the USIA. Increasingly disenchanted by what he saw in television, Murrow was ready to leave broadcasting and he accepted the president's offer. He was unanimously confirmed by the U.S. Senate and sworn in as director by Kennedy himself on March 21. Despite his health, he traveled to Europe and Asia on behalf of the USIA. On October 2, he collapsed in Teheran. He was flown home where doctors examined him and found a spot on his left lung. They did not think it was cancerous.

Shortly after Kennedy was assassinated on November 22, 1963, Murrow submitted his resignation from the USIA to the new president, Lyndon B. Johnson. His health continued to fail and on November 8, 1964, he was admitted to New York Hospital where a tumor was found near his brain and removed, on November 18. Despite objections from his doctors, he was released from the hospital on December 24 and returned to his beloved farm on Quaker Hill. On April 25, 1965, Edward R. Murrow turned fifty-seven. He died two days later.

Among the thousands of broadcasts Murrow made, many of them dealing with critical issues, the ones that affected America most were those dealing with Joseph McCarthy. The following five excerpts were broadcast between March 10, 1950, and May 2, 1957. They were all broadcast on CBS radio, with the exception of the March 9, 1954 excerpt—the conclusion to Murrow's legendary half-hour *See It Now* television program on McCarthy. The material is excerpted from *In Search of Light: The Broadcasts of Edward R. Murrow 1938–1961*, edited by Edward Bliss, Jr.

SOURCES. Bliss, Edward, Jr., editor, *In Search of Light: The Broadcasts of Edward R. Murrow 1938–1961*, Macmillan, London, 1968; Finkelstein, Norman H., *With Heroic Truth: The Life of Edward R. Murrow*, Clarion Books, New York, 1997; Friendly, Fred W., *Due To Circumstances Beyond Our Control ...*, Vintage Books, New York, 1967; Gates, Gary Paul, *Air Time: The Inside Story of CBS News*, Berkley Books, New York, 1979; Kendrick, Alexander, *Prime Time: The Life of Edward R. Murrow*, Little, Brown & Co., Boston, 1969; Murrow, Edward R. and Fred W. Friendly, editors, *See It Now*, Simon & Schuster, New York, 1955; Persico, Joseph E., *Edward R. Murrow: An American Original*, McGraw-Hill Publishing Co., New York, 1988; Smith, R. Franklin, *Edward R. Murrow: The War Years*, New Issues Press, Western Michigan University, Kalamazoo, Michigan, 1978; Sperber, A. M., *Murrow: His Life and Times*, Freundlich Books, New York, 1986; Winfield, Betty Houchin and Lois B. DeFleur, *The Edward R. Murrow Heritage: Challenge for the Future*, Iowa State University Press, Ames, 1986.

CBS News Broadcasts
Edward R. Murrow

MARCH 10, 1950[1]

Today's *New York Times*, in an unusually free-swinging lead editorial, thinks maybe we are not sufficiently grateful for people like Senator McCarthy; he may cause us to think about this matter of guilt by association. And anybody who does much thinking on the principle of the right to join things is likely to find that it is pretty closely tied up with ancient American traditions and liberties....

The *Times* concludes its editorial in this fashion: "If these good old American principles are again generally accepted, some of us may feel like organizing an organization to raise money to set up a plaque, or something, in honour of Senator McCarthy. We will just have to hope that no communists, or fellow-travelers, will join this organization. But if they should, we do not believe the other members of the organization can properly be denounced in Congress, or subjected to other cruel and unusual punishment."

I don't know about that suggestion of raising money to set up a plaque, or something, in honour of Senator McCarthy, but in my opinion the *New York Times* deserves a scroll, or something, for having used the Senator as the rather unsubstantial peg on which to hang an editorial with a good cutting edge, reminding us in these rather hysterical days that "guilt by association" is, in the true sense, an un-American doctrine.

FEBRUARY 23, 1954[2]

When the transcript of a sensational attack by Senator McCarthy on a witness is published, it is natural to expect it to supply the reason for the attack. Senator McCarthy last night read passages from the transcript of his examination of General Ralph Zwicker, commandant of Fort Kilmer. That was in a speech accepting a gold medal from the Sons of the American Revolution. Now the whole transcript of the general's examination has been published. It fails to answer the question that needs clarification if the public is to judge whether Senator McCarthy was justified in denouncing the general.

The senator at the hearing was trying to show that General Zwicker should have delayed the honourable discharge of Major Irving Peress, a dental officer, which he had been ordered to give. The senator thought he should have done it because of evidence about Peress heard by his subcommittee. This evidence had been heard after the General had received orders to give the honourable discharge. The senator passionately denied General Zwicker's fitness for command on the ground that he did not postpone the action.

What needs to be made clear, if possible, is why the General did not act. He said it was because the evidence of the McCarthy subcommittee on Peress was about matters already known to those who ordered the honourable discharge. Senator McCarthy at the hearing presented the General with this analogy. Suppose a major was about to be honourably discharged, and someone brought him evidence the day before that he had committed a fifty-dollar theft. Would the General delay the honourable discharge? The General said he would, so as to check the facts. Then why not do it if the allegation was membership in a Communist conspiracy, Senator McCarthy asked. The way the question was put made it sound as though the general did not think that membership in a Communist conspiracy was as bad as a fifty-dollar theft. But the general patiently explained that he did not postpone the discharge on his own initiative because he knew of no evidence before the McCarthy committee which had not been known to those who ordered the discharge. That is, without new evidence, he couldn't interfere. He had not heard of any new evidence. And even the statement of an undercover agent that Major Peress had been the liaison between his [the agent's] Communist cell and the American Labour Party was not, he said, substantially new.

Surely the issue insofar as General Zwicker is concerned is whether the McCarthy subcommittee had produced evidence the Army had not known, so that the general would be justified in postponing the discharge. The transcript does not show that Senator McCarthy tried to establish that the evidence it had produced was of this kind. New or not, he used it as a basis to attack the fitness of General Zwicker for command.

Last night Senator McCarthy told his audience that he had been too temperate in the attack, and if he had it to do over again he would be even more vigorous. But he did not attempt to show that the General had been given the new facts he needs for action. All he did was to strengthen his attack. It is a familiar stratagem to strengthen an accusation without strengthening the evidence. In present-day America, charges are easily mistaken for evidence, something Senator McCarthy well knows.

People who have read only of the abuse heaped on General Zwicker may not realize what Army Secretary Stevens last week wrote Senator McCarthy about the Peress case. He told the Senator new procedures had been ordered so that another Peress case would not occur. He also told the Senator that he did not believe a man should be given a commission who refused to answer properly asked questions about his loyalty. This is what Dr. Peress had done in pleading the Fifth Amendment at the McCarthy hearing. It can't happen again, Mr. Stevens assured the Senator. But he also told him that what had been done could not well be undone. "The separation of an officer under circumstances such as this," he wrote, "is a final action, and there is no means of which I am aware by which the action could be successfully reversed." He said the only new fact available to the Army on which charges could be based was the refusal to answer questions before the committee. A previous case based on a similar charge, he told the Senator, had failed in courts-martial. All this General Zwicker knew before he testified. And so did Senator McCarthy. So what the Senator was trying to do was to maneuver the General into criticizing his orders and those who issued them. The General did say that he thought Communists should not receive commissions or honourable discharges. But he was under presidential orders not to testify on security matters, and when pressed to violate the order, he refused. When he refused, he was abused.

There may not be any permanent harm in this abuse, but more is at stake than a scolding by Senator McCarthy. What is at issue is whether a senator is to delve into departmental matters, goad subordinates into criticism of their superiors, taint them with insinuations of Communist sympathies and impugn their judgment and integrity to the demoralization of the department. This is not the way Senate investigations are supposed—or entitled—to function. They do have a proper and important role in our system of government. This is not the role.

MARCH 9, 1954[3]

Editor Edward Bliss, Jr., writes: A half-hour See It Now *broadcast was devoted to a report on Senator McCarthy told mainly in words used by the Senator while campaigning and sitting as chairman of his investigating committee. The purpose, and achievement, of the CBS television program produced by Murrow and Fred W. Friendly was to document publicly McCarthy's methods. Viewers heard Murrow say in conclusion:*

No one familiar with the history of this country can deny that congressional committees are useful. It is necessary to investigate before legislating. But the line between investigation and persecution is a very fine one, and the junior senator from Wisconsin has stepped over it repeatedly. His primary achievement has been in confusing the public mind as between the internal and the external threat of Communism. We must not confuse dissent with disloyalty. We must remember always that accusation is not proof and that conviction depends upon evidence and due process of law. We will not walk in fear, one of another. We will not be driven by fear into an age of unreason if we dig deep in our history and our doctrine and remember that we are not descended from fearful men, not from men who feared to write, to speak, to associate and to defend causes which were for the moment unpopular.

This is no time for men who oppose Senator McCarthy's methods to keep silent, *or* for those who approve. We can deny our heritage and our history, but we cannot escape responsibility for the result. As a nation we have come into our full inheritance at a tender age. We proclaim ourselves, as indeed we are, the defenders of freedom—what's left of it—but we cannot defend freedom abroad by deserting it at home. The actions of the junior senator from Wisconsin have caused alarm and dismay amongst our allies abroad and given considerable comfort to our enemies. And whose fault is that? Not really his; he didn't create this situation of fear, he merely exploited it and rather successfully. Cassius was right. "The fault, dear Brutus, is not in our stars but in ourselves."

JUNE 10, 1954[4]

Yesterday, after Senator McCarthy had named Mr. Fisher as a member of an organization which he termed "the legal arm of the Communist Party," Army Counsel [Joseph N.] Welch, of whose law firm Fisher is a member, became

JESSICA MITFORD

Although she was born into British aristocracy, raised in a castle, educated by a governess, debuted in an aristocratic yearlong "coming out" in London, and presented at Buckingham Palace, Jessica Mitford eventually rejected her royal heritage. She ran away to fight Fascism in the Spanish Civil War, became a dedicated Communist, and ended up in America achieving her own royalty as "Queen of the Muckrakers."

Jessica Mitford was born September 11, 1917 in Batsford, Gloucestershire, England, to Lord and Lady Redesdale. They had six daughters and a son. The Honorable Jessica Lucy Mitford, called Decca, was the fourth daughter. They lived in what some might feel was a fairytale existence, but Mitford felt it was as oppressive as a prison.

None of the Mitford girls attended a formal school. Only her older brother Tom was given that opportunity, as was the custom at the time. The girls were taught by their mother until they were eight or nine and then turned over to a governess who tutored them at home. In later years, when asked what education she received, Mitford would delightedly respond, "Nil."

By the time she was twelve years old, she started to develop a sense of outrage over the way poorer people had to live. She had been disturbed by the distinct differences between poverty and wealth she observed when her mother took her into the village to deliver small gifts of charity to the poor. It was also at the age of twelve that she decided to leave home as soon as she could; she opened a "Running-Away Account" at Drummond's Bank.

Growing up during the early 1930s, Mitford's political attitudes were influenced by the Depression, widespread unemployment, and hunger marches. Reading pacifist literature and following the left-wing press, Mitford first became a pacifist and then a socialist. Her political beliefs were also fashioned partly in reaction to her older sisters: Diana and Unity supported the Fascists. Diana would eventually marry Sir Oswald Mosely, head of the British Fascist movement, and Unity would move to Germany in hopes of marrying Adolph Hitler. Mitford, for her part, was attracted to her younger second cousin (and Winston Churchill's nephew), Esmond Romilly, who wrote anti-Fascist tracts. He completely won her heart when he went to Spain to fight the Fascists while he was still a teenager.

Finally, at the age of nineteen, Mitford rejected her family and social privilege, took her "running away" money, and fled to France to meet Romilly. From there they went to Spain where Romilly worked as a journalist for the Loyalist press. Despite her father's efforts to bring her back—he once sent a destroyer to Spain after her—Mitford and Romilly went to France where they were married in 1937.

They returned to England where they lived sparingly on what Romilly earned from his job at an advertising agency and what she made as a market-research pollster. In 1939, depressed over the signs of Hitler's progress in Europe and the death of their infant daughter from pneumonia a few days after she was born, the couple emigrated to the United States to start a new life.

For a while, they both did odd jobs in New York, New England, Washington, D.C., and Miami, where they ran a bar. When Hitler launched his offensive against Western Europe in 1940, they returned to Washington, D.C., where a pregnant Mitford stayed with friends. Romilly traveled on to Canada to join the Royal Canadian Air Force. In November 1941, he was killed in action while flying over the Atlantic. He was 23 years old.

It was while giving birth to her daughter Constancia in a Washington hospital that Mitford organized her first mass social action. When the nurses were particularly slow answering call bells, Mitford asked for all her fellow patients to wet their beds. The "bedpan protest" was successful.

Her hopes to attend journalism school were dashed because she did not have an undergraduate degree. Instead, she went to work at the Office of Price Administration (OPA) in Washington, where she met Bob Treuhaft, an enforcement attorney who shared her political beliefs. They both transferred to the OPA office in San Francisco in February 1943, and were married later that year.

They had one son, who died at age ten, and later, a second, Benjamin, born in 1947. Mitford and Treuhaft became increasingly active in fighting for civil rights and joined the Communist Party in 1943. In 1947, they moved to Oakland, California, where Bob joined a law firm whose clients included the CIO and the Communist Party. Soon afterward, Mitford was subpoenaed to appear before the California State Committee on Un-American Activities in San Francisco in 1951, where she "politely and quite elegantly" refused to answer questions about the Communist Party.

In 1956, Mitford wrote her first published work, a satire of the language of the communist left. The mini-book was patterned after her older sister Nancy's *Noblesse Oblige*, a collection of essays satirizing the language of the upper class. Mitford expected to sell about a hundred copies of *Lifeitself-manship, or How to Become a Precisely-Because Man*; instead, it sold some twenty-five hundred copies.

Mitford and Treuhaft remained members of the Communist Party until 1958. They left the Party because they felt it no longer was an effective force for democracy, peace, and socialism, and, even worse, it had become boring.

Emboldened by her first publishing success, Mitford started to write a book in 1957 based on the letters she had received from Romilly during the war. She expanded the book into a full autobiography and *Daughters and Rebels* was published in spring 1960. *Daughters and Rebels* brought Mitford certain respectability in publishing circles and she started writing a series of investigative articles that exposed a wide variety of society's "cherished" institutions. These included The Famous Writers School, the expensive Sign of the Dove restaurant in New York, Elizabeth Arden's Maine Chance spa in Arizona, onerous personnel procedures at San Jose State University in California, and NBC's censorship of a two-part episode on the dangers of syphilis. These articles appeared in *McCall's*, the *Atlantic*, and *New York*.

Mitford had begun a battle with censorship and corruption that would win her respect as one of the nation's foremost investigative journalists. It also inspired the *New York Times* to note that "Mitford's pen is mightier than the sword." And following the publication of "Let Us Now Appraise Famous Writers" in the *Atlantic*, which led to the demise of the Famous Writers School, *Time* magazine crowned Mitford "Queen of the Muckrakers" in 1970.

Her success with *Daughters and Rebels* and investigative articles encouraged her to pursue writing as a full-time endeavor. She wrote *The American Way of Death*, a scathing indictment of the funeral industry; The *Trial of Dr.*

Spock (1969), a harsh look at the prosecution of the famous pediatrician and four other anti-war activists known as "The Boston Five"; *Kind and Usual Punishment: The Prison Business* (1973), a devastating portrayal of the prison system in the United States; *A Fine Old Conflict* (1977), a sequel to *Daughters and Rebels*; *Poison Penmanship: The Gentle Art of Muckraking* (1979), a compilation of her investigative articles; and *The American Way of Birth* (1992), which warned of the increasing number of problems associated with high-tech dehumanized birth procedures and supported the use of midwives.

Mitford was working on an updated version of *The American Way of Death* when she died on July 23, 1996 at her home in Oakland at the age of seventy-eight. The revised edition, *The American Way of Death Revisited*, was published in 1998.

Her memorial service was an ironic tribute to the person who revolutionized the funeral industry. When asked what kind of funeral she would want for herself, Mitford always jokingly replied that she wanted six black horses with plumes and an embalmer who would make her look twenty years younger. While a carriage with six black horses and plumes at her memorial service was arranged for by friends with a Mitford sense of humor, the actual process was a $475 cremation, and no embalming.

The American Way of Death sold more than any of her other books and had the greatest impact on society. It started when she published an article entitled "St. Peter, Don't You Call Me" that appeared in November 1958 in *Frontier*, a small, liberal Los Angeles magazine. The article was prompted by her husband Treuhaft's efforts to provide affordable funerals for members of the trade unions he represented and his formation of the Bay Area Memorial Foundation.

A televized debate between Mitford and two undertakers followed, generating some good local reviews. Next came a call from Roul Tunley, a staff writer with the *Saturday Evening Post*, who had heard about the debate. He interviewed Mitford and wrote an article, "Can You Afford to Die?" for the *Post* in June 1961. Almost immediately, there was a national furor and more mail came into the *Post* than any other article in the magazine's history had provoked.

When Mitford suggested that Tunley write a book on the subject, he said she should write it herself. With the strong full-time research help of her husband, she started to write *The American Way of Death*. Early queries to publishers brought rejections, complaining that Mitford's sense of humor was inappropriate to the subject matter. Nonetheless, an editor at Simon & Schuster appreciated her wit and finally offered her an advance. It was published in 1963.

It was an overnight publishing sensation, partially because of the publicity the funeral industry itself had generated in a foolish effort to prevent people from reading the book. It went to the top of the *New York Times* bestseller list and stayed there for a year. The reviews were almost all glowing and the book became a major topic in the media. CBS made a documentary based on the book, called *The Great American Funeral*, and newspapers across the country did their own surveys of local funeral costs and practices. It was also a leading subject for radio talk shows, and funeralistic cartoons were syndicated in hundreds of newspapers.

Mitford went on a six-week book tour that generated large crowds after the funeral industry had tried to discredit her by exposing her Communist background, a fact she had never hidden.

More importantly, the book helped to change the way Americans thought about death, funerals, and burial practices. A forewarned public was no longer an easy target for funeral directors hoping to exploit personal grief. Because of the massive public outrage it generated, the Federal Trade Commission established funeral industry standards where none had existed before: The various costs would now be detailed and an acknowledgment made that embalming was not always required.

Mitford once told aspiring writers, "You may not be able to change the world but at least you can embarrass the guilty." She did both.

The following is a reprint of the first chapter of *The American Way of Death*. The selection reflects the caustic wit, wisdom, and poisoned pen she used so successfully to attack her subjects.

SOURCES. McCreery, Laura, "Queen of the Muckrakers: Jessica Mitford's Contribution to American Journalism," unpublished M.S. thesis, San Jose State University, 1995; Mitford, Jessica, *A Fine Old Conflict*, Alfred A. Knopf, New York, 1977; Mitford, Jessica, *Daughters and Rebels: An Autobiography*, Holt, Rinehart and Winston, New York, 1960; Mitford, Jessica, *Kind and Usual Punishment: The Prison Business*, Alfred A. Knopf, New York, 1973; Mitford, Jessica, *Poison Penmanship: The Gentle Art of Muckraking*, Alfred A. Knopf, New York, 1979; Mitford, Jessica, *The American Way of Death*, Simon & Schuster, New York, 1963.

The American Way of Death

Jessica Mitford

Chapter One:
MYTH OF THE TWENTIETH-CENTURY
AMERICAN FUNERAL RITE

O Death, where is thy sting? O grave, where is thy victory? Where indeed. Many a badly stung survivor, faced with the aftermath of some relative's funeral, has ruefully concluded that the victory has been won hands down by a funeral establishment—in disastrously unequal battle.

Much as been written of late about the affluent society in which we live, and much fun poked at some of the irrational "status symbols" set out like golden snares to trap the unwary consumer at every turn. Until recently, little has been said about the most irrational and weirdest of the lot, lying in ambush for all of us at the end of the road—the modern American funeral.

If the Dismal Traders (as an eighteenth-century English writer calls them) have traditionally been cast in a comic role in literature, a universally recognized symbol of humor from Shakespeare to Dickens to Evelyn Waugh, they have successfully turned the tables in recent years to perpetrate a huge, macabre and expensive practical joke on the American public. It is not consciously conceived of as a joke, of course; on the contrary, it is hedged with admirably contrived rationalizations.

Gradually, almost imperceptibly, over the years the funeral men have constructed their own grotesque cloud-cuckoo-land where the trappings of Gracious Living are transformed, as in a nightmare, into the trappings of Gracious Dying. The same familiar Madison Avenue language, with its peculiar adjectival range designed to anesthetize sales resistance to all sorts of products, has seeped into the funeral industry in a new and bizarre guise. The emphasis is on the same desirable qualities that we have all been schooled to look for in our daily search for excellence: comfort, durability, beauty, craftsmanship. The attuned ear will recognize too the convincing quasi-scientific language, so reassuring even if unintelligible.

So that this too, too solid flesh might not melt, we are offered "solid copper—a quality casket which offers superb value to the client seeking long-lasting protection," or, "the Colonial Classic Beauty—eighteen-gauge lead-coated steel, seamless top, lap-jointed welded body construction." Some are equipped with foam rubber, some with innerspring mattresses. Elgin offers "the revolutionary 'Perfect-Posture' bed." Not every casket need have a silver lining, for one may choose between "more than sixty color-matched shades, magnificent and unique masterpieces" by the Cheney casket-lining people. Shrouds no longer exist. Instead, you may patronize a grave-wear couturière who promises "handmade original fashions—styles from the best in life for the last memory—dresses, men's suits, negligees, accessories." For the final, perfect grooming: "Nature-Glo—the ultimate in cosmetic embalming." And, where have we heard that phrase "peace-of-mind protection" before? No matter. In funeral advertising, it is applied to the Wilbert Burial Vault, with its three-eighths-of-an-inch precast asphalt inner liner plus extra-thick, reinforced concrete—all this "guaranteed by *Good Housekeeping*." Here again the Cadillac, status symbol par excellence, appears in all its gleaming glory, this time transformed into a pastel-colored funeral hearse.

You, the potential customer for all this luxury, are unlikely to read the lyrical descriptions quoted above, for they are culled from *Mortuary Management* and *Casket and Sunnyside*, two of the industry's eleven trade magazines. For you there are ads in your daily newspaper, generally found on the obituary page, stressing dignity, refinement, high-caliber professional service and that intangible quality, *sincerity*. The trade advertisements are, however, instructive, because they furnish an important clue to the frame of mind into which the funeral industry has hypnotized itself.

A new mythology, essential to the twentieth-century American funeral rite, has grown up—or rather has been built up step by step—to justify the peculiar customs surrounding the disposal of our dead. And, just as the witch doctor must be convinced of his own infallibility in order to maintain a hold over his clientele, so the funeral industry has had to "sell itself" on its articles of faith in the course of passing them along to the public.

The first of these is the tenet that today's funeral procedures are founded in "American tradition." The story comes to mind of a sign on the freshly sown lawn of a brand-new Midwest college: "There is a tradition on this campus that students never walk on this strip of grass. This tradition goes into effect next Tuesday." The most cursory look at American funerals of past times will establish the parallel. Simplicity to the point of starkness, the plain pine box, the laying out of the dead by friends and family who also bore the coffin to the grave—these were the hallmarks of the traditional funeral until the end of the nineteenth century.

Secondly, there is the myth that the American public is only being given what it wants—an opportunity to keep up with the Joneses to the end. "In keeping with our high standard of living, there should be an equally high standard of dying," says the past president of the Funeral Directors of San Francisco. "The cost of a funeral varies according to individual taste and the niceties of living the family has been accustomed to." Actually, choice doesn't enter the picture for the average individual, faced, generally for the first time, with the necessity of buying a product of which he is totally ignorant, at a moment when he is least in a position to quibble. In point of fact the cost of a funeral almost always varies, not "according to individual taste" but according to what the traffic will bear.

Thirdly, there is an assortment of myths based on half-digested psychiatric theories. The importance of the "memory picture" is stressed—meaning the last glimpse of the deceased in open casket, done up with the latest in embalming techniques and finished off with a dusting of makeup. A newer one, impressively authentic-sounding, is the need for "grief therapy," which is beginning to go over big in mortuary circles. A historian of American funeral directing hints at the grief-therapist idea when speaking of the new role of the undertaker—"the dramaturgic role, in which the undertaker becomes a stage manager to create an appropriate atmosphere and to move the funeral party through a drama in which social relationships are stressed and an emotional catharsis or release is provided through ceremony."

Lastly, a whole new terminology, as ornately shoddy as the satin rayon casket liner, has been invented by the funeral industry to replace the direct and serviceable vocabulary of former times. Undertaker has been supplanted by "funeral director" or "mortician." (Even the classified section of the telephone directory gives recognition to this; in its pages you will find "Undertakers—

see Funeral Directors.") Coffins are "caskets"; hearses are "coaches," or "professional cars"; flowers are "floral tributes"; corpses generally are "loved ones," but mortuary etiquette dictates that a specific corpse be referred to by name only—as, "Mr. Jones"; cremated ashes are "cremains." Euphemisms such as "slumber room," "reposing room," and "calcination—the kindlier heat" abound in the funeral business.

If the undertaker is the stage manager of the fabulous production that is the modern American funeral, the stellar role is reserved for the occupant of the open casket. The decor, the stagehands, the supporting cast are all arranged for the most advantageous display of the deceased, without which the rest of the paraphernalia would lose its point—*Hamlet* without the Prince of Denmark. It is to this end that a fantastic array of costly merchandise and services is pyramided to dazzle the mourners and facilitate the plunder of the next of kin.

Grief therapy, anyone? But it's going to come high. According to the funeral industry's own figures, the average undertaker's bill in 1961 was $708 for casket and "services," to which must be added the cost of a burial vault, flowers, clothing, clergy and musician's honorarium, and cemetery charges. When these costs are added to the undertaker's bill, the total average cost for an adult's funeral is, as we shall see, closer to $1,450.

The question naturally arises, is this what most people want for themselves and their families? For several reasons, this has been a hard one to answer until recently. It is a subject seldom discussed. Those who have never had to arrange for a funeral frequently shy away from its implications, preferring to take comfort in the thought that sufficient unto the day is the evil thereof. Those who have acquired personal and painful knowledge of the subject would often rather forget about it. Pioneering "Funeral Societies" or "Memorial Associations," dedicated to the principle of dignified funerals at reasonable cost, have existed in a number of communities throughout the country, but their membership has been limited for the most part to the more sophisticated element in the population—university people, liberal intellectuals—and those who, like doctors and lawyers, come up against problems in arranging funerals for their clients.

Some indication of the pent-up resentment felt by vast numbers of people against the funeral interests was furnished by the astonishing response to an article by Roul Tunley, titled "Can You Afford to Die?" in the *Saturday Evening Post* of June 17, 1961. As though a dike had burst, letters poured in from every part of the country to the *Post*, to the funeral societies, to local news-papers. They came from clergymen, professional people, old-age pensioners, trade unionists. Three months after the article appeared, an estimated six thousand had taken pen in hand to comment on some phases of the high cost of dying. Many recounted their own bitter experiences at the hands of funer-al directors; hundreds asked for advice on how to establish a consumer orga-nization in communities where none exists; others sought information about pre-need plans. The membership of the funeral societies skyrocketed. The funeral industry, finding itself in the glare of public spotlight, has begun to engage in serious debate about its own future course—as well it might.

Is the funeral inflation bubble ripe for bursting? A few years ago, the Unit-ed States public suddenly rebelled against the trend in the auto industry towards ever more showy cars, with their ostentatious and nonfunctional fins, and a demand was created for compact cars patterned after European models. The all-powerful auto industry, accustomed to *telling* the customer what sort of car he wanted, was suddenly forced to *listen* for a change. Overnight, the little cars became for millions a new kind of status symbol. Could it be that the same cycle is working itself out in the attitude towards the final return of dust to dust, that the American public is becoming sickened by ever more ornate and costly funerals, and that a status symbol of the future may indeed be the simplest kind of "funeral without fins?"

BETTY FRIEDAN

In the late 1950s, Betty Friedan appeared to be a happy housewife and mother living a traditional middle-class life in the suburbs north of New York City. A decade later, she wrote a book that would change her life and the lives of women to come.

Betty Friedan was born Bettye Naomi Goldstein in Peoria, Illinois, on February 4, 1921, just a year after U.S. women won the right to vote. The eldest of three children, she grew up in a financially secure environment. Her father owned a jewelry store and her mother had given up her job as society editor of the local paper in order to raise the children. Bettye was encouraged by her mother to work on the school newspaper in junior high, and started a literary magazine in high school. Above all, her mother wanted Bettye to get the college education she never had. When the time came, her father encouraged her to leave Peoria for college.

At Smith College she was editor of the student newspaper, elected to Phi Beta Kappa in her junior year, and graduated summa cum laude. At Smith, Friedan used her journalistic skills and the school newspaper to promote political activism and took on the student government, the administration, and campus social clubs. She also published controversial critiques of professors' teaching.

When she left Smith for graduate school, she dropped the "e" from her first name, probably to separate herself from the small town image of Peoria.

In her first year of graduate school at Berkeley, she was offered a prestigious teaching fellowship. She decided to reject the fellowship because she feared she would end up as an "old maid college teacher." The feminine mystique, she later said, had claimed one of its first victims.

After leaving Berkeley, she did some social science research and freelance writing for magazines. Between October 1943 and July 1946, she was a staff writer for the Federated Press, a left-wing wire service that provided stories for newspapers, especially union papers, across the nation. For six years beginning in July, 1946, she was a reporter for the *UE News*, a union paper.

Friedan's work in the labor movement gave her a personal education in sexual discrimination and helped shape her emergence as a feminist. She lost her job at the Federated Press because she became pregnant, and her job at the *UE News* to a man who had more seniority.

In 1947, she married Carl Friedan, a returning World War II veteran who first attempted to make a career in the theatre and then switched to advertising and public relations. She kept writing under the name Betty Goldstein until 1955 when she started writing for women's magazines as Betty Friedan. In addition to being an acknowledgment of the change in her marital status, the Friedan name marked a significant shift from her being a political activist writer for left-wing labor papers to a free-lance writer for mass circulation magazines reflecting suburban middle-class ideals.

Between 1948 and 1956, she gave birth to three children, Daniel, Jonathan, and Emily. After the birth of her third child, the Friedans left the urban bohemian lifestyle they had in New York for a trendy stone barn in Sneden's Landing on the west side of the Hudson River in Rockland County, New York, just above the New Jersey border. A year later they settled in nearby Grandview in an eleven-room Addams family–type Victorian house. Between driving her children to school, participating in the PTA, reading Dr. Spock, putting on buffet dinners with the help of *The Joy of Cooking*, she started to feel trapped in her role as a traditional suburbanite. This manifested itself most visibly when the Federal census form asked for her occupation. She would put down "housewife"—but always felt discontented and somewhat guilty.

It was this sense of dissatisfaction, combined with an inspiration of what might be, that led her to write *The Feminine Mystique*, a task that would take five years. As she put it, "All the pieces of my own life came together for the first time." She recalled the discontent she had always sensed in her mother; the success and confidence she experienced from her journalism and political activism at Smith, her education in Gestalt psychology that led her to understand the wholeness of the situation, and to seek self-fulfillment. Also, her work as a labor journalist and political activist after Smith provided her with first-hand insights about the inequities in life. Finally, her own discontent as a wife and mother helped her understand the frustrations felt by millions of other women. All together, they led to her emergence as a leading feminist in the 1960s.

With the publication of *The Feminine Mystique* in 1963, the Women's Liberation Movement was finally underway, with the theory that women's unhappiness was caused by a society which "does not permit women to accept or gratify their basic need to grow and fulfill their potentialities as human beings."

Despite the success of the book (it has sold three million copies), it soon became apparent to Friedan that nothing was going to happen for women until there was an organized movement, similar to the black movement, to fight for equality for women. On October 29, 1966, Friedan launched the National Organization for Women (NOW). Like the book, NOW became a success and a major influence in the national, social, and political fabric of America.

In her second book, *It Changed My Life*, Friedan recounted the influences on her life that led to her all-consuming battle for the rights of women. Recognizing the need to reinvigorate the then listless women's movement, Friedan called for yet another massive campaign: women's participation in political power. On July 10, 1971, she opened the National Women's Political Caucus, which urged women to start taking leadership roles in the political process. She correctly predicted that it would not be long before women would have a significant impact in Congress, statehouses, and city and county offices.

Shortly after she was divorced in 1969, Friedan realized that opposing sex discrimination was only part of a woman's problem. She encountered the trials of single parenthood. She was concerned that the women's liberation movement didn't allow for the traditional aspects of women's experience such as "clothes, food, home decor, entertaining, hairdos, kids, and even happiness with men."

In *The Second Stage* (1981) Friedan declared the end of the first stage of the women's movement she had herself launched, undoing the feminine mystique and organizing to confront sex discrimination. It was time, she wrote, to "get on to the second stage: the restructuring of our institutions on a basis of real equality for women and men."

She challenged the direction of some leaders within the women's movement who contributed to the image of the anti-male, anti-family, bra-burning feminist. In essence, she criticized the movement she created, and separated herself from radical elements within NOW, which she felt no longer represented mainstream feminism. Radical feminists accused her of selling out while other feminists embraced her new thesis with relief.

In the 1980s and 1990s, Friedan focused her writing on aging, the economy, and the family. In *The Fountain of Age* (1993), aware of growing older, she acknowledged that while the problems of women were not all solved, it also was time for a transformation of consciousness about aging. She had found a new group of disenfranchised Americans who could benefit from her powerful advocacy. She attacked the "aging mystique" with the same intensity she had used against the "feminine mystique."

In *Beyond Gender: The New Politics of Work and Family* (1997), Friedan surveys the social order in the late nineties and calls for a new paradigm. She concludes it is time to move beyond identity-based, single-issue political activism to a more unified world of work, family, and community.

Betty Friedan revolutionized America's social structure and reshaped American attitudes toward women's lives and rights. In addition to NOW and the National Women's Political Caucus, she founded the National Abortion Rights Action League (NARAL), worked to pass Title VII of the Civil Rights Act of 1964, and campaigned for the Equal Rights Amendment.

As a visiting scholar at many universities and think tanks around the world, she had an impact on women's rights internationally. She has lectured to Irish feminists, won a debate at Cambridge University on whether feminism was good for men, and helped launch the Israeli women's movement with her contributions to the American Jewish Congress Dialogue on Women in Israel in August 1984. She has been named Humanist of the Year, Author of the Year, and in 1989 she received the Eleanor Roosevelt Leadership Award.

In 1999, a national panel of journalists and historians cited the publication of *The Feminine Mystique* as one of the top one hundred events that changed history during the twentieth century.

The Feminine Mystique set off a second American revolution creating shockwaves felt around the world. It exposed the "housewife's malaise" and examined the frustrating lives of countless American women who had been expected to find fulfillment primarily through the achievements of their husbands and children. It forced women and men to rethink how women were defined and what their roles and responsibilities were.

Below is a controversial excerpt from *The Feminine Mystique* that compares the conditions of the "housewife's malaise" with those of prisoners in the Nazi concentration camps during World War II.

SOURCES. *Beyond Gender: The New Politics of Work and Family*, The Woodrow Wilson Center Press, Washington, D.C., 1997; Friedan, Betty, *It Changed My Life: Writings on the Women's Movement*, Random House, New York, 1976; Friedan, Betty, *The Feminine Mystique*, Norton, New York, 1963; Friedan, Betty, *The Fountain of Age*, Simon & Schuster, New York, 1993; Friedan, Betty, *The Second Stage*, Summit Books, New York, 1981; Horowitz, Daniel, "Rethinking Betty Friedan and The Feminine Mystique," *American Quarterly* 48.1, 1996.

The Feminine Mystique

Betty Friedan

From Chapter Twelve, Progressive Dehumanization: THE COMFORTABLE CONCENTRATION CAMP[1]

I think it [progressive dehumanization] will not end, as long as the feminine mystique masks the emptiness of the housewife role, encouraging girls to evade their own growth by vicarious living, by non-commitment. We have gone on too long blaming or pitying the mothers who devour their children, who sow the seeds of progressive dehumanization, because they have never grown to full humanity themselves. If the mother is at fault, why isn't it time to break the pattern by urging all these Sleeping Beauties to grow up and live their own lives? There never will be enough Prince Charmings, or enough therapists to break that pattern now. It is society's job, and finally that of each woman alone. For it is not the strength of the mothers that is at fault but their weakness, their passive childlike dependency and immaturity that is mistaken for "femininity." Our society forces boys, insofar as it can, to grow up, to endure the pains of growth, to educate themselves to work, to move on. Why aren't girls forced to grow up—to achieve somehow the core of self that will end the unnecessary dilemma, the mistaken choice between femaleness and humanness that is implied in the feminine mystique?

It is time to stop exhorting mothers to "love" their children more, and face the paradox between the mystique's demand that women devote themselves completely to their home and their children, and the fact that most of the problems now being treated in child-guidance clinics are solved only when the mothers are helped to develop autonomous interests of their own, and no longer need to fill their emotional needs through their children. It is time to stop exhorting women to be more "feminine" when it breeds a passivity and dependence that depersonalizes sex and imposes an impossible burden on their husbands, a growing passivity in their sons.

It is not an exaggeration to call the stagnating state of millions of American housewives a sickness, a disease in the shape of a progressively weaker core of human self that is being handed down to their sons and daughters at a time when the dehumanizing aspects of modern mass culture make it necessary for men and women to have a strong core of self, strong enough to retain human individuality through the frightening, unpredictable pressures of our changing environment. The strength of women is not the cause, but the cure for this sickness. Only when women are permitted to use their full strength, to grow to their full capacities, can the feminine mystique be shattered and the progressive dehumanization of their children be stopped. And most women can no longer use their full strength, grow to their full human capacity, as housewives.

It is urgent to understand how the very condition of being a housewife can create a sense of emptiness, non-existence, nothingness, in women. There are aspects of the housewife role that make it almost impossible for a woman of adult intelligence to retain a sense of human identity, the firm of self or "I" without which a human being, man or woman, is not truly alive. For women of ability, in America today, I am convinced there is something about the housewife state itself that is dangerous. In a sense that is not as far-fetched as it sounds, the women who "adjust" as housewives, who grow up wanting to be "just a housewife," are in as much danger as the millions who walked to their own death in the concentration camps—and the millions more who refused to believe that the concentration camps existed.

In fact, there is an uncanny, uncomfortable insight into why a woman can so easily lose her sense of self as a housewife in certain psychological observations made of the behavior of prisoners in Nazi concentration camps. In these settings, purposely contrived for the dehumanization of man, the prisoners literally became "walking corpses." Those who "adjusted" to the conditions of the camps surrendered their human identity and went almost indifferently to their deaths. Strangely enough, the conditions which destroyed the human identity of so many prisoners were not the torture and the brutality, but conditions similar to those which destroy the identity of the American housewife.

In the concentration camps the prisoners were forced to adopt childlike behavior, forced to give up their individuality and merge themselves into an amorphous mass. Their capacity for self-determination, their ability to predict the future and to prepare for it, was systematically destroyed. It was a gradual process which occurred in virtually imperceptible stages—but at the end, with the destruction of adult self-respect, of an adult frame of reference, the dehumanizing process was complete. This was the process as observed by Bruno Bettelheim, psychoanalyst and educational psychologist, when he was a prisoner at Dachau and Buchenwald in 1939.[2]

When they entered the concentration camp, prisoners were almost traumatically cut off from their past adult interests. This in itself was a major blow to their identity over and above their physical confinement. A few, though only a few, were able to work privately in some way that had interested them in the past. But to do this alone was difficult; even to talk about these larger adult interests, or to show some initiative in pursuing them, aroused the hostility of other prisoners. New prisoners tried to keep their old interests alive, but "old prisoners seemed mainly concerned with the problem of how to live as well as possible inside the camp."

To old prisoners, the world of the camp was the only reality. They were reduced to childlike preoccupation with food, elimination, the satisfaction of primitive bodily needs; they had no privacy, and no stimulation from the outside world. But above all, they were forced to spend their days in work which produced great fatigue—not because it was physically killing, but because it was monotonous, endless, required no mental concentration, gave no hope of advancement or recognition, was sometimes senseless and was controlled by the needs of others or the tempo of machines. It was work that did not emanate from the prisoner's own personality; it permitted no real initiative, no expression of the self, not even a real demarcation of time.

And the more the prisoners gave up their adult human identity, the more they were preoccupied with the fear that they were losing their sexual potency, and the more preoccupied they became with the simplest animal needs. It brought them comfort, at first, to surrender their individuality, and lose themselves in the anonymity of the mass—to feel that "everyone was in the same boat." But strangely enough, under these conditions, real friendships did not grow. Even conversation, which was the prisoners' favorite pastime and did much to make life bearable, soon ceased to have any real meaning. So rage mounted in them. But the rage of the millions that could have knocked down the barbed wire fences and the SS guns were turned instead against themselves, and against the prisoners even weaker than they. Then they felt even more powerless than they were, and saw the SS and the fences as even more impregnable than they were.

It was said, finally, that not the SS but the prisoners themselves became their own worst enemy. Because they could not bear to see their situation as it really was—because they denied the very reality of their problem, and finally "adjusted" to the camp itself as if it were the only reality—they were caught in the prison of their own minds. The guns of the SS were not powerful enough to keep all those prisoners subdued. They were manipulated to trap themselves; they imprisoned themselves by making the concentration camp the whole world, by blinding themselves to the larger world of the past, their responsibility for the present, and their possibilities for the future. The ones who survived, who neither died nor were exterminated, were the ones who retained in some essential degree the adult values and interests which had been the essence of their past identity.

All this seems terribly remote from the easy life of the American suburban housewife. But is her house in reality a comfortable concentration camp? Have not women who live in the image of the feminine mystique trapped themselves within the narrow walls of their homes? They have learned to "adjust" to their biological role. They have become dependent, passive, childlike; they have given up their adult frame of reference to live at the lower human level of food and things. The work they do does not require adult capabilities; it is endless, monotonous, unrewarding. American women are not, of course, being readied for mass extermination, but they are suffering a slow death of mind and spirit. Just as with the prisoners in the concentration camps, there are American women who have resisted that death, who have managed to retain a core of self, who have not lost touch with the outside world, who use their abilities to some creative purpose. They are women of spirit and intelligence who have refused to "adjust" as housewives.

It has been said time and time again that education has kept American women from "adjusting" to their role as housewives. But if education, which serves human growth, which distills what the human mind has discovered and created in the past, and gives man the ability to create his own future—if education has made more and more American women feel trapped, frustrated, guilty as housewives, surely this should be seen as a clear signal that *women have outgrown the housewife role.*

It is not possible to preserve one's identity by adjusting for any length of time to a frame of reference that is in itself destructive to it. It is very hard indeed for a human being to sustain such an "inner" split—conforming outwardly to one reality, while trying to maintain inwardly the values it denies. The comfortable concentration camp that American women have walked into, or have been talked into by others, is just such a reality, a frame of reference that denies woman's adult human identity. By adjusting to it, a woman stunts her intelligence to become childlike, turns away from individual identity to become an anonymous biological robot in a docile mass. She becomes less than human, preyed upon by outside pressures, and herself preying upon her husband and children. And the longer she conforms, the less she feels as if she really exists. She looks for her security in things, she hides the fear of losing her human potency by testing her sexual potency, she lives a vicarious life through mass daydreams or through her husband and children. She does not want to be reminded of the outside world; she becomes convinced there is nothing she can do about her own life or the world that would make a difference. But no matter how often she tries to tell herself that this giving up of personal identity is a necessary sacrifice for her children and husband, it serves no real purpose. So the aggressive energy she should be using in the world becomes instead the terrible anger that she dare not turn against her husband, is ashamed of turning against her children, and finally turns against herself, until she feels as if she does not exist. And yet in the comfortable concentration camp as in the real one, something very strong in a woman resists the death of herself.

---

1. From *The Feminine Mystique* by Betty Friedan (New York: Laurel, 1984, pages 304–309). Copyright © 1983, 1974, 1973, 1963 by Betty Friedan. Reprinted by permission of W. W. Norton & Company, Inc.
2. Bruno Bettelheim, *The Informed Heart—Autonomy in a Mass Age*, Glencoe, Illinois, 1960.

MALCOLM X

He was called Malcolm Little, Big Red, Satan, Homeboy, El-Hajj Malik El-Shabazz, and other names, but he was best known as Malcolm X, one of the most hated, feared, reviled, and despised men of the turbulent 1950s and 1960s. He also was one of the most beloved, admired, respected, and influential men of his time.

Malcolm X opens his autobiography with a story his mother told him. She said she was pregnant with Malcolm in Omaha, Nebraska, when a party of hooded Ku Klux Klan riders galloped up to their home brandishing burning torches, shotguns, and rifles. When they learned his father wasn't home, they shouted threats at his mother and warned her to get out of town because "the good Christian white people" were not going to stand for his father's "spreading trouble" among the "good" Negroes of Omaha with his "back-to-Africa" preaching. While the story may have been apocryphal, it was one Malcolm told many times, and the first of a number of encounters, real or imagined, that would give rise to his early deep-rooted hatred for white men.

Malcolm Little was born on May 19, 1925, in Omaha, Nebraska, to Louise, an educated light-skinned woman from Grenada, the British West Indies, and Earl Little, an under-educated dark-skinned Baptist minister from Reynolds, Georgia. Louise's mother had been raped by a white man in Grenada and Malcolm was born with a light complexion and red hair. Malcolm "learned to hate every drop of that white rapist's blood" that was in him.

Malcolm had four brothers, Wilfred, Philbert, Reginald, and Wesley, and two sisters, Hilda and Yvonne. The Littles lived briefly in Milwaukee before settling in Lansing, Michigan. In 1929, the Little's home burned down after being firebombed by whites, according to Malcolm. Earl Little himself was accused of arson, but that charge was later dropped.

In September 1931, Malcolm returned home from school one day to find his parents engaged in one of their many arguments (his father would sometimes beat his mother). Earl Little stormed angrily out of the house and walked up the road toward town. Later that evening, he was found dying on the trolley tracks. Malcolm believed his father had been murdered by whites and left on the tracks to be run over. The police closed the case as an accident.

After her husband's death, Louise slowly deteriorated physically, emotionally, and mentally from the stress of trying to raise seven children at the height of the Depression. In 1939, she was committed to a mental institution in Kalamazoo, Michigan, where she would remain for more than two decades until another of her sons arranged for her release.

When she was institutionalized, the younger children were placed in foster homes. Malcolm, who had committed a variety of petty thefts and school pranks that ended in his suspension, was already in foster care for juvenile delinquency. At the age of thirteen, he was sent to a county juvenile home in Mason, Michigan. Malcolm attended the eighth grade at Mason Junior High School where he was the only black student in his class.

Malcolm was a little older than his classmates—already well over six feet tall—and he earned the respect of his peers. Showing early evidence of his leadership skills, he was elected class president in his second semester. He felt better about who he was and started to involve himself in both his studies and sports, and excelled.

Near the end of the eighth grade, Malcolm's growing aspirations were suddenly dashed when an English teacher he respected asked him if had given any thought to a career. When he said he had been thinking about becoming a lawyer, the teacher said, "That's no realistic goal for a nigger." Malcolm later wrote that "It was then that I began to change—inside." Where before he wasn't overly bothered by the term "nigger," he was growing to resent it, and started to let people know how he felt.

When he had graduated from the eighth grade, Malcolm wrote his older half-sister Ella and asked if he could come to live with her in Roxbury, a black section of Boston. Several months after his arrival, Shorty, a stocky young man who racked balls at the local pool hall, got Malcolm a job as a shoeshine boy at the Roseland Ballroom in Boston's Back Bay section. Under Shorty's tutelage, Malcolm became a zoot suit–wearing small-time hustler, playing the numbers, and smoking marijuana.

Tiring of the petty gambling in Roxbury, and attracted by the sights and sounds of New York, he soon moved to Harlem where, by his own admission, he learned to be "one of the most depraved parasitical hustlers among New York's eight million people." He was a bootlegger, drug dealer, addict, thief, pimp, male prostitute, and gambler. In the ghetto, he was transformed into "an animal, a vulture."

After about a year in Harlem, he returned to Boston at the age of twenty, where he formed his own gang, along with his old mentor, Shorty. After a series of successful robberies, he was arrested in February 1946, convicted on several counts, and sentenced to ten years in Charlestown State Prison. The penitentiary had small cells, no running water, rats, lice, and had not been renovated since its construction during Jefferson's presidency. Prisoners did, however, have access to books and Malcolm launched an effort at self-improvement, taking correspondence courses in English while reading a variety of books in the prison library. He immersed himself in history, politics, and philosophy. He also joined a debating club in the prison and trained himself to be a persuasive speaker and debater.

While he was in prison, his brothers and sisters in Detroit and Chicago had converted to a new "natural religion for the black man." They persuaded him to write to Elijah Muhammad, the leader of the Nation of Islam, an Islam-based religion. Muhammad responded and Malcolm started writing him almost daily. By early 1949, he was converted to the Nation of Islam, which decried the domination of whites and the oppression of blacks. Malcolm would frequently refer to the "devil white man" and the "brainwashed black man."

After his parole from prison in 1952, he met with Elijah Muhammad, and officially joined the Nation of Islam under Elijah Muhammad's personal guidance. He also received the name "X." To Malcolm, the X replaced the "white slave-master name of Little."

Malcolm moved to Detroit where he stayed with his brother, Wilfred, and joined the Detroit Temple Number One of the Nation of Islam, the religion's first temple, started in 1931. He was inspired to proselytize and applied his persuasive skills to converting blacks he met in Detroit's ghetto bars, poolrooms, and street corners. Within a few months, Temple Number One tripled its membership and Malcolm X again attracted the attention of Elijah Muhammad. Before long, Malcolm X was named Detroit Temple Number One's assistant minister, and Elijah was treating him like a son.

After his success in Detroit, Elijah sent Malcolm X to Boston and Philadelphia, where he established new temples. In June 1954, Elijah named him minister of the fledgling storefront Temple Seven in New York City, which had the largest black population in the country.

By 1956, the Nation of Islam had grown sizably, due mostly to the recruiting skills of Malcolm X. Its membership soared from a few hundred to tens of thousands. Malcolm's role within the Nation of Islam had also grown rapidly. Elijah Muhammad announced, "Thank Allah for my brother minister, Malcolm," and named him the chief minister and top administrator of the Nation of Islam.

During a trip to his home temple in Detroit, Malcolm X met a young member of the temple named Sister Betty X. She was a tall, intelligent young woman with a regal bearing. He was immediately attracted to her, courted her briefly, and, with Elijah Muhammad's approval, they were married in January 1958. They had six children.

Malcolm X promoted black power in his temple talks, his newspaper column that appeared first in Harlem's *Amsterdam News* and later in the *Los Angeles Herald Dispatch*, and in radio and television interviews. To further reach people, he launched *Muhammad Speaks*, the first national black Muslim newspaper. It eventually reached a circulation of 900,000.

It wasn't until mid-July 1959 that the black Muslim movement attracted the attention of white America. An interview on *The Mike Wallace Show*, a CBS television documentary series, entitled "The Hate That Hate Produced," focused national attention on Malcolm X and his campaign for black rights.

With his contentious charge that all whites were devils and slave masters, and that the only solution was black separatism, Malcolm became a popular guest on radio and television programs and a standing room–only speaker on college campuses. He came to be perceived as the leader of the black Muslim movement, an impression not lost on Elijah Muhammad.

Meanwhile, Elijah Muhammad's health started to decline. When speaking he would be seized by severe coughing spells and was increasingly unable to attend mass meetings planned in advance. Malcolm X often filled in for him at these rallies. As a result of this, as well as the press Malcolm was getting, some of Elijah Muhammad's close associates, including his children, who were jealous of the attention their father had given him, started to spread rumors about Malcolm X. He was accused of trying to oust Elijah to take over the Nation of Islam. At the same time, there was an increasing number of rumors that Elijah Muhammad was an adulterer. Disappointed by the criticism leveled at him by the Nation of Islam's hierarchy and disillusioned by his mentor's reported infidelity, Malcolm X became critical of Elijah Muhammad.

The real break came on December 1, 1963, just nine days after the assassination of President Kennedy. In a question-and-answer session following a talk at the Manhattan Center, Malcolm X was asked about Kennedy's assassination. He immediately replied, "Chickens coming home to roost never did make me sad; they've always made me glad." The irreverent remark received national media coverage and widespread criticism and prompted Elijah Muhammad to call Malcolm X to Chicago for a meeting. He said that negative comments about Kennedy had damaged the Nation of Islam's image, and he ordered Malcolm X not to make any more public statements, even forbidding him from speaking at his own temple.

Shortly thereafter, Malcolm announced he was leaving the Nation of Islam. After being released from the constraints of the "silencing," Malcolm X held a press conference. He said, "I am going to organize and head a new mosque in New York City known as the Muslim Mosque, Inc."

From his new base, Malcolm started to make conciliatory gestures toward the Civil Rights movement and began to articulate a more political black nationalism. He argued that blacks should control the politics within their own communities and encouraged his followers to use the ballot to effect change.

Feeling the need for a spiritual renewal, he then decided to go to Mecca to remake himself into an authentic Muslim. The 1964 pilgrimage marked the next significant period in his life. After nearly a lifetime of hating "white devils," he started to reappraise his attitude: "In the Muslim world, I had seen that men with white complexions were more genuinely brotherly than anyone else had ever been." It was the start of his "radical alteration" on the topic of white men.

He began to rethink his ideas about separatism and integration. After his epiphany, he wrote a letter to his wife about his new understanding of America's racial dilemma. Considering it an important letter, he sent copies of the letter to his friends, colleagues, and his assistants at the newly formed Muslim Mosque, Inc. in Harlem. It came to be known as the "Letter From Mecca." He signed it with his new Muslim name, El-Hajj Malik El-Shabazz.

After a visit to Africa, he returned home to preach his new beliefs and to "destroy the racist cancer that is malignant in the body of America."

Seeing that the Muslim Mosque, Inc., was faltering, he established a new organization, the Organization of Afro-American Unity (OAAU). The OAAU was to be Malcolm's vehicle for forging strong links between blacks in America and Africa. But it was not to be. Malcolm X had become increasingly concerned about his safety, and with good reason. He had received several death threats, and his home in Queens, New York, was firebombed on February 14, 1965. He accused the Nation of Islam of attempting to kill him. He also predicted that his next talk, scheduled for the Audubon Ballroom on Sunday, February 21, would be one of his last.

At 3:10 p.m., on Sunday, February 21, Malcolm X strode onto the stage of the Audubon Ballroom in Harlem and greeted the audience with his customary "Assalaam alaikum." Suddenly there was a scuffle in the audience. A smoke bomb went off and, amidst the confusion, a man in the front row stood up and fired a shot directly at Malcolm's chest. He fell to the floor. Two other men joined the original assailant emptying their guns into his motionless body. He was rushed to the nearby Columbia-Presbyterian Hospital where he was declared dead at 3:30 p.m.

On March 11, 1966, three men were convicted of first-degree murder and sentenced to life imprisonment: Talmadge Hayer, Norman 3X Butler and Thomas 15X Johnson. In March 1998, Louis Farrakhan, now leader of the Nation of Islam, would appoint Butler, now Muhammad Abdul Aziz, to head Temple Seven, the same Harlem house of worship that Malcolm X had founded. Butler, who denied any role in the assassination, served nineteen years in prison for killing Malcolm X before being paroled in 1985.

For all of the controversy that swirled around him throughout his life, Malcolm X, El-Hajj Malik El-Shabazz, left a legacy that assures his place in history. Malcolm X raised the consciousness of twenty-two million blacks in America. He caused black Americans to look at themselves in a new way and taught them to be proud of their race. He mobilized a dormant rage into a strong and effective political force. He helped black Americans find personal strength, courage, and pride.

His influence was not on blacks alone. He had an enormous impact on white Americans as well. He exposed the dangers of white supremacy and facilitated some of the successes of the civil rights movement that were to come.

Malcolm X was 39 years old when he died, a martyr. *The Autobiography of Malcolm X*, written with the assistance of Alex Haley, author of *Roots*, was published in 1965. In 1999, it was named one of the top one hundred nonfiction books of the twentieth century by Modern Library.

The following two excerpts were selected as reflections of two stages of Malcolm X's life as a Muslim. The first is excerpted from the famous *Playboy* interview in May 1963 with Alex Haley, representing the period when Malcolm X was preaching segregation and hatred of whites. The second, "Letter from Mecca," was written by El-Hajj Malik El-Shabazz in April 1964, and shows his changing attitudes toward whites and integration. In *The Autobiography of Malcolm X*, as told to Alex Haley, he prefaces the letter with the words, "Here is what I wrote... from my heart."

SOURCES. Breitman, George, editor, *Malcolm X Speaks: Selected Speeches and Statements*, Grove Press, Inc., New York, 1965; Bruce, Perry, *Malcolm: The Life of a Man Who Changed Black America*, Station Hill, Barrytown, New York, 1991; Clark, Kenneth B., *King, Malcolm, Baldwin: Three Interviews*, Wesleyan University Press, Hanover, New Hampshire, 1985; Cleage, Rev. Albert and George Breitman, *Myths About Malcolm X: Two Views*, Merit Publishers, New York, 1968; Epps, Archie, editor, *The Speeches of Malcolm X at Harvard*, William Morrow & Co., New York, 1968; Gallen, David, editor, *Malcolm X, As They Knew Him*, Carroll & Graf, New York, 1992; Haley, Alex and Malcolm X, *The Autobiography of Malcolm X*, Grove Press, Inc., New York, 1964.

From Alex Haley's Playboy Interview
(May 1963)

PLAYBOY: In a recent interview, Negro author-lecturer Louis Lomax said, "Eighty percent, if not more, of America's twenty million negroes vibrate sympathetically with the muslims' indictment of the white power structure. But this does not mean we agree with them in their doctrines of estrangement or with their proposed resolutions of the race problem." Does this view represent a consensus of opinion among negroes? And if so, is it possible that your separationist and anti-Christian doctrines have the effect of alienating many of your own race?

MALCOLM X: Sir, you make a mistake listening to people who tell you how much our stand alienates black men in this country. I'd guess actually we have the sympathy of ninety percent of the black people. There are twenty million dormant Muslims in America. A Muslim to us is somebody who is for the black man; I don't care if he goes to the Baptist Church seven days a week. The Honorable Elijah Muhammad says that a black man is born a Muslim by nature. There are millions of Muslims not aware of it now. All of them will be Muslims when they wake up; that's what's meant by the resurrection.

Sir, I'm going to tell you a secret: The black man is a whole lot smarter than white people think he is. The black man has survived in this country by fooling the white man. He's been dancing and grinning and white men never guessed what he was thinking. Now you'll hear the bourgeois negroes pretending to be alienated, but they're just making the white man think they don't go for what Mr. Muhammad is saying. This negro that will tell you he's so against us, he's just protecting the crumbs he gets from the white man's table. This kind of negro is so busy trying to be like the white man that he doesn't know what the real masses of his own people are thinking. A fine car

177

and house and clothes and liquor have made a lot think themselves different from their poor black brothers. But Mr. Muhammad says that Allah is going to wake up all black men to see the white man as he really is, and see what Christianity has done to them. The black masses that are waking up don't believe in Christianity anymore. All it's done for black men is help to keep them slaves....

PLAYBOY: Isn't it true that many gentiles have also labored with dedication to advance integration and economic improvement for the Negro, as volunteer workers for the NAACP, CORE and many other interracial agencies?

MALCOLM X: A man who tosses worms in the river isn't necessarily a friend of the fish. All the fish who take him for a friend, who think the worm's got no hook in it, usually end up in the frying pan. All these things dangled before us by the white liberal posing as a friend and benefactor have turned out to be nothing but bait to make us think we're making progress....

PLAYBOY: Is there anything then, in your opinion, that could be done—by either whites or blacks—to expedite the social and economic progress of the negro in America?

MALCOLM X: First of all, the white man must finally realize that he's the one who has committed the crimes that have produced the miserable condition that our people are in. He can't hide this guilt by reviling us today because we answer his criminal acts—past and present—with extreme and uncompromising resentment. He cannot hide his guilt by accusing us, his victims, of being racists, extremists and black supremacists. The white man must realize that the sins of the fathers are about to be visited upon the heads of the children who have continued those sins, only in more sophisticated ways. Mr. Elijah Muhammad is warning this generation of white people that they, too, are also facing a time of harvest in which they will have to pay for the crime committed when their grandfathers made slaves out of us.

But there is something the white man can do to avert this fate. He must atone—and this can only be done by allowing black men, those who choose, to leave this land of bondage and go to a land of our own. But if he doesn't want a mass movement of our people away from this house of bondage, then he should separate this country.

The Autobiography of Malcolm X

LETTER FROM MECCA
(From Chapter Seventeen: Mecca)[1]

Never have I witnessed such sincere hospitality and the overwhelming spirit of true brotherhood as is practiced by people of all colors and races here in this Ancient Holy Land, the home of Abraham, Muhammad, and all the other prophets of the Holy Scriptures. For the past week, I have been utterly speechless and spellbound by the graciousness I see displayed all around me by people *of all colors*.

I have been blessed to visit the Holy City of Mecca. I have made my seven circuits around the Ka'ba, led by a young *Mutawaf* named Muhammad. I drank water from the well of Zem Zem. I ran seven times back and forth between the hills of Mt. Al-Safa and Al-Marwah. I have prayed in the ancient city of Mina, and I have prayed on Mt. Arafat.

There were tens of thousands of pilgrims, from all over the world. They were of all colors, from blue-eyed blonds to black-skinned Africans. But we were all participating in the same ritual, displaying a spirit of unity and brotherhood that my experiences in America had led me to believe never could exist between the white and the non-white.

America needs to understand Islam, because this is the one religion that erases from its society the race problem. Throughout my travels in the Muslim world, I have met, talked to, and even eaten with people who in America would have been considered "white"—but the "white" attitude was removed from their minds by the religion of Islam. I have never before seen *sincere* and *true* brotherhood practiced by all colors together, irrespective of their color.

You may be shocked by these words coming from me. But on this pilgrimage, what I have seen, and experienced, has forced me to *rearrange* much of my thought patterns previously held, and to *toss aside* some of my previous conclusions. This was not too difficult for me. Despite my firm convictions, I have been always a man who tries to face facts, and to accept the reality of life as new experience and new knowledge unfolds it. I have always kept an open mind, which is necessary to the flexibility that must go hand in hand with every form of intelligent search for truth.

During the past eleven days here in the Muslim world, I have eaten from the same plate, drunk from the same glass, and slept in the same bed (or on the same rug)—while praying to the *same God*—with fellow Muslims, whose eyes were of the bluest of blue, whose hair was the blondest of blond, and whose skin was the whitest of white. And in the *words* and in the *actions* and in the *deeds* of the "white" Muslims, I felt the same sincerity that I felt among the black African Muslims of Nigeria, Sudan, and Ghana.

We were *truly* all the same (brothers)—because their belief in one God had removed the "white" from their *minds*, the "white" from their *behavior*, and the "white" from their *attitude*.

I could see from this, that perhaps if white Americans could accept the Oneness of God, then perhaps, too, they could accept *in reality* the Oneness of Man—and cease to measure, and hinder, and harm others in terms of their "differences" in color.

With racism plaguing America like an incurable cancer, the so-called "Christian" white American heart should be more receptive to a proven solution to such a destructive problem. Perhaps it could be in time to save America from imminent disaster—the same destruction brought upon Germany by racism that eventually destroyed the Germans themselves.

Each hour here in the Holy Land enables me to have greater spiritual insights into what is happening in America between black and white. The American Negro never can be blamed for his racial animosities—he is only reacting to four hundred years of the conscious racism of the American whites. But as racism leads America up the suicide path, I do believe, from the experiences that I have had with them, that the white of the younger generation, in the colleges and universities, will see the handwriting on the wall and many of them will turn to the *spiritual* path of *truth*—the *only* way left to America to ward off the disaster that racism inevitably must lead to.

Never have I been so highly honored. Never have I been made to feel more humble and unworthy. Who would believe the blessings that have been heaped upon an *American Negro*? A few nights ago, a man who would be called in America a "white" man, a United Nations diplomat, an ambassador, a companion of kings, gave me *his* hotel suite, *his* bed. By this man, His Excellency Prince Faisal, who rules this Holy Land, was made aware of my presence here in Jedda. The very next morning, Prince Faisal's son, in person, informed me that by the will and decree of his esteemed father, I was to be a State Guest.

The Deputy Chief of Protocol himself took me before the Hajj Court. His Holiness Sheik Muhammad Harkon himself okayed my visit to Mecca. His Holiness gave me two books on Islam, with his personal seal and autograph, and he told me that he prayed that I would be a successful preacher of Islam in America. A car, a driver, and a guide, have been placed at my disposal, making it possible for me to travel about this Holy Land almost at will. The government provides air-conditioned quarters and servants in each city that I visit. Never would I have even thought of dreaming that I would ever be a recipient of such honors—honors that in America would be bestowed upon a King—not a Negro.

All praise is due to Allah, the Lord of all the Worlds.

Sincerely,
El-Hajj Malik El-Shabazz (Malcolm X)

---

1. From *The Autobiography of Malcolm X* by Malcolm X, with the assistance of Alex Haley (New York: Ballantine, 1992, pages 390–393). Copyright © 1964 by Malcolm X and Alex Haley. Copyright © 1965 by Alex Haley and Betty Shabazz. Reprinted by permission of Random House, Inc.

MICHAEL HARRINGTON

A self-described "long-distance runner," Michael Harrington's modest goal was to make the world a better place to live in for everyone. For his efforts, he was widely criticized for being a radical and a socialist, and was relegated to the fringes of political power. Nonetheless, in "going the distance," he got the attention of two presidents, sparked the War on Poverty, and radically changed the course of the nation's history.

Michael Harrington was born February 24, 1928, in the midwestern Irish American culture of St. Louis, Missouri. His mother was an idealistic teacher and his father was a patent attorney who had fought in World War I. He was a child of the Depression who grew up in a pro-labor, middle-class home. His grandfather, a high school dropout, lived in the classic Irish American world of his immigrant generation. He was an Irish Catholic Democrat and proud of it.

While Harrington died an atheist, he was raised as a Catholic and attended St. Rose's School in St. Louis. He was taught by liberal Jesuits who were militant union supporters. It was while in kindergarten at St. Rose's at the age of four that he first felt compassion for the poor: He gave his lunch money to the missions "to help save a baby in China for Christ." Later, looking back at his life, he said this moment was when his destiny was shaped.

Harrington attended St. Louis University High School where the curriculum included four years of Latin and two years of Greek. At the age of 16, he started at the College of the Holy Cross in Worcester, Massachusetts. He went on to the University of Chicago where he earned a master's degree in English literature in 1949. He also attended Yale Law School for a year from 1947 to 1948. Years later, in June 1971, he would return to Holy Cross to deliver the commencement address and receive an honorary doctorate.

With his master's in hand, he returned to St. Louis in 1949 and threw himself into his work with the Public Welfare Department of the St. Louis Public Schools. His dream was to save up enough money to move to New York and be a poet, writer, and bohemian. One rainy day, his work took him into an old, decayed house near the Mississippi River; it smelled of "stopped-up toilets, dead rats, and human misery." The poverty-stricken life of human beings living in such filth and without hope was a shock to his "privileged, middle-class nostrils." It also led to an epiphany. He suddenly knew he was to dedicate the rest of his life to working to end poverty. His long-distance race had started.

In the fall of 1949, he moved east to Greenwich Village where he worked as a writer for the *Columbia Encyclopedia*, as a soda jerk, a machine operator, and a freelance writer and researcher for a foundation. He took a job as a writer-trainee with *Life* in 1950. When he discovered that *Life* did not like employees to join the American Newspaper Guild, he immediately joined the journalists' union. He quit *Life* six months later.

For the next ten years he would lead a bohemian life. He would start touring the Greenwich Village bars at midnight, sleep until eleven or twelve, and work for the next twelve hours, reading, writing, or doing socialist organizing. Other regulars in that 1950s scene included Dylan Thomas, Norman Mailer, James Baldwin, Jules Feiffer, Bob Dylan, William Styron, and Allen Ginsberg.

During the Korean War, he first joined the Army Medical Reserve and later declared himself a conscientious objector. In 1951, he joined the Catholic Worker movement, a radical left organization that advocated pacifism. As associate editor of the *Catholic Worker* magazine, he focused his efforts on promoting the unions and eliminating poverty. He was a self-confessed young radical under the spell of Karl Marx, who believed that the working class would eventually save humanity. Harrington's life, dedicated to eliminating poverty, revolved around the socialist and labor movements. His idealism would earn him a spot on President Richard Nixon's enemies list.

After more than a decade working with the victims of poverty, Harrington was persuaded by an editor of *Commentary* to write an article about poverty for the magazine. "Our Fifty Million Poor" was published in 1959 and provoked inquiries from three book publishers. Harrington agreed to write a book on the topic and moved to Paris to work on it. He married Stephanie Gervis, a reporter at the *Village Voice*.

The Other America: Poverty in the United States was published by Macmillan in March 1962. It persuasively argued that there were tens of millions of Americans who, though employed, lived below the poverty level, and were unseen and neglected by the government. A remarkable forty-page review of the book in the *New Yorker* brought it additional attention and made poverty a topic of discussion in the intellectual-political world. Ironically, the book about poverty was an unexpected overnight success that transformed Harrington's life, lifting him out of the bohemian poverty he had been living in. It also brought him national recognition and requests for speaking engagements across the country.

Returning from France in January 1963, he worked with a number of progressive socialist organizations, including the League for Industrial Democracy and the Socialist International. He had originally joined the Socialist Party in 1948 and subsequently served on its national executive board and as co-chair. He resigned from the Socialist Party in 1972 disillusioned by its infighting.

As a result of the hectic pace of lecturing, political organizing, traveling, and writing, Harrington suffered a nervous breakdown in March 1965. After working with a psychoanalyst for four years, he came to understand the pressures of overnight success and financial reward that had led to his breakdown. He even managed to put a political spin on his illness, referring to the general law of capitalist insecurity cited by Marx in *The Communist Manifesto*. Although the breakdown was serious, causing him to cancel speaking engagements, he never stopped writing.

Both his public and private life revolved around his leadership roles in the Democratic Socialist Organizing Committee and the New American Movement (which combined in 1982 to form the Democratic Socialists of America (DSA)). He was the founding chairman of the DSA and was later co-chairman of the group.

Through his participation with those organizations he encountered a number of other social issues. Some of these included feminism, Black and Hispanic racism, the anti-draft movement, Central American intervention, the Israeli-Palestinian conflict, and Vietnam. In the mid-eighties, he organized a national Justice for All day to foster consciousness about poverty in the United States.

He and Stephanie had two sons, Alexander Gervis and Edward Michael III. By 1972, the financial pressures of raising a family in the city forced Harrington to reevaluate his bohemian lifestyle. Until 1971, they had health insurance from Stephanie's job at the *Village Voice*, but when she left her job to spend more time with the children, they lost their coverage. Confronted with the high cost of health insurance, Harrington looked for a teaching job. In 1972, he was appointed professor of political science at Queens College.

While born out of need, his move to teaching proved to be a fortuitous transition. Concerned about his lack of a Ph.D., Harrington worked hard to educate himself to become a good professor. As it turned out, he was a born teacher who loved to explore, motivate, and share new ideas with his students. Queens College also provided him with a secure home base. He was given tenure after a couple of years, and in 1988 he was named a Distinguished Professor of Political Science. His years at Queens also confirmed his belief that higher mass education should be made available to all who respond to it.

In 1979, Harrington moved his family out of Manhattan to the small, middle-class suburban community of Larchmont. Criticized by the media as being a left-wing hypocrite for fleeing the problems of the city for the suburbs, he defended his decision: Manhattan was not the same place it was when he moved there in 1949, "a place with a stable working-class population in a period of exceptional nonviolence." He also noted that rent in Manhattan was too high, the public schools too dangerous, and the streets too grim.

In November 1984, while driving to a symposium at Princeton University to celebrate the hundredth birthday of Norman Thomas, one of his mentors, he discovered a lump on the side of his neck. At first it was diagnosed as a swollen gland, but a biopsy proved it was cancerous. In the final years of his life, while undergoing periods of surgery, radiation, and chemotherapy, he kept up a full schedule of travel, research, and writing. He finished his autobiography and wrote two other books during this difficult period.

In the epilogue to his autobiography, Harrington wonders about how little he had accomplished. Despite his efforts, socialism was still an alien and un-American idea to most Americans. Perhaps, he thought, he should have abandoned the romantic futurism of socialism and settled for good left-wing liberalism. But no, he concluded, these are difficult times and "if the best values of humanity are to survive, then we will have to go down the road upon which I have been running."

On July 31, 1989, Michael Harrington died of cancer of the esophagus at the age of sixty-one in his home in Larchmont.

If Harrington had questions about his accomplishments, history didn't. In addition to teaching, lecturing, and political organizing, he wrote sixteen books that challenged America to look at itself in a different light. Perhaps, he suggested, there *was* more to life than capitalism and greed. His impact went beyond the philosophical. The first book he wrote, *The Other America*, had a direct effect on millions of Americans living today.

President Kennedy was so impressed by the book that he made it required reading in his administration, and made abolition of poverty a major domestic goal. Before Kennedy could launch any specific programs, he was assassinated. President Johnson then picked up the challenge. Harrington suddenly found himself called to the capitol as an advisor to the president on poverty and *The Other America* became the genesis for the War on Poverty. Harrington, once a radical socialist, suddenly recognized that he had an opportunity "to actually influence the course of events in the most powerful capitalist society history has ever known."

On the twenty-fifth anniversary of the publication of *The Other America* in 1987, the *New York Times* compared it to Thomas Paine's *Common Sense*, Harriet Beecher Stowe's *Uncle Tom's Cabin*, and Sinclair's *The Jungle* as books that influenced the course of the nation's history: "More than any other single work, historians say, it inspired the landmark antipoverty measures— Medicare, Medicaid, federal aid to education and the expansion of Social Security and food stamp benefits, to name a few—that became engrained in the American system."

The following excerpt from *The Other America* describes the tens of millions of hidden Americans who are suffering in the midst of the "affluent society."

SOURCES. Harrington, Michael, *Fragments of the Century*, Saturday Review Press/E. P. Dutton & Co., New York, 1973; Harrington, Michael, *The Accidental Century*, Macmillan, New York, 1965; Harrington, Michael, *The Long-Distance Runner: An Autobiography*, Henry Holt & Co., New York, 1988; Harrington, Michael, *The New American Poverty*, Holt, Rinehart & Winston, New York, 1984; Harrington, Michael, *The Other America: Poverty in the United States*, Macmillan, New York, 1962.

The Other America: Poverty in the United States

Michael Harrington

From Chapter One:
THE INVISIBLE LAND[1]

There is a familiar America. It is celebrated in speeches and advertised on television and in the magazines. It has the highest mass standard of living the world has ever known.

In the 1950s this America worried about itself, yet even its anxieties were products of abundance. The title of a brilliant book was widely misinterpreted, and the familiar America began to call itself "the affluent society." There was introspection about Madison Avenue and tail fins; there was discussion of the emotional suffering taking place in the suburbs. In all this, there was an implicit assumption that the basic grinding economic problems had been solved in the United States. In this theory the nation's problems were no longer a matter of basic human needs, of food, shelter, and clothing. Now they were seen as qualitative, a question of learning to live decently amid luxury.

While this discussion was carried on, there existed another America. In it dwelt somewhere between forty million and fifty million citizens of this land. They were poor. They still are.

To be sure, the other America is not impoverished in the same sense as those poor nations where millions cling to hunger as a defense against starvation. This country has escaped such extremes. That does not change the fact that tens of millions of Americans are, at this very moment, maimed in body and spirit, existing at levels beneath those necessary for human decency. If these people are not starving, they are hungry, and sometimes fat with

189

hunger, for that is what cheap foods do. They are without adequate housing and education and medical care.

The government has documented what this means to the bodies of the poor, and the figures will be cited throughout this book. But even more basic, this poverty twists and deforms the spirit. The American poor are pessimistic and defeated, and they are victimized by mental suffering to a degree unknown in suburbia.

This book is a description of the world in which these people live; it is about the other America. Here are the unskilled workers, the migrant farm workers, the aged, the minorities, and all the others who live in the economic underworld of American life. In all this, there will be statistics, and that offers the opportunity for disagreement among honest and sincere men. I would ask the reader to respond critically to every assertion, but not to allow statistical quibbling to obscure the huge, enormous, and intolerable fact of poverty in America. For, when all is said and done, that fact is unmistakable, whatever its exact dimensions, and the truly human reaction can only be outrage. As W. H. Auden wrote:

Hunger allows no choice
To the citizen or the police;
We must love one another or die.

The millions who are poor in the United States tend to become increasingly invisible. Here is a great mass of people, yet it takes an effort of the intellect and will even to see them.

I discovered this personally in a curious way. After I wrote my first article on poverty in America, I had all the statistics down on paper. I had proved to my satisfaction that there were around fifty million poor in this country. Yet, I realized I did not believe my own figures. The poor existed in the government reports; they were percentages and numbers in long, close columns, but they were not part of my experience. I could prove that the other America existed, but I had never been there.

My response was not accidental. It was typical of what is happening to an entire society, and it reflects profound social changes in this nation. The other America, the America of poverty, is hidden today in a way that it never was before. Its millions are socially invisible to the rest of us. No wonder that so many misinterpreted Galbraith's title and assumed that "the affluent society" meant that everyone had a decent standard of life. The misinterpretation was true as far as the actual day-to-day lives of two-thirds of the nation were concerned. Thus, one must begin a description of the other America by understanding why we do not see it.

There are perennial reasons that make the other America an invisible land.

Poverty is often off the beaten track. It always has been. The ordinary tourist never left the main highway, and today he rides interstate turnpikes. He does not go into the valleys of Pennsylvania where the towns look like movie sets of Wales in the thirties. He does not see the company houses in rows, the rutted roads (the poor always have bad roads whether they live in the city, in towns, or on farms), and everything is black and dirty. And even if he were to pass through such a place by accident, the tourist would not meet the unemployed men in the bar or the women coming home from a runaway sweatshop.

Then, too, beauty and myths are perennial masks of poverty. The traveler comes to the Appalachians in the lovely season. He sees the hills, the streams, the foliage—but not the poor. Or perhaps he looks at a run-down mountain house and, remembering Rousseau rather than seeing with his eyes, decides that "those people" are truly fortunate to be living the way they are and that they are lucky to be exempt from the strains and tensions of the middle class. The only problem is that "those people," the quaint inhabitants of those hills, are undereducated, underprivileged, lack medical care, and are in the process of being forced from the land into a life in the cities, where they are misfits.

These are normal and obvious causes of the invisibility of the poor. They operated a generation ago; they will be functioning a generation hence. It is more important to understand that the very development of American society is creating a new kind of blindness about poverty. The poor are increasingly slipping out of the very experience and consciousness of the nation.

If the middle class never did like ugliness and poverty, it was at least aware of them. "Across the tracks" was not a very long way to go. There were forays into the slums at Christmas time; there were charitable organizations that brought contact with the poor. Occasionally almost everyone passed through the negro ghetto or the blocks of tenements, if only to get downtown to work or to entertainment.

Now the American city has been transformed. The poor still inhabit the miserable housing in the central area, but they are increasingly isolated from contact with, or sight of, anybody else. Middle-class women coming in from suburbia on a rare trip may catch the merest glimpse of the other America on the way to an evening at the theater, but their children are segregated in suburban schools. The business or professional man may drive along the fringes of slums in a car or bus, but it is not an important experience to him. The failures, the unskilled, the disabled, the aged, and the minorities are right there, across the tracks, where they have always been. But hardly anyone else is.

In short, the very development of the American city has removed poverty from the living emotional experience of millions upon millions of middle-class Americans. Living out in the suburbs, it is easy to assume that ours is, indeed, an affluent society.

This new segregation of poverty is compounded by a well-meaning ignorance. A good many concerned and sympathetic Americans are aware that there is much discussion of urban renewal. Suddenly, driving through the city, they notice that a familiar slum has been torn down and that there are towering, modern buildings where once there had been tenements or hovels. There is a warm feeling of satisfaction, of pride in the way things are working out: the poor, it is obvious, are being taken care of.

The irony in this ... is that the truth is nearly the exact opposite to the impression. The total impact of the various housing programs in postwar America has been to squeeze more and more people into existing slums. More often than not, the modern apartment in a towering building rents at forty dollars a room or more. For, during the past decade and a half, there has been more subsidization of middle- and upper-income housing than there has been of housing for the poor.

Clothes make the poor invisible too: America has the best-dressed poverty the world has ever known. For a variety of reasons, the benefits of mass production have been spread more evenly in this area than in many others. It is much easier in the United States to be decently dressed than it is to be decently housed, fed, or doctored. Even people with terribly depressed incomes can look prosperous.

This is an extremely important factor in defining our emotional and existential ignorance of poverty. In Detroit the existence of social classes became much more difficult to discern the day the companies put lockers in the plants. From that moment on, one did not see men in work clothes on the way to the factory, but citizens in slacks and white shirts. This process has been magnified with the poor throughout the country. There are tens of thousands of Americans in the big cities who are wearing shoes, perhaps even a stylishly cut suit or dress, and yet are hungry. It is not a matter of planning, though it almost seems as if the affluent society had given out costumes to the poor so that they would not offend the rest of society with the sight of rags.

Then, many of the poor are the wrong age to be seen. A good number of them (over eight million) are sixty-five years of age or better; an even larger number are under eighteen. The aged members of the other America are often sick, and they cannot move. Another group of them live out their lives in loneliness and frustration: they sit in rented rooms, or else they stay close to a house in a neighborhood that has completely changed from the old days. Indeed, one of the worst aspects of poverty among the aged is that these people are out of sight and out of mind, and alone.

The young are somewhat more visible, yet they too stay close to their neighborhoods. Sometimes they advertise their poverty through a lurid tabloid story about a gang killing. But generally they do not disturb the quiet streets of the middle class.

And finally, the poor are politically invisible. It is one of the cruelest ironies of social life in advanced countries that the dispossessed at the bottom of society are unable to speak for themselves. The people of the other America do not, by far and large, belong to unions, to fraternal organizations, or to political parties. They are without lobbies of their own; they put forward no legislative program. As a group, they are atomized. They have no face; they have no voice.

Thus, there is not even a cynical political motive for caring about the poor, as in the old days. Because the slums are no longer centers of powerful political organizations, the politicians need not really care about their inhabitants. The slums are no longer visible to the middle class, so much of the idealistic urge to fight for those who need help is gone. Only the social agencies have a really direct involvement with the other America, and they are without any great political power.

To the extent that the poor have a spokesman in American life, that role is played by the labor movement. The unions have their own particular idealism, an ideology of concern. More than that, they realize that the existence of a reservoir of cheap, unorganized labor is a menace to wages and working conditions throughout the entire economy. Thus, many union legislative proposals —to extend the coverage of minimum wage and social security, to organize migrant farm laborers—articulate the needs of the poor.

That the poor are invisible is one of the most important things about them. They are not simply neglected and forgotten as in the old rhetoric of reform; what is much worse, they are not seen.

---

1. Reprinted with the permission of Simon & Schuster, Inc., from *The Other America: Poverty in the United States* by Michael Harrington (New York: Macmillan, 1962, pages 1–8). Copyright © 1962, 1969, 1981 by Michael Harrington.

PAUL BRODEUR

During his thirty-eight years as a staff writer at the *New Yorker*, Paul Brodeur was called an alarmist by captains of the asbestos industry, a scaremonger by detergent manufacturers, a muckraker by the makers of chlorofluorocarbons, and an environmental terrorist by spokesmen for the electric utility industry. Along the way he helped prolong the lives of tens of thousands of American workers and other people in the general community.

Paul Brodeur was born May 16, 1931, in Boston and grew up in its suburbs. His father, Paul, who had fought the Germans in World War I as a member of the French Foreign Legion, was an orthodontist and sculptor, and his mother, Sarah Marjorie, a former actress, was a drama teacher. He had a younger brother, David, and a sister, Valjeanne.

In the fall of 1945, Brodeur was sent off to Phillips Academy in Andover, Massachusetts, an elite prep school for boys. While at Phillips, he was both a reporter and editor for the school newspaper and discovered his aptitude for writing. By the time he entered Harvard in the fall of 1949, he knew he wanted to be a writer.

While at Harvard, the Cold War between Russia and the United States was in full swing with international intrigue, espionage, threats of atomic warfare, and the "police action" in Korea. Upon his graduation, Brodeur enlisted in the Army Counterintelligence Corps. After basic training at Fort Dix, New Jersey, and counterintelligence training at Fort Holabird in Maryland, he was sent to Germany where he spent the rest of his military career guarding nuclear warheads stored in an underground depot near the French border.

In the summer of 1955, Brodeur was asked to interrogate a young Polish American soldier, Adam Warshawsky, from the coal fields south of Pittsburgh. Warshawsky's loyalty was being questioned by the FBI because he had attended dances at a Ukrainian American club in Pennsylvania when was he was seventeen. Brodeur was convinced of Warshawsky's loyalty and made every effort to clear him, but despite this, Warshawsky's security clearance was lifted and he was transferred to a tank outfit to finish out his military service.

Disturbed by this development, Brodeur asked for an early discharge and went off to Paris to embark upon his dream of becoming a writer. While in Paris, he wrote a short story, "The Sick Fox," which was published in the *New Yorker* in the spring of 1956. Shortly thereafter, he was hired as the magazine's "newsbreak" editor. In this job he was responsible for sifting through the hundreds of newspaper gaffes and non sequiturs sent in by readers each week to select the best and funniest to which E. B. White would append his famed taglines.

During the next few years, Brodeur expanded "The Sick Fox" into a novel and became a writer for the *New Yorker*'s popular "Talk of the Town" section. His first major assignment was to write about Werner Heisenberg, the German Nobel Prize-winning physicist. *New Yorker* editor William Shawn liked the piece enough to ask Brodeur to cover scientific subjects from then on. Around this time, Brodeur married his sweetheart from his Harvard days and they had a son and a daughter.

Brodeur spent nearly forty years at the *New Yorker*, during which time he published two novels—*The Sick Fox* and *The Stunt Man*—a book of short stories, *Downstream*, and eight books of nonfiction. *The Stunt Man* was made into a movie starring Peter O'Toole and Barbara Hershey

Brodeur wrote his first long article about asbestos, "The Magic Mineral," in 1968. It was the first of a dozen articles he wrote about the massive public health hazard posed by asbestos. It marked a major turning point in his professional life. "During the next twenty-five years," Brodeur said, "I would devote myself almost exclusively to chronicling environmental and occupational hazards, and in doing so, would uncover and expose the secrecy and callous disregard for life that formed corporate conduct at almost every level in the United States."

After asbestos, Brodeur turned his attention to the hazards of the stain-eating enzymes that had recently been added to laundry detergents. In January of 1971, the *New Yorker* published his lengthy article investigating the enzymes, which he proved were associated with pulmonary disease, asthma, and skin rashes. Within a few weeks, the three largest manufacturers, Proctor and Gamble, Colgate-Palmolive, and Lever Brothers, withdrew the enzymes from their products.

Another corporate target Brodeur took aim at was the giant chemical manufacturer, E. I. du Pont de Nemours, the world's leading producer of chlorofluorocarbons. Brodeur reported on research indicating that manmade chlorofluorocarbons, used as aerosol propellants and coolants in refrigerators and air conditioners, were contributing to the depletion of the ozone layer. Du Pont initially denied the risk, claiming there was no evidence that the ozone layer was being destroyed. But chlorofluorocarbons were eventually banned. In 1989, the United Nations Environment Programme added Brodeur's name to its Global 500 Honour Roll, for bringing the problem of ozone depletion to public attention.

Brodeur then wrote about the dangers posed by microwave and radio-frequency radiation in the *New Yorker* in December 1976, bringing national attention to the effects of electromagnetic rays for the first time. The hazards were further detailed in his widely-read book, *The Zapping of America*, published in 1977.

During his tenure at the *New Yorker*, Brodeur wrote about the health hazards associated with exposure to a number of widely used chemicals. His last and most controversial project was a series of articles about the cancer hazard posed to hundreds of thousands of people by exposure to the electromagnetic fields (EMF) given off by high-voltage and high-current power lines. A three-part series appeared in the *New Yorker* in June 1989 and was published as the book *Currents of Death* that same year. Subsequent articles on the subject were published in 1993 as *The Great Power-Line Cover-Up*.

The national reaction was extraordinary. Brodeur discussed the EMF issue on more than fifty television and radio programs and received more than two thousand letters and phone calls from people concerned about EMF hazards. Dozens of citizens' groups were formed to protest the presence and/or construction of high voltage and high-current lines near their neighborhoods.

In the winter of 1990, EPA officials released a detailed 367-page report concluding that power-frequency magnetic fields were a "probable" cause of cancer in humans. Within days, Bush administration officials forced the EPA to delete the word "probable" and replace it with "possible." As Brodeur says, "Thus began the official cover-up of the power-line hazard that inspired the title of my book, and that continues to this day."

Brodeur's investigative reports on the misconduct of the renegade asbestos industry led to congressional hearings, regulatory measures, and White House initiatives. His articles and books on asbestos encouraged victims to sue asbestos manufacturers and their insurers, and were used by attorneys to win huge settlements against the industry. Some of the hundreds of millions of dollars accrued through successful litigation were later used to finance a legal assault on the tobacco industry. Such suits have encouraged others to sue firearm manufacturers, the lead paint industry, and, most recently, the managed health care industry.

In 1987, after having been divorced for many years, Brodeur met Milane Christiansen, a bookstore owner in Southern California and they married in 1992.

Brodeur remained with the *New Yorker* until 1996, when he reached retirement age. By that time, Tina Brown, former editor of *Vanity Fair*, had become editor of the magazine and, according to Brodeur, had steered it away from its tradition of investigating matters of environmental health which began when the magazine had published Rachel Carson's *Silent Spring*.

The dozen articles Brodeur wrote on asbestos were published as several books, including *Asbestos and Enzymes, Expendable Americans,* and *Outrageous Misconduct: The Asbestos Industry on Trial.* As a result of his exposés, asbestos manufacturing plants where thousands of workers had become disabled with deadly diseases were shut down as some of the nation's leading asbestos manufacturers, including Johns-Manville, were forced into bankruptcy. Legislation was passed banning the manufacture and use of asbestos products in the United States. Tens of thousands of lives were undoubtedly prolonged by these actions.

In his 1997 memoir, *Secrets: A Writer in the Cold War*, Brodeur describes himself as a "kind of literary entomologist, one who overturns rocks in the dank garden of the private enterprise system as it presently exists and describes what he sees crawling out from underneath." In a *New York Times Book Review*, Lewis Lapham, editor of *Harper's Magazine*, described Brodeur's "rocks" as "large corporations, manufacturers of asbestos, proteolytic enzymes or chlorofluorocarbons, that earned a rich return on capital by fouling the atmosphere, poisoning the water, delivering as byproducts new and improved forms of leukemia and pulmonary disease."

The following excerpt from Brodeur's *Expendable Americans*, published in 1974, reveals the passion and investigative skills Brodeur brought to his pursuit of corporations involved in asbestos manufacturing. (Anthony Mazzocchi, cited here, was director of the legislative department at the Oil, Chemical, and Atomic Workers International Union.)

SOURCES. Brodeur, Paul, *Currents of Death: Power Lines, Computer Terminals, and the Attempt to Cover Up Their Threat to Your Health*, Simon & Schuster, New York, 1989; Brodeur, Paul, *Expendable Americans*, Viking, New York, 1974; Brodeur, Paul, *The Great Power-Line Cover-Up: How the Utilities and the Government Are Trying to Hide the Cancer Hazards Posed by Electromagnetic Fields*, Little, Brown & Co., New York, 1993; Brodeur, Paul, *Outrageous Misconduct: The Asbestos Industry on Trial*, Pantheon, New York, 1985; Brodeur, Paul, *Secrets: A Writer in the Cold War*, Faber & Faber, Boston, 1997; Brodeur, Paul, *The Zapping of America: Microwaves, Their Deadly Risk, and the Cover-Up*, Norton, New York, 1977.

Expendable Americans

Paul Brodeur

THE DUST THAT ATE US UP[1]

The Tyler, Texas asbestos plant, owned by Pittsburgh Corning, was in the region supervised by the Dallas office of the U.S. Occupational Safety and Health Administration. Brodeur met with the administrator and his assistant who denied there were safety problems at the plant, adding, "How can there be a serious danger [from asbestos dust] if it doesn't hurt you right away?"

I first heard about the Tyler plant when I attended the press conference that Anthony Mazzocchi held in Washington, D.C., on February 10, 1972. Later, at my request, he provided me with copies of all the inspection reports, surveys, and studies that had been made of the factory over the years, and, after studying them, I decided to go to Texas and talk with some of the people who had been involved in the whole sad affair....

Half an hour later, I was driving a rented car east on Interstate 20 toward Tyler, about a hundred miles away. For the first fifty or sixty miles, the country was flat and dotted with grazing cattle; then it became hilly and wooded. Here and there, a pale-green wash of buds on bushes growing in wet draws signaled the approach of spring, but the hint seemed lost against a larger background of brown fields, skeletal trees, red clay soil, and a vast sky filled with circling buzzards. At about four-thirty in the afternoon, I turned off Interstate 20 and drove south on U.S. Highway 69 to a motel on the outskirts of Tyler, where I had made a reservation. At the turnoff, there was a large billboard, erected by the Peoples National Bank of Tyler, that read "Life Is a Bed of Roses."

When I got to the motel, I telephoned Dr. George Hurst, superintendent of the East Texas Chest Hospital, and made an appointment to see him the next afternoon. Then I got in touch with Herman Yandle, the local union chairman, who lives in Hawkins, a small town eighteen miles north of Tyler. Yandle has no telephone, but his wife's grandmother's house is next door, and she went over to get him. I had called him from New York and told him I wanted to talk with him, and when he came to the phone a few minutes later he said he would be along within an hour. While I waited for him, I drew up a list of questions for Charles Van Horne, Pittsburgh Corning's plant manager, whom I planned to see the following day.

Yandle, who arrived shortly before six o'clock, proved to be a tall, heavyset man with an engaging grin and an easygoing manner. He came into the room, stuck out a hand, and plopped down in an easy chair. I asked him to tell me something about himself and his work history, and he said he was thirty-six years old and had gone to work at the Tyler plant in the autumn of 1961. He had spent three and a half years in the production department, he went on, working on the feeder and scrap machines, and for the past seven years he had been in the shipping department. The first time he had ever worn a respirator was in July of 1971, he told me, and it was also the first time he had ever seen any of his co-workers wearing respirators except for a short period in the spring of 1969, when two or three men working in very dusty areas had requested them. "It was more or less voluntary in 1969," he explained. "And after a few weeks the guys stopped wearing them."

I asked Yandle when he had first been told that asbestos was hazardous to work with, and he said it was in August of 1971, when Dr. Lee Grant came down to give the men a talk. "We were real mad about the masks," he said. "Heck, I'd been working there ten years without one, and they were a pain in the neck to wear, especially in the summer, when it got so hot in there you'd sweat and couldn't get enough air through to breathe. So when Dr. Grant called my shift into the shipping supervisor's office, the first thing we asked him was how long we were going to have to wear the respirators. He said no longer than a year, because the company was going to shift over from asbestos to mineral wool. He had a blackboard set up in there with a lot of complicated words and numbers on it that none of us could make head or tail of. I remember he said that the company could make the whole plant dust-free but they couldn't make the finished product safe for the insulators to use. When somebody asked him about better dust collectors, he said that profits wouldn't allow them now. He said that the amosite mines in South Africa were running out and that the rates were getting too high for the company to bear the cost. He also said it had been known since 1963 that asbestos could hurt us. At the same time, he said that amosite asbestos didn't cause trouble if you didn't smoke—that it wasn't proved medically that it could cause trouble. He had it written on the blackboard that seventeen percent of the people who work with asbestos have lung cancer, but he told us that was another kind of asbestos. He claimed that if you didn't smoke you didn't have any more chance of catching cancer in the plant than you did walking out in the street. He also wrote a word I can't pronounce—meso-something."

"Mesothelioma?" I asked.

"That's it," Yandle replied. "Dr. Grant said for us not to worry about that, either. Especially if we didn't smoke. Cigarettes and asbestos don't go together is what he told us. Next thing we knew, they were sending us over to Dr. Hurst at the East Texas Chest Hospital for X-rays, lung-function tests, and blood tests."

I asked Yandle if he had ever been X-rayed before then, and he said he had, on two occasions. "Both times, it was at a Medical and Surgical Clinic in Tyler," he told me. "They're the ones who handled all the accident work and medical stuff for Pittsburgh Corning. The first time I got X-rayed was in 1961, when I went to work there, and the next time was in the spring of 1969, not long after the Department of Labor people inspected the plant. According to Van Horne, all the X-rays they took of us in the spring of 1969 were good. We never saw them, of course, and wouldn't have known what to make of them if we had. I came across them, just by accident, last October, though, when the NIOSH boys were down here making their big inspection. I was taking them through the plant as the union representative, and I spotted a whole stack of something on a shelf high up in the men's room. So I climbed up there and took a look. It turned out to be our 1969 X-rays, but they were so old and cracked and covered with dust and dirt you couldn't have made out a thing."

I asked Yandle what he and his fellow workers were told about the X-rays and tests that Dr. Hurst had performed the previous August, and he said they were not told anything until a few weeks before the NIOSH inspection in October. "Early in October, two of us went over to the hospital to ask Dr. Hurst for our medical reports," he went on. "Dr. Hurst said that he had sent them to Van Horne and Dr. Grant. He explained that he was obligated to Pittsburgh Corning, because he had done the tests for them, but that, as a medical doctor, he was also obligated to us. He said we had no asbestosis on our diagnosis, and that if there were shadows on the X-rays they were probably not related to asbestosis. He said that as far as he could tell there were no health problems that were related to our work, but there were people who had emphysema and bronchitis, which he said was on account of smoking. When a NIOSH doctor examined me a few weeks later, though, he said he was sure I had a good dose of asbestosis. Also, I'd begun to think back on things and to wise up on my own. I remembered when Willie Hurtt had to quit a few years ago because he was spitting up blood. And Robert Thomas, a neighbor of mine up in Hawkins, who hasn't been able to breathe good for a long time now. And Ed Land, with the same trouble. And Bill Morris, who was spitting up blood, too, and took himself over to the Gladewater Municipal Hospital in 1969, where they found spots on his lungs and made a biopsy. And a whole bunch of others I could name. So when Steve Wodka and I went over to the East Texas Chest Hospital in January to meet with Hurst, Grant, Farkos, Spiegel, and Lemen, and I heard that seven of us who'd worked in the plant for ten years had symptoms of asbestosis, I wasn't surprised. Wodka and I asked for a thorough medical reading on the health problems of each and every man in the plant, and after that we began to hear a different tune. Early in February, Van Horne put up a notice on the factory bulletin board scheduling appointments with Dr. Hurst for twenty-three of us, who, it turned out, had something wrong on our medical tests. I went over there on the ninth with Arthur Bearden, who'd worked in the plant for about sixteen years. I went in first, and Dr. Hurst read off a lot of numbers and said that after a recheck of my tests they'd made a new diagnosis. He told me that I had symptoms of early asbestosis but that my condition wasn't so bad as some of the others. He said that a few more weeks in the plant wouldn't hurt but that after it shut down I shouldn't try to find work in a foundry or a welding shop, or anyplace where it's dusty, and he advised me to look for a truck-driving job. He told the exact same thing to Arthur Bearden. Naturally, one of the things I asked Dr. Hurst was what I could do for myself. And that's when it dawned on me that I was in real bad trouble, because he said that there was no medicine or cure for asbestosis, and that I had to keep coming back every two years for another examination to see if it was getting worse."

I asked Yandle how he felt these days, and he said not bad. "It's kind of hard to explain," he went on. "But if I exert myself real fast, I kind of just give out." Yandle added that in addition to Bearden and himself, Robert Thomas, Mitchell Walker, Tom Belcher, and Harold Spencer had been told by

Dr. Hurst that they had symptoms of early asbestosis, and had been advised not to work in dusty places. "There's a seventh guy with the same trouble, but he's a supervisor and he won't talk about it," Yandle said. "We hear that the company settled six months' pay on all the supervisors. These other fellows I told you about, though—they'll talk, and if you want I can introduce you to some of them."

I told Yandle I would like to meet them, and anyone else he could think of who could help to give me a clear picture of what had gone on in the Tyler plant.

"Well, then, you ought to talk to Frank Spencer," he said. "He's Harold's father, and the interesting thing about him is that he used to work at the old Union Asbestos & Rubber Company plant in McGregor, down by Waco. Old Frank's got an awful problem breathing these days, so he's almost always at home. Why don't I call him up now? I might as well call Ray Barron, too. Ray lives right close, and he's part of the maintenance crew they've kept on to clean up the plant."

Yandle telephoned Spencer and arranged for us to visit him at his house later in the evening. Then he called Barron and invited him to come to the motel. When he had hung up, I asked him to tell me what he knew about the burlap bags that asbestos was shipped to Tyler in and that were later sold to nurseries in the Dallas-Tyler area.

"That's a real laugh," he said. "I mean about them recalling thirty-five thousand of those bags from the local nurseries. You see, the amosite came in hundred-pound bags from South Africa to New Orleans and Houston, and then it was freighted over here on the Cotton Belt Route. Now, I happen to know from 1963 to 1967 Pittsburgh Corning sold those bags to the Coastal Bag & Bagging Corporation, of Houston. Then, after 1967, they started selling them locally—mostly to the nurseries. Anyway, what I'm getting at is that the thirty-five thousand bags are just a drop in the bucket. Look at it this way. We used two hundred sacks of amosite a day in production, and we worked a five-day week. That makes a thousand bags a week, and fifty-two thousand bags a year. Is that right?"

"Right," I said.

"Okay," Yandle went on. "Fifty-two thousand bags a year for ten years give you how much?"

"More than half a million," I replied.

"More than half a million," Yandle said quietly. "And you know what? They leaked like crazy—all of them. I know because I used to help unload them from the freight cars. They leaked like crazy, and they were dusty as could be."

Later in his exhaustive investigation of the asbestos industry, Brodeur observed, "By this time, I was beginning to understand how multiple and intricate were the reasons for the appalling casualty rate in the nation's workplaces, and how intertwined and pervasive were the activities of the medical-industrial complex, which was apparently bent on perpetuating the situation. What seemed more and more incredible to me as the months passed, however, was how such a situation could be—indeed, was being—tolerated at the highest levels of the federal government."

---

1. From Part Two: "The Dust that Ate Us Up" in *The Expendable Americans* by Paul Brodeur (New York: The Viking Press, 1974). Reprinted by permission of Sterling Lord Literistic, Inc. Copyright © 1974 by Paul Brodeur.

PAUL EHRLICH

He began as an entomologist studying butterflies, and became an internationally controversial expert on population growth and the environment. Paul Ehrlich's words ignited an academic and public debate that focused world attention on overpopulation. Some critics refer to him as America's most shameless scaremonger, a sour misanthrope, and one of the great hysterics of our time. Others say he is saving the planet.

Paul Ralph Ehrlich was born in Philadelphia on May 29, 1932, to William and Ruth Ehrlich. As a teenager he was fascinated by nature, and his room was filled with butterfly collections and tropical fish. His concern for nature grew as he saw butterfly habitats replaced by housing developments. He started finding it impossible to raise caterpillars on local plants because of the pesticides on their leaves. He would later donate his collection of thousands of butterflies to the American Museum of Natural History. A mentor at the museum had been the first to encourage him to study butterflies and publish papers when he was still in high school.

Following high school, Ehrlich went on to study zoology at the University of Pennsylvania where he received his A.B. degree in 1953. As an undergraduate, he read two books that gave him a global framework for what he had observed as a young naturalist: *Our Plundered Planet*, by Fairfield Osborn, and *Road to Survival*, by William Vogt. During his college years, he adopted the Malthusian perspective of the world, that if the population continued to grow at this pace, its needs would eventually exceed what the world's resources could provide. If the birthrate weren't controlled, he felt war, famine, and poverty would have to serve as natural restrictions to an increasing population.

He went to the University of Kansas to do graduate work in entomology. His first job was studying the evolution of DDT resistance in fruit flies. He received his M.A. in 1955 and his Ph.D. in entomology in 1957.

While he was in graduate school at the University of Kansas, he met and married a fellow student, Anne Fitzhugh Howland. Anne, who would come to co-author many books with him, was an art and French major who shared his fascination with nature and science. They had one daughter, Lisa Marie. Several years later Ehrlich, in keeping with his population-control beliefs, had a vasectomy.

Ehrlich became a postdoctoral research associate at the Chicago Academy of Sciences, and in 1959, he joined the faculty at Stanford, where he started his thirty-five-year study of local checkerspot butterfly populations, the most thorough research ever done on the ecology and evolution of a single animal species. In the 1960s, the Ehrlichs' butterfly research on population dynamics and resource limitations led to a deepening understanding of such processes for other species. At the time, the human population was growing at its highest rate in history, more than two percent annually. Ehrlich paid progressively more attention to the complex interconnections between ecology, ecosystems, and human population, and soon began lecturing on these subjects to alumni and civic groups as well as to his students at Stanford.

In his first sabbatical year, 1965-1966, Paul and Anne took a field trip around the world to gain a global perspective on the taxonomy, evolution, and ecology of butterflies, the natural system that was the focus of their scientific interest. "Around the world," they later wrote in *Betrayal of Science and Reason* (1996), "we have watched humanity consuming its natural capital and degrading its own life-support systems. Virtually everywhere—be it the Comoros Islands or California, Delhi or Detroit, Antarctica or Alaska, Fiji or Florence, Tanzania or Tokyo, Australia or the Amazon, Beijing or Bora Bora— we've seen the result of gradually building pressures caused by increasing human numbers, over-consumption, and the use of environmentally damaging technologies and practices."

Ehrlich explained his transition from the study of butterflies to human population as a natural progression. "The evolution and ecology of butterflies and of people just sort of naturally go together because it's the same system," he said. "We're all subject to exactly the same laws. Butterfly populations and human populations can only grow beyond carrying capacity for a short time."

By the mid-1960s, Ehrlich was giving public lectures about the population problem. After a well-publicized speech to the Commonwealth Club in San Francisco, David Brower (then director of the Sierra Club) and Jan Ballantine (of Ballantine Books) persuaded him to write the book that made him famous overnight. *The Population Bomb* turned out to be what may be the all time ecological bestseller. It has sold more than three million copies.

People's initial reaction to the book was shock, often on a religious basis, at the thought that there could ever be "too many people." While there was some initial denial on the part of "Cornucopians," it was not until the 1980s that Ehrlich became a primary target for anti-Malthusians.

In *Betrayal of Science and Reason*, Paul and Anne Ehrlich persuasively argue with critics who believe the world's natural resources are infinite, population growth good for the environment, and global warming a hoax. Ehrlich responds to those who say the earth can sustain an ever-growing population by pointing out that with "death control" through modern medicine and without birth control, war or hunger would be the penalty of failing to control population growth, and not the means to do it. There could come a time when there is no room for more human beings on earth. "After 1900 years, the mass of human population would equal the mass of the earth," Ehrlich asserts.

When Paul Ehrlich wrote *The Population Bomb* it helped reinvigorate an international movement that already existed to promote family planning in less developed regions. It also stimulated national concern about environmental problems. Before Ehrlich's book there was no Environmental Protection Agency, no Council on Environmental Quality, no National Environmental Policy Act, no Endangered Species Act, no Superfund for toxic wastes, no recycling, and no Earth Day Celebration. Ehrlich's warnings set the stage for long-lasting social changes.

In July 1998, Brian Atwood, administrator of the U.S. Agency for International Development, reported on the progress made by the international fight against poverty in the developing world in the past thirty years. The progress includes a fifty percent rise in literacy; the average woman worldwide now has three children; infant mortality has been cut fifty percent; malnutrition has been cut fifty percent; life expectancy has risen by more than ten years; and per capita income has risen by fifty percent. The Green Revolution produced a near miraculous increase in crop yields.

World Population Prospects: The 1996 Revision, a reference book published by the United Nations, reported that the total fertility rate (TFR) worldwide had decreased from 5 in 1970 to just below 3 in 1995. In 1998, the TFR was estimated at 2.8 and still dropping.

With the support of grassroots organizations like Zero Population Growth in the United States and Planned Parenthood, with its international impact, people everywhere have been changing their minds about the number of children to have. The "replacement level," estimated at 2.1 (the number of children a woman must have to maintain but not increase or decrease the population), has been achieved in an increasing number of countries.

Ehrlich is an activist as well as an academic whose words put the issue of population control on the international agenda for more than thirty years. His crusade for population control has not been limited to academic journals. He appeared on *The Tonight Show with Johnny Carson* twenty-five times in the 1970s. He was nominated for an Emmy in 1990 for his twelve NBC feature reports on global ecological issues. He has been a featured keynote speaker at annual Earth Day rallies, and was profiled in a PBS documentary, *Paul Ehrlich and the Population Bomb*, that traced his career from his early field work in the Arctic to his successful campaign for population control.

In 1968, the world discovered that the human species was reproducing itself uncontrollably with possibly ominous consequences. Today, while pleased with the progress made over the past three decades, Ehrlich continues his crusade, warning the public not to become complacent. He warns of the dangers of energy consumption, urban sprawl, air and water pollution, and disappearing farmland. Noting that the problem of overpopulation is accompanied and intensified by overconsumption, he calls for an end to population growth and implores the rich to spend less to assure ecological sustainability. He also strongly supports the empowerment and education of women, not only as a means to ending over-reproduction, but also because their participation is an essential component of successful economic development.

Today Ehrlich is Bing Professor of Population Studies, Professor of Biological Sciences, and founder and president of the Center for Conservation Biology at Stanford University. His honors and awards include the first Scientific American Prize for Science in the Service of Humanity, the Crafoord Prize in Population Biology and the Conservation of Biological Diversity, a MacArthur Fellowship, the Volvo Environment Prize, the International Center for Tropical Ecology's World Ecology Medal, the World Wildlife Federation Medal, the United Nations/Saskawa Environment Prize, the Heinz Environmental Prize, the International Ecology Institute Prize, and the Tyler Award. Ehrlich has written more than seven hundred books, papers, and articles. His first book, *How to Know the Butterflies*, was published in 1961.

In 1999, the Clinton administration announced a major shift in federal population policy that would move the nation from its decades-old pro-growth position to a controlled-growth stance. A billion-dollar program was proposed to help communities protect open space and farmland in an effort to stop runaway suburban sprawl.

Ehrlich reminds his supporters, as well as his critics, that if he is right about what must be done, we have a chance to save civilization. If he is wrong, people will still be better fed, better housed, and happier. Not a bad deal.

Meanwhile, on October 12, 1999, U.N. Secretary-General Kofi Annan symbolically welcomed Adnan, a Sarajevan baby boy, as the six billionth person in the world. When Ehrlich published *The Population Bomb* in 1968, there were fewer than four billion people on earth. The following excerpts from *The Population Bomb* highlight the issues of population growth, food scarcity, and environmental deterioration the world faced even then.

SOURCES. Ehrlich, Paul, *The Population Bomb*, Ballantine Books, New York, 1968; Ehrlich, Paul and Anne Ehrlich, *Betrayal of Science and Reason: How Anti-Environmental Rhetoric Threatens Our Future*, Island Press, Washington, D.C., 1996; Ehrlich, Paul and Anne Ehrlich, *Extinction: The Causes and Consequences of the Disappearance of Species*, Random House, New York, 1981; Ehrlich, Paul and Anne Ehrlich, *Healing the Planet: Strategies for Resolving the Environmental Crisis*, Addison-Wesley Publishing Co., New York, 1991; Ehrlich, Paul and Anne Ehrlich, *The Population Explosion*, Simon & Schuster, New York, 1990.

The Population Bomb

Dr. Paul R. Ehrlich

TOO MANY PEOPLE[1]

Americans are beginning to realize that the undeveloped countries of the world face an inevitable population–food crisis. Each year food production in undeveloped countries falls a bit further behind burgeoning population growth, and people go to bed a little bit hungrier. While there are temporary or local reversals of this trend, it now seems inevitable that it will continue to its logical conclusion: mass starvation. The rich are going to get richer, but the more numerous poor are going to get poorer. Of these poor, a minimum of three and one-half million will starve to death this year, mostly children. But this is a mere handful compared to the numbers that will be starving in a decade or so. And it is now too late to take action to save many of those people.

In a book about population there is a temptation to stun the reader with an avalanche of statistics. I'll spare you most, but not all, of that. After all, no matter how you slice it, population is a numbers game. Perhaps the best way to impress you with numbers is to tell you about the "doubling time"—the time necessary for the population to double in size.

It has been estimated that the human population of 6000 b.c. was about five million people, taking perhaps one million years to get there from two and a half million. The population did not reach five hundred million until almost 8,000 years later—about 1650 a.d. This means it doubled roughly once every thousand years or so. It reached a billion people around 1850, doubling in some two hundred years. It took only 80 years or so for the next doubling, as the population reached two billion around 1930. We have not completed the next doubling to four billion yet, but we now have well over three billion people. The doubling time at present seems to be about 37 years. Quite a reduction in doubling times: 1,000,000 years, 1,000 years, 200 years, 80 years, 37 years....

Of course, population growth is not occurring uniformly over the face of the Earth. Indeed, countries are divided rather neatly into two groups: those with rapid growth rates, and those with relatively slow growth rates. The first group, making up about two-thirds of the world population, coincides closely with what are known as the "undeveloped countries" (UDCs). The UDCs are not industrialized, tend to have inefficient agriculture, very small gross national products, high illiteracy rates and related problems. That's what UDCs are technically, but a short definition of undeveloped is "starving." Most Latin American, African, and Asian countries fall into this category. The second group consists, in essence, of the "developed countries" (DCs). DCs are modern industrial nations, such as the United States, Canada, most European countries, Israel, Russia, Japan, and Australia. Most people in these countries are adequately nourished.

Doubling times in the UDCs range around 20 to 35 years.... Think of what it means for the population of a country to double in 25 years. In order just to keep living standards at the present inadequate level, the food available for the people must be doubled. Every structure and road must be duplicated. The amount of power must be doubled. The capacity of the transport system must be doubled. The number of trained doctors, nurses, teachers, and administrators must be doubled. This would be a fantastically difficult job in the United States—a rich country with a fine agricultural system, immense industries, and rich natural resources. Think of what it means to a country with none of these....

Doubling times for the populations of the DCs tend to be in the 50- to 200-year range.... These are industrialized countries that have undergone the so-called demographic transition—a transition from high to low growth rate. As industrialization progressed, children became less important to parents as extra hands to work on the farm and as support in old age. At the same time they became a financial drag—expensive to raise and educate. Presumably these are the reasons for a slowing of population growth after industrialization. They boiled down to a simple fact—people just want to have fewer children....

As you are well aware, however, urban concentrations are creating serious problems even in America. In the United States, one of the more rapidly growing DCs, we hear constantly of the headaches caused by growing population:

not just garbage in our environment, but overcrowded highways, burgeoning slums, deteriorating school systems, rising crime rates, riots, and other related problems....

In summary, the world's population will continue to grow as long as the birth rate exceeds the death rate; it's as simple as that. When it stops growing or starts to shrink, it will mean that either the birth rate has gone down or the death rate has gone up or a combination of the two. Basically, then, there are only two kinds of solutions to the population problem. One is a "birth rate solution," in which we find ways to lower the birth rate. The other is a "death rate solution," in which ways to raise the death rate—war, famine, pestilence—*find us*. The problem could have been avoided by *population control*, in which mankind consciously adjusted the birth rate so that a "death rate solution" did not have to occur.

TOO LITTLE FOOD[2]

Why did I pick on the next nine years instead of the next nine hundred for finding a solution to the population crisis? One answer is that the world, especially the undeveloped world, is rapidly running out of food. And famine, of course, could be one way to reach a death rate solution to the population problem. In fact, the battle to feed humanity is already lost, in the sense that we will not be able to prevent large-scale famines in the next decade or so. It is difficult to guess what the exact scale and consequences of the famines will be. But there *will be* famines. Let's look at the situation today.

Everyone agrees that at least half of the people of the world are undernourished (have too little food) or malnourished (have serious imbalances in their diet). The number of deaths attributable to starvation is open to considerable debate. The reason is threefold. First, demographic statistics are often incomplete or unreliable. Second, starving people don't necessarily die of starvation. They often fall victim to some disease as they weaken. When good medical care is available, starvation can be a long, drawn-out process indeed. Third, and perhaps more important, starvation is undramatic. Deaths from starvation go unnoticed, even when they occur as close as Mississippi. Many Americans are under the delusion that an Asian can live happily "on a bowl of rice a day." Such a diet means slow starvation for an Asian, just as it would for an American. A *New Republic* article estimated that five million Indian children die each year of malnutrition. The Population Crisis Committee estimates that three and one-half million people will starve to death this year, mostly children....

All of this boils down to a few elementary facts. There is not enough food today. How much there will be tomorrow is open to debate. If the optimists are correct, today's level of misery will be perpetuated for perhaps two decades into the future. If the pessimists are correct, massive famines will occur soon, possibly in the early 1970s, certainly by the early 1980s. So far most of the evidence seems to be on the side of the pessimists, and we should plan on the assumption that they are correct. After all, some two billion people aren't being properly fed in 1968!

A DYING PLANET[3]

Our problems would be much simpler if we needed only to consider the balance between food and population. But in the long view the progressive deterioration of our environment may cause more death and misery than any conceivable food-population gap. And it is just this factor, environmental deterioration, that is almost universally ignored by those most concerned with closing the food gap.

It is fair to say that the environment of every organism, human and non-human, on the face of the Earth has been influenced by the population explosion of *Homo sapiens*. As direct or indirect results of this explosion, some organism, such as the passenger pigeon, are now extinct. Many others, such as the larger wild animals of all continents, have been greatly reduced in members. Still others, such as sewer rats and house flies, enjoy much enlarged populations. But these are obvious results and probably less important than more subtle changes in the complex web of life and in delicately balanced natural chemical cycles. Ecologists—those biologists who study the relationships of plants and animals with their environments—are especially concerned about these changes. They realize how easily disrupted are ecological systems (called ecosystems), and they are afraid of both the short- and long-range consequences for these ecosystems of many of mankind's activities.

Environmental changes connected with agriculture are often striking. For instance, in the United States we are paying a price for maintaining our high level of food production. Professor LaMonte Cole recently said, "...even our own young country is not immune to deterioration. We have lost many thousands of acres to erosion and gullying, and many thousands more to strip mining. It has been estimated that the agricultural value of Iowa farmland, which is about as good land as we have, is declining by one percent per year. In our irrigated lands of the West there is the constant danger of salinization from rising water tables, while, elsewhere, from Long Island to Southern California, we have lowered water tables so greatly that in coastal regions salt water is seeping into the aquifers. Meanwhile, an estimated two thousand irrigation dams in the United States are now useless impoundments of silt, sand, and gravel.".…

Plans for increasing food production invariably involve large-scale efforts at environmental modification. These plans involve the "inputs" so beloved of the agricultural propagandist—especially fertilizers to enrich soils and pesticides to discourage our competitors. Growing more food also may involve the clearing of forests from additional land and the provision of irrigation water. There seems to be little hope that we will suddenly have an upsurge in the level of responsibility or ecological sophistication of persons concerned with increasing agricultural output. I predict that the rate of soil deterioration will accelerate as the food crisis intensifies. Ecology will be ignored more and more as things get tough. It is safe to assume that our use of synthetic pesticides, already massive, will increase. In spite of much publicity, the intimate relationship between pesticides on the one hand and environmental deterioration on the other is not often recognized.…

In spite of all the efforts of conservationists, all the propaganda, all the eloquent writing, all the beautiful pictures, the conservation battle is presently being lost. In my years of interest in this question I've come to the conclusion that it is being lost for two powerful reasons. The first, of course, is that nothing "undeveloped" can long stand in the face of the population explosion. The second is that most Americans clearly don't give a damn. They've never heard of the California condor and would shed no tears if it became extinct. Indeed, many Americans would compete for the privilege of shooting the last one. Our population consists of two groups: a comparatively small one dedicated to the preservation of beauty and wildlife, and a vastly larger one dedicated to the destruction of both (or at least apathetic toward it). I am assuming that the first group is with me and that the second cannot be moved to action by an appeal to beauty, or a plea for mercy for what may well be our only living companions in a vast universe.

I have just scratched the surface of the problem of environmental deterioration, but I hope that I have at least convinced you that subtle ecological effects may be much more important than the obvious features of the problem. The causal chain of the deterioration is easily followed to its source. Too many cars, too many factories, too much detergent, too much pesticide, multiplying contrails, inadequate sewage treatment plants, too little water, too much carbon dioxide—all can be traced easily to *too many people.*

---

1. From *The Population Bomb* by Dr. Paul R. Ehrlich, pages 17–18, 22–23, 23–25, 34–35. Copyright © 1968, 1971 by Paul R. Ehrlich. Reprinted by permission of Ballantine Books, a Division of Random House.

2. Ehrlich, *The Population Bomb*, pages 36–37, 44–45.

3. Ehrlich, *The Population Bomb*, pages 46–47, 48–49, 65–67.

RALPH NADER

Ralph Nader is six feet four inches tall and speaks with a quiet intensity. He shuns publicity, jealously guards his privacy, and has few close friends. He is nearly fanatical in his fight for justice. As America's leading scourge of fat cats in politics and business, he has taken on many of their idols and exposed their frailties. He was the David to General Motors' Goliath. He taught America that you can fight city hall and win. Your life today is better because of him.

Ralph Nader was born in Winsted, northwestern Connecticut, on February 27, 1934, to Nadra and Rose Bouziane Nader, immigrants from Lebanon. He was one of four children—two boys and two girls.

His father owned a restaurant and bakery, The Highland Arms, which came to be Winsted's main eatery and town gathering place. His mother, a homemaker and active citizen, was known for her gourmet Mediterranean meals. She would tell her children stories about heroes while they shared kitchen chores. In 1991, she would write a cookbook, *It Happened in the Kitchen: Recipes for Food and Thought*, where she blended her philosophy of child rearing with her recipes. His father, who often spoke out on public issues, taught the children the significance of civic responsibility in a democracy. Both Naders were active in Winsted community affairs and taught their children the importance of education and civic self-esteem.

Nader attributed his passion for activism to his father, who once held a march in Winsted to protest a congressional salary increase. Talks around the dinner table often centered on national and international events. Ralph was reading the *Congressional Record* by the time he was twelve, and his list of heroes ranged from Pericles to Thomas Jefferson. He also admired muckrakers such as Upton Sinclair and Ida Tarbell. In fact, his interest in social issues was sparked by Sinclair's *The Jungle*. In the mid-1950s, Ralph witnessed a gruesome auto crash that would have an enduring impact on him.

As a youngster, Ralph was a big Yankees fan. Lou Gehrig was his hero. He was impressed by Gehrig's stamina (he played 2,130 consecutive games) and admired his demeanor, modesty, and self-control. As it turned out, this was a fairly good description of the person Nader was to become.

Nader graduated from Gilbert School, the secondary school in Winsted, in 1951. He was an excellent student and limited his extracurricular activities to dramatics, where he worked backstage.

With the strong encouragement of his parents, he attended Princeton University. He was a voracious reader with an exceptional memory and graduated magna cum laude with a bachelor degree in government and economics in 1955. He started at Harvard Law School at age twenty-one. In his first year at Harvard, he joined the staff of the *Record*, the student newspaper, and by his second semester, he was named editor-in-chief. He tried to turn the focus of the paper to controversial social issues and subsequently left the paper after a disagreement over his plan to make the *Record* a national legal newspaper. In 1958, he received his LL.B.

In late 1958 and early 1959, he fulfilled his military service requirements by serving six months in the Army at Fort Dix, New Jersey. He was also in the inactive reserve for five years. In April 1959, he published an article in *The Nation* that documented the auto manufacturers' responsibility for highway accident deaths and injuries.

Nader was admitted to the Connecticut Bar in 1958, and to the Massachusetts Bar in 1959. He was approved to practice before the U.S. Supreme Court. He had an office in Hartford, Connecticut as an attorney in private practice, starting in 1959. During the early years of his law practice, Nader handled several auto accident cases and became increasingly interested in highway mortality statistics.

He taught history and government at the University of Hartford from 1961 to 1963. During the early 1960s, he traveled throughout the Soviet Union, Scandinavia, Africa, and South America as a freelance journalist.

In 1963, Nader left his Hartford practice and hitchhiked to Washington, D.C. He was hired the following year by then-Assistant Secretary of Labor Daniel Moynihan to be a consultant on auto safety issues and later shared his findings on automobile safety with a congressional committee.

Since 1956, he had been compiling his research on auto safety for a book that would catapult him into national fame. *Unsafe at Any Speed: The Designed-in Dangers of the American Automobile*, a relentless attack on the auto industry, was published in late November 1965. The book charged that the Chevrolet Corvair was an unsafe car, and that General Motors was aware of its design flaws, but ignored them in order to increase its profits. Nader's exposé might have been ignored if General Motors, in its deluded outrage over the accusations, hadn't decided to try to discredit Nader and his book.

General Motors hired a private investigator to tail Nader and dig up dirt on him. The tactic backfired. General Motors ended up with the tarnished image. There was no dirt to be found in Nader's private life, as he led a modest, near-monastic existence, living alone in a rented room. His life was his work, and his work was unassailable. Nader sued General Motors for invasion of privacy, and the case was settled out of court for $425,000 and a public apology. General Motor's embarrassed apology, delivered in front of a Senate committee, brought Nader a national folk-hero image and made him a media star. Ironically, the cash settlement helped Nader create a national consumer movement that would successfully challenge General Motors again.

He became a sought-after public speaker and inspired college students to support consumer issues on campuses from coast to coast. He was also a lecturer at Princeton University from 1967 to 1968.

Nader used his speaking fees, foundation grants, contributions, and proceeds from the sale of reports and publications to create a unique national network of organizations that still employs thousands of people in consumer protection. Many of his young proteges, known as "Nader's Raiders," mostly college students or recent law graduates, spread out across the country investigating the affairs of business and government. One of his main organizations, the Center for the Study of Responsive Law, was started just a few blocks from the White House in Washington, D.C.

Despite his fame, Nader continued to live a frugal life, eschewing many modern conveniences, including credit cards. He once remarked that he did not own a car because he "could never find a safe car to drive."

When there was talk of his running for president, Nader initially rejected the idea. It wasn't until 1992 that he appeared as a write-in candidate in New Hampshire and on the ballot in the Massachusetts presidential primaries. Nader encouraged voters elsewhere to write "none of the above" on the ballot. In 1996, in an effort to challenge the power of the two ruling political parties, Nader agreed to be the presidential candidate on the Green Party slate. He ran a low-key campaign, using his platform to rail against the influence of money in the political process. He spent less than five thousand dollars on his campaign and attracted about seven hundred thousand votes. Nader ran on the Green ticket again in 2000.

Ralph Nader started changing America in 1965 with *Unsafe at Any Speed*. The book was the landmark event of a new public interest movement focused on consumer affairs. It was a bestseller that led to 1966 legislation requiring the federal government to set auto safety standards for the first time. President Johnson invited Nader to the White House for the signing ceremony. When asked, in 1985, to describe the impact of the book since its publication, Nader responded with one impressive result, "There are tens of thousands of people that we've saved every year because of the federal highway safety program."

On the twentieth anniversary of the publication of the book, *Maclean's* described it as "a book that changed America—and, therefore, the world." Michael Kinsley, then editor of the *New Republic*, said no living American was responsible for "more concrete improvement in the society we actually do inhabit," than Nader. Since *Unsafe at Any Speed*, Nader has sponsored, edited, and written dozens of books, manuals, and guides for consumer action.

While Nader may be best known for his victory over General Motors, he is not a "one trick pony." Over the years, his activism has covered a wide range of subjects, including law, freedom of information, access to justice, health, energy, purchasing, lobbying, litigation, aviation, auto safety, nutrition, air and water pollution, children, disability rights, banks, insurance, food additives, nursing homes, pension rights, federal regulation agencies, anti-trust enforcement, the Internet and computer industry, and telecommunications.

Nader once described himself as a "Johnny Appleseed getting consumer groups started and letting them grow on their own." Some of the consumer advocacy groups he founded include Center for the Study of Responsive Law, Public Citizen, Inc., National Insurance Consumer Organization, Public Interest Research Group, Citizen Utility Boards, Aviation Consumer Action Project, Center for Auto Safety, Connecticut Citizen Action Group, Critical Mass Energy

Project, Project for Corporate Responsibility, Health Research Group, Clean Water Action Project, Disability Rights Center, Appleseed Centers for Law & Justice, and the Pension Rights Center. In 1973, he provided seed money to start the Capitol Hill News Service to encourage more critical news coverage of Congress.

His advocacy helped push through wide-ranging legislation to upgrade standards for meat and poultry, promote natural gas pipeline safety and underground safety, and establish the Occupational Safety and Health Administration, the Consumer Product Safety Commission, and the Environmental Protection Agency. A few of the laws he helped pass include the National Traffic and Motor Vehicle Safety Act, the Clean Air Act, the National Consumer Cooperative Bank Act, the 1974 Freedom of Information Act, and the Radiation Control Act. In 1989, he led a successful campaign to block members of Congress from approving a fifty-one percent pay raise for themselves.

One of Nader's most satisfying achievements may have come in 1989 when his old nemesis, General Motors, announced it would install airbags as standard equipment in hundreds of thousands of 1990 cars. In fact, if you have ever benefited from seatbelts, crash-worthy cars, better labeling on food, lower levels of lead in the environment, reduced auto insurance rates, non-smoking sections, cleaner water, you have Ralph Nader to thank.

Always seeking new foes to conquer, in 1998, at the age of sixty-four, Ralph Nader was leading a national army of more than one hundred consumer and environmental organizations, rallying them to defeat the utility companies' efforts to pass billions of dollars of bad investments along to electric utility consumers.

With all of the material benefits he has brought American society, Nader believes that one of his greatest achievements is an intangible one. "Most important, I think," Nader said, "is to give people heart. If you show them what can be done, they believe that maybe they can do it on a different scale in their communities, that they can strengthen citizen-style democracy. It's an enabling function that we have given visibility to, you know, you *can* fight city hall and Exxon."

The following preface from *Unsafe at Any Speed* summarizes the depth of the problem of highway accidents and depicts the economic forces that had developed over the years to thwart efforts to reduce those accidents. The excerpts from "The Sporty Corvair" chapter, describe the human consequences of designing cars for profit, not safety.

SOURCES. Isaac, Katherine, *Ralph Nader's Practicing Democracy 1997: A Guide to Student Action*, St. Martin's Press, New York, 1997; McCarry, Charles, *Citizen Nader*, Saturday Review Press, New York, 1972; Nader, Ralph and Donald Ross, *Action for a Change: A Student's Manual for Public Interest Organizing*, revised edition, Grossman Publishers, New York, 1972; Nader, Ralph and Wesley J. Smith, *Collision Course: The Truth About Airline Safety*, Tab Books/McGraw-Hill, Blue Ridge Summit, Pennsylvania, 1994; Nader, Ralph and William Taylor, *The Big Boys: Power and Position in American Business*, Pantheon Books, New York, 1986; Nader, Ralph, Clarence Ditlow, and Joyce Kinnard, *The Lemon Book*, Caroline House Publishers, Ottawa, Illinois, 1980; Nader, Ralph, *Unsafe at Any Speed: The Designed-In Dangers of the American Automobile*, Grossman Publishers, New York, 1965; Nader, Ralph, *Updated: Unsafe at Any Speed: The Designed-In Dangers of the American Automobile*, Grossman Publishers, New York, 1972.

Unsafe at Any Speed

Ralph Nader

WHO BENEFITS FROM
AUTO ACCIDENTS?

For over half a century the automobile has brought death, injury, and the most inestimable sorrow and deprivation to millions of people. With Medea-like intensity, this mass trauma began rising sharply four years ago, reflecting new and unexpected ravages by the motor vehicle. A 1959 Department of Commerce report projected that fifty-one thousand persons would be killed by automobiles in 1975. That figure will probably be reached in 1965, a decade ahead of schedule.

A transportation specialist, Wilfred Owen, wrote in 1946, "There is little question that the public will not tolerate for long an annual traffic toll of forty to fifty thousand fatalities." Time has shown Owen to be wrong. Unlike aviation, marine, or rail transportation, the highway transport system can inflict tremendous casualties and property damage without in the least affecting the viability of the system. Plane crashes, for example, jeopardize the attraction of flying for potential passengers and therefore strike at the heart of the air transport economy. They motivate preventative efforts. The situation is different on the roads.

Highway accidents were estimated to have cost this country in 1964, $8.3 billion in property damage, medical expenses, lost wages, and insurance overhead expenses. Add an equivalent sum to comprise roughly the indirect costs and the total amounts to over two percent of the gross national product. But these are not the kind of costs which fall on the builders of motor vehicles (excepting a few successful law suits for negligent construction of the vehicle)

225

and thus do not pinch the proper foot. Instead, the costs fall to users of vehicles, who are in no position to dictate safer automobile designs.

In fact, the gigantic costs of the highway carnage in this country support a service industry. A vast array of services—medical, police, administrative, legal, insurance, automotive repair, and funeral—stand equipped to handle the direct and indirect consequences of accident injuries. Traffic accidents create economic demands for these services running into billions of dollars. It is in the post-accident response that lawyers and physicians and other specialists labor. This is where the remuneration lies and this is where the talent and energies go. Working in the area of prevention of these casualties earns few fees. Consequently our society has an intricate organization to handle direct and indirect aftermaths of collisions. But the true mark of a humane society must be what it does about *prevention* of accident injuries, not the cleaning up of them afterward.

Unfortunately, there is little in the dynamics of the automobile accident industry that works for its reduction. Doctors, lawyers, engineers and other specialists have failed in their primary professional ethic: to dedicate themselves to the prevention of accident-injuries. The roots of the unsafe vehicle problem are so entrenched that the situation can be improved only by the forging of new instruments of citizen action. When thirty practicing physicians picketed for safe auto design at the New York International Automobile Show on April 7, 1965, their unprecedented action was the measure of their desperation over the inaction of the men and institutions in government and industry who have failed to provide the public with the vehicle safety to which it is entitled. The picketing surgeons, orthopedists, pediatricians and general practitioners marched in protest because the existing medical, legal and engineering organizations have defaulted.

A great problem of contemporary life is how to control the power of economic interests which ignore the harmful effects of their applied science and technology. The automobile tragedy is one of the most serious of these man-made assaults on the human body. The history of that tragedy reveals many obstacles which must be overcome in the taming of any mechanical or biological hazard which is a by-product of industry or commerce. Our society's obligation to protect the "body rights" of its citizens with vigorous resolve and ample resources requires the precise, authoritative articulation and front-rank support which is being devoted to civil rights.

This country has not been entirely laggard in defining values relevant to new contexts of a technology laden with risks. The postwar years have witnessed a historic broadening, at least in the courts, of the procedural and substantive rights of the injured and the duties of manufacturers to produce a safe product. Judicial decisions throughout the fifty states have given living meaning to Walt Whitman's dictum, "If anything is sacred, the human body is sacred." Mr. Justice Jackson in 1953 defined the duty of the manufacturers by saying, "Where experiment or research is necessary to determine the presence of the degree of danger, the product must not be tried out on the public, nor must the public be expected to possess the facilities of the technical knowledge to learn for itself of inherent but latent dangers. The claim that a hazard was not foreseen is not available to one who did not use foresight appropriate to his enterprise."

It is a lag of almost paralytic proportions that these values of safety concerning consumers and economic enterprises, reiterated many times by the judicial branch of government, have not found their way into legislative policy-making for safer automobiles. Decades ago legislation was passed, changing the pattern of private business investments to accommodate more fully the safety value on railroads, in factories, and more recently on ships and aircraft. In transport, apart from the motor vehicle, considerable progress has been made in recognizing the physical integrity of the individual. There was a period when railroad workers were killed by the thousands and the editor of *Harper's* could say late in the last century: "So long as brakes cost more than trainmen, we may expect the present sacrificial method of car-coupling to be continued." But injured trainmen did cause the railroads some operating dislocations; highway victims cost the automobile companies next to nothing and the companies are not obliged to make use of developments in science-technology that have demonstrably opened up opportunities for far greater safety than any existing safety features lying unused on the automobile companies' shelves.

A principal reason why the automobile has remained the only transportation vehicle to escape being called to meaningful public account is that the public has never been supplied the information nor offered the quality of competition to enable it to make effective demands through the marketplace and through government for a safe, non-polluting and efficient automobile that can be produced economically. The consumer's expectations regarding automotive innovations have been deliberately held low and mostly oriented to very gradual annual style changes. The specialists and researchers outside the industry who could have provided the leadership to stimulate this flow of information by and large chose to remain silent, as did government officials.

The persistence of the automobile's immunity over the years has nourished the continuance of that immunity, recalling Francis Bacon's insight: "He that will not apply new remedies must expect new evils, for time is the great innovator."

The accumulated power of decades of effort by the automobile industry to strengthen its control over car design is reflected today in the difficulty of even beginning to bring it to justice. The time has not come to discipline the automobile for safety; that time came over four decades ago. But that it not cause to delay any longer what should have been accomplished in the 1920s.

THE SPORTY CORVAIR:
THE 'ONE-CAR' ACCIDENT

John F. Gordon, president of General Motors, was the keynote speaker before the annual National Safety Congress in October 1961. He talked about the "diversionary forces" undermining safety progress and warned the safety professionals about self-styled experts with radical and ill-conceived proposals. His unabashed pro-industry version of auto safety was widely publicized in the national media.

Mrs. Rose Pierini did not read about Mr. Gordon's complaints. She was learning to adjust to the loss of her left arm which was severed two months earlier when the 1961 Chevrolet Corvair she was driving turned over on its top just beyond the San Marcos overpass on Hollister Street in Santa Barbara, California. Exactly thirty-four months later, in the same city, General Motors decided to pay Mrs. Pierini seventy thousand dollars rather than continue a trial which for three days threatened to expose on the public record one of the greatest acts of industrial irresponsibility in the present century.

Mrs. Pierini's experience with a Corvair going unexpectedly and suddenly out of control was not unique. There simply are too many Corvairs with such inclinations for her case to be singular. What was distinctive about the "accident" was the attempt to find the cause of it on the basis of investigation, instead of resorting to the customary, automatic placing of blame on the driver.

As described by a California Highway Patrol officer, John Bortolozzo, who witnessed the flip-over while motoring in the opposite direction, the Pierini vehicle was traveling about thirty-five miles per hour in a thirty-five miles per hour zone in the right lane headed towards Goleta. He saw the car move towards the right side of the road near the shoulder and then "all of a sudden the vehicle made a sharp cut to the left and swerved over." Bortolozzo testified at the trial that he rushed over to the wreck and saw an arm with a wedding band and wristwatch lying on the ground. Two other men came over quickly and began to help Mrs. Pierini out of the vehicle while trying to stop the torrent of blood gushing forth from the stub of her arm. She was very calm, observed Bortolozzo, only saying that "something went wrong with my steering."

After helping Mrs. Pierini to the ambulance, the officer made a check of the vehicle while it was on its top. He noticed that the left rear tire was deflated because of an air-out. Looking at the road, he noticed some gouge marks made by the metal rim of the left rear tire. He gave his opinion at the trial that the distinctive design features of the Corvair caused it to go out of control and flip over as had other Corvairs in accidents he had investigated. It was during the cross-examination of Officer Bortolozzo by defense lawyers that General Motors decided to settle the case....

The notoriety attached to the Corvair would have soiled the General Motors image of product leadership carefully shaped over the years by a superbly managed program of public relations. For a car to have gone on trial and have been struck down by "twelve men good and pure" would have profoundly shaken even this goliath of American industry. And finally, what about the possible spillover into that dreaded chasm, public regulation? What would legislators think—men long nourished on the diet that "it's all because of the nut behind the wheel"—when court-sanctioned investigations of evidence brought out into the open the facts about an American car that abruptly decides to do the driving *for* the driver in a wholly untoward manner? Against such prospects of ill omen, the alternative—pay and delay—was much more attractive.

Delay can do many things when a large corporation is doing battle with an injured person. The corporation can hang on much longer. Furthermore, the offending Corvairs—primarily 1960–1963 models—can only diminish in number with each passing month; the cause of their collisions and waywardness can continue to go undetected by victims, next of kin, accident investigators, and lawyers.

SEYMOUR HERSH

Seymour Hersh's family, along with millions of other innocent civilians, suffered from the atrocities of the Holocaust during World War II. Less than three decades later, he exposed the horrific atrocities committed by his own government against innocent civilians. His exposé shook America's faith in the military and helped bring an end to the Vietnam War. While he is respected as one of the nation's best investigative journalists, he may also be one of the most reviled journalists of his time.

Seymour Myron Hersh was born April 8, 1937 to Isadore and Dorothy Hersh on the South Side of Chicago. He has a twin brother, Alan, a physicist, and older twin sisters, Marcia, a psychotherapist, and Phyllis, a homemaker. Seymour is a first-generation American. His father, who ran a dry-cleaning business, was born in Russia, and his mother, a housewife, was born in Poland.

Hersh had a typical first-generation upbringing in a middle-class family. "We weren't wealthy," he has said, "but I never knew we weren't wealthy." As a youngster, baseball was his passion, and he was a Chicago White Sox fan. He attended public schools in Chicago: Shakespeare Grammar School and Hyde Park High School. He then studied English and history at the University of Chicago. An average student, he graduated with a bachelor degree in 1958. He started law school but dropped out after one year, realizing that he "hated law school."

After leaving the University of Chicago, he heard about a job at the City News Bureau in Chicago. In 1959, after nine months on the waiting list, the twenty-two-year-old Hersh was hired as a copyboy, starting his journalistic career at the bottom.

Before long, he became a police reporter where he learned the rudiments of journalism and gained a reputation as a tough, go-getting reporter. He left the City News Bureau in 1960 to join the Army where he continued working as a journalist. He wrote for the base newspaper in Fort Riley, Kansas, and after his basic training, he wrote speeches for a general.

After completing his military service, he edited a small weekly newspaper in a Chicago suburb, but after a year of tediously trying to sell ads and arguing with the owner, he quit. He then landed a job with UPI in 1962 and he began working as a correspondent in Pierre, South Dakota. Pierre didn't quite fulfill his aspirations of covering top-level Washington politics. Hersh quit in 1963, and soon joined the Associated Press (AP).

His journalism career was now on the fast track. He first worked as a correspondent in Chicago where he married Elizabeth Sarah Klein, a psychiatrist, in 1964. (They have three children, Matthew, Melissa, and Joshua, and live in Washington's Cleveland Park neighborhood.) In 1965, AP sent him to Washington, D.C., and within a year, he was asked to cover the Department of Defense. He quickly started to develop his reputation as an "outsider." While most reporters were impressed or intimidated by the military, often only reporting the official line, Hersh wasn't. Instead of dutifully taking notes at the regularly scheduled, staged press conferences, or rewriting press releases, he would wander the halls of the Pentagon searching for anyone who would talk to him. Many of them, never having been approached by the press before, would tip Hersh off about stories not discussed at the press conferences.

It was while covering the Pentagon and listening to the lies the military told about the Vietnam War that Hersh became a cynic. He became a popular anti-war speaker at campuses across the country where he would galvanize students with his insider impressions. During this time, he met his mentor, I. F. Stone, who had seen some of his reporting and the two became friends. "Stone showed me how to report," Hersh said. Stone advised him that he couldn't write without reading. A major critic of the Vietnam War, Stone would read everything. Hersh learned to read everything, too. "It's all there if you look," he said.

While at the AP, Hersh gathered damaging information about the American stockpiling of deadly chemical and biological weapons. His series of potentially explosive stories was rewritten by the AP and cut to one short piece. Angered by the AP's refusal to tell the whole story, he quit to write a book. His first investigative book, *Chemical and Biological Warfare: America's Hidden Arsenal*, was published in 1967.

Disappointed by the lack of response to the alarming charges in his book, and hoping to make a difference, he went to work for Senator Eugene McCarthy, who was then seeking the Democratic presidential nomination in 1968. He joined the campaign in New Hampshire as McCarthy's press secretary and speechwriter for his "children's crusade against the Vietnam War." It wasn't long before Hersh became disillusioned with politics altogether and returned to freelancing.

In October 1969, Hersh got a tip about a U.S. Army officer who had reportedly led an attack on innocent civilians in a Vietnamese village. Hersh tracked down Lieutenant William Calley, who was being court-martialed at Fort Benning, Georgia. Calley granted him an exclusive interview about the massacre, and Hersh wrote what became the infamous My Lai story. Several major magazines, including *Life* and *Look*, rejected his story because they believed it could not be true. Finally, he distributed a series of five volatile newspaper stories through the small Dispatch News Service, owned by a friend of his. After the major media were persuaded the story was true, they started to publish his articles, and suddenly Hersh's reputation as a super-journalist was established. His My Lai stories earned him a Pulitzer Prize for international reporting in 1970. Hersh followed up his exposé with two books, *My Lai 4: A Report on the Massacre and Its Aftermath* (1970); and *Cover-Up: The Army's Secret Investigation of the Massacre of My Lai 4* (1972).

With a Pulitzer in hand and his growing reputation as an investigative reporter, the *New York Times* was eager to add Hersh to its award-winning staff in 1972. He spent seven years at the *Times*, mostly as a correspondent in its Washington bureau. While with the *Times*, he broke a number of significant Watergate stories, revealed how Henry Kissinger bugged his own aides, and continued to shake up the military establishment with exposés about covert CIA operations in Cambodia, Pakistan, Chile, and Angola.

Despite his successes at the *Times*, Hersh tired of the newsroom culture and politics and quit in 1979. As a freelance writer, Hersh became a regular contributor to *Atlantic Monthly* and the *New Yorker*, and then wrote a series of controversial books that drew the anger of his targets and generated skepticism on the part of some of his colleagues in journalism. One of his first books as a freelancer was *The Price of Power: Kissinger in the Nixon White House*, published in 1983. Based on more than 1,000 interviews, it seriously tarnished the credibility of Henry Kissinger, National Security Advisor and Secretary of State under President Nixon. It also won the *Los Angeles Times* Book Prize, the National Book Critics Circle Award, and the Investigative Reporters and Editors prize, all in 1983. *The Target Is Destroyed: What Really Happened to Flight 007 and What America Knew About It* was published in 1986 despite warnings from the CIA. This controversial account of the downing of Korean Air Lines (KAL) Flight 007—all 269 people were killed—pleased few readers. He angered the Soviet government by reporting that KAL 007 was not on a CIA espionage mission, as they had claimed. He irritated President Reagan by saying that the flight's destruction was not a wanton act of murder, as President Reagan had alleged. And he disappointed others by not revealing some international conspiracy. Hersh concluded that KAL 007 was simply lost over the USSR, and the Soviet government failed to correctly identify the aircraft.

The Samson Option: Israel's Nuclear Arsenal and America's Foreign Policy (1991) brought Hersh another award from the Investigative Reporters and Editors. The book revealed how the U.S. government covered up its secret approval of Israel's acquisition of nuclear weapons.

The Dark Side of Camelot, published in 1997, probably generated the most criticism of any of his books. His revisionist work about John F. Kennedy's White House years drew both praise and ire from historians and the general public. The book explored how Kennedy's private life and personal obsessions affected both domestic and foreign policy during his presidency. The book's credibility was severely tarnished when a chapter reporting that Kennedy paid Marilyn Monroe to win her silence was found to be fraudulent and had to be removed. His source was later found guilty of selling forged documents.

Hersh also alienated conspiracy theorists by concluding that the Warren Commission was right: Lee Harvey Oswald had acted alone.

Hersh took on the military establishment with *Against All Enemies—Gulf War Syndrome: The War Between America's Ailing Veterans and Their Government*, published in 1998. He hoped to force the government to recognize that Gulf War Syndrome was a legitimate illness, and that veterans deserved medical treatment and compensation.

Hersh has brought public attention to the government's malfeasance on any number of issues. Starting with his revelation of government misconduct with chemical and biological warfare weapons in 1967, and continuing through to his powerful message about the government's failure to help its suffering veterans in 1998, Hersh has proven to be one of the nation's leading political and military watchdogs. In most cases, his words provoked a national discussion and, in some cases, they have led to direct governmental action and altered U.S. policy. His 1967 stories led to a presidential order to stop production and storage of biological weapons. In 1975, his stories about covert American assistance to Angolan rebels led the U.S. Senate to cut off its aid to the rebels.

His most powerful exposé of the My Lai massacre of hundreds of civilians by American soldiers came at the peak of the Vietnam War and contributed significantly to failing public support for the war. It made Americans look upon the war with a new skepticism. In one interview, Hersh shocked America by suggesting that we weren't much better than the Japanese and Nazis when it came to military atrocities.

Hersh has been vilified by some colleagues and critics as being brash, relentless, profane, abrasive, and always contemptuous of protocol. He acknowledges he has made enemies, but insists, "I couldn't see anything so wrong in holding the men at the top to the highest possible standard."

During a time when journalism has tarnished its own reputation with the sensational and relentless reporting of subjects like the O. J. Simpson trial and Bill Clinton's sex life, Hersh has maintained his reputation as one of America's leading hard-news investigative reporters. His My Lai exposé helped establish the standard for modern-day investigative reporting.

When Hersh was asked what he had to say to aspiring journalists, he replied, "You have to not be afraid to tell the truth," modifying George Seldes's advice, which was "Tell the truth and run."

What follows is Seymour Hersh's description of what happened on March 16, 1968, in a tiny Vietnamese hamlet, excerpted from *My Lai 4: A Report on the Massacre and its Aftermath.*

SOURCES. Hersh, Seymour M., *Chemical and Biological Warfare: America's Hidden Arsenal*, Bobbs-Merrill, New York, 1968; Hersh, Seymour M., *Cover-Up: The Army's Secret Investigation of the Massacre at My Lai 4*, Random House, New York, 1972; Hersh, Seymour M., *My Lai 4: A Report on the Massacre and Its Aftermath*, Random House, New York, 1970; Hersh, Seymour M., *The Dark Side* *of Camelot*, Little, Brown & Co., New York, 1997; Hersh, Seymour M., *The Price of Power: Kissinger in the Nixon White House*, Summit Books, New York, 1983; Hersh, Seymour M., *"The Target is Destroyed:" What Really Happened to Flight 007 and What America Knew About It*, Vintage Books, New York, 1986.

My Lai 4
Seymour Hersh

The My Lai massacre occurred on the morning of March 16, 1968. It was not until April 1969, after repeated congressional requests for an investigation, that the Army started to look into the My Lai case. By early 1970, the investigators recommended that charges be placed against fifteen officers, including two generals, two colonels, two lieutenant colonels, four majors, two captains, and two first lieutenants. Of the fifteen, fourteen were charged with the crime. Of the fourteen, thirteen had the charges dismissed. Only one of the defendants, a young lieutenant named William L. Calley, Jr., was charged with murder. He was found guilty, court-martialed, and sentenced to life imprisonment. With the support of President Nixon, Calley was paroled in 1975. He moved to Columbus, Georgia, married the daughter of a jewelry store owner, and lives a quiet life there.

From Chapter Three:
THE DAY—PART I[1]

The hamlet itself had a population of about seven hundred people, living either in flimsy thatch-covered huts—"hootches," as the GIs called them—or in solidly made red-brick homes, many with small porches in front. There was an east-west footpath just south of the main cluster of homes; a few yards further south was a loose surface road that marked a hamlet boundary. A deep drainage ditch and then a rice paddy marked the eastern boundary. To the south of My Lai 4 was a large center, or plaza area—clearly the main spot for mass meetings. The foliage was dense: there were high bamboo trees, hedges and plant life everywhere. Medina couldn't see thirty feet into the hamlet from the landing zone.

The first and second platoons lined up carefully to begin the hundred-meter advance into My Lai 4. Walking in line is an important military concept;

if one group of men gets too far in front, it could be hit by bullets from behind—those fired by colleagues. Yet even this went wrong. Ron Grzesik was in charge of a small first-platoon fire team of riflemen and a machine gunner; he took his job seriously. His unit was supposed to be on the right flank, protecting Calley and his men. But Grzesik's group ended up on Calley's left.

As Brooks' second platoon cautiously approached the hamlet, a few Vietnamese began running across a field several hundred meters on the left. They may have been Viet Cong, or they may have been civilians fleeing the artillery shelling or the bombardment from the helicopter gunships. Vernado Simpson, Jr., of Jackson, Mississippi, saw a man he identified as a Viet Cong soldier running with what seemed to be a weapon. A woman and a small child were running with him. Simpson fired... again and again. He killed the woman and the baby. The man got away. Reporter Roberts saw a squad of GIs jump off a helicopter and begin firing at a group of people running on a nearby road. One was a woman with her children. Then he saw them "shoot two guys who popped up from a rice field. They looked like military-age men.... When certain guys pop up from rice fields, you shoot them." This was the young reporter's most dangerous assignment. He had never been in combat before. "You're scared to death out there. We just wanted to go home."

The first two platoons of Charlie Company, still unfired upon, entered the hamlet. Behind them, still in the rice paddy, were the third platoon and Captain Medina's command post. Calley and some of his men walked into the plaza area in the southern part of the hamlet. None of the people was running away; they knew that U.S. soldiers would assume that anyone running was a Viet Cong and would shoot to kill. There was no immediate sense of panic. The time was about 8 a.m. Grzesik and his fire team were a few meters north of Calley; they couldn't see each other because of the dense vegetation. Grzesik and his men began their usual job of pulling people from their homes, interrogating them, and searching for Viet Cong. The villagers were gathered up, and Grzesik sent Meadlo, who was in his unit, to take them to Calley for further questioning. Grzesik didn't see Meadlo again for more than an hour.

Some of Calley's men thought it was breakfast time as they walked in; a few families were gathered in front of their homes cooking rice over a small fire. Without a direct order, the first platoon also began rounding up the villagers. There still was no sniper fire, no sign of a large enemy unit. Sledge remembered thinking that "if there were V.C. around, they had plenty of time to leave before we came in. We didn't tiptoe in there."

The killings began without warning. Harry Stanley told the C.I.D. that one young member of Calley's platoon took a civilian into custody and then "pushed the man up to where we were standing and then stabbed the man in the back with his bayonet.... The man fell to the ground and was gasping for breath." The GI then "killed him with another bayonet thrust or by shooting him with a rifle.... There were so many people killed that day it is hard for me to recall exactly how some of the people died." The youth next "turned to where some soldiers were holding another forty- or fifty-year-old man in custody." He "picked this man up and threw him down a well. Then [he] pulled the pin from a M26 grenade and threw it in after the man." Moments later Stanley saw "some old women and some little children—fifteen or twenty of them—in a group around a temple where some incense was burning. They were kneeling and crying and praying, and various soldiers ... walked by and executed these women and children by shooting them in the head with their rifles. The soldiers killed all fifteen or twenty of them...."

There were few physical protests from the people; about eighty of them were taken quietly from their homes and herded together in the plaza area. A few hollered out, "No V.C. No V.C." But that was hardly unexpected. Calley left Meadlo, Boyce and a few others with the responsibility of guarding the group. "You know what I want you to do with them," he told Meadlo. Ten minutes later—about 8:15 a.m.—he returned and asked, "Haven't you got rid of them yet? I want them dead." Radioman Sledge, who was trailing Calley, heard the officer tell Meadlo to "waste them." Meadlo followed orders: "We stood about ten to fifteen feet away from them and then he [Calley] started shooting them. Then he told me to start shooting them. I started to shoot them. So we went ahead and killed them. I used more than a whole clip—used four or five clips." There are seventeen M16 bullets in each clip. Boyce slipped away, to the northern side of the hamlet, glad he hadn't been asked to shoot. Women were huddled against their children, vainly trying to save them. Some continued to chant, "No V.C." Others simply said, "No. No. No."

Do Chuc is a gnarled forty-eight-year-old Vietnamese peasant whose two daughters and an aunt were killed by the GIs in My Lai 4 that day. He and his family were eating breakfast when the GIs entered the hamlet and ordered them out of their homes. Together with other villagers, they were marched a few hundred meters into the plaza, where they were told to squat. "Still we had no reason to be afraid," Chuc recalled. "Everyone was calm." He watched as the GIs set up a machine gun. The calm ended. The people began crying and begging. One monk showed his identification papers to a soldier, but the American simply said, "Sorry." Then the shooting started. Chuc was wounded in the leg, but he was covered by dead bodies and thus spared. After waiting an hour, he fled the hamlet....

Now it was nearly nine o'clock and all of Charlie Company was in My Lai 4. Most families were being shot inside their homes, or just outside the doorways. Those who had tried to flee were crammed by GIs into the many bunkers built throughout the hamlet for protection—once the bunkers became filled, hand grenades were lobbed in. Everything became a target. Gary Garfolo borrowed someone's M79 grenade launcher and fired it point-blank at a water buffalo: "I hit that sucker right in the head; went down like a shot. You don't get to shoot water buffalo with an M79 every day." Others fired the weapon into the bunkers full of people.

Jay Roberts insisted that he saw Medina in My Lai 4 most of the morning: "He was directing the operations in the village. He was in the village the whole time I was—from nine o'clock to eleven o'clock."

Carter recalled that some GIs were shouting and yelling during the massacre: "The boys enjoyed it. When someone laughs and jokes about what they're doing, they have to be enjoying it." A GI said, "Hey, I got me another one." Another said, "Chalk up one for me." Even captain Medina was having a good time, Carter thought: "You can tell when someone enjoys their work." Few members of Charlie Company protested that day. For the most part, those who didn't like what was going on kept their thoughts to themselves.

Herbert Carter also remembered seeing Medina inside the hamlet well after the third platoon began its advance: "I saw all those dead people laying there. Medina came right behind me." At one point in the morning one of the members of Medina's CP joined in the shooting. "A woman came out of a hut with a baby in her arms and she was crying," Carter told the C.I.D. "She was crying because her little boy had been in front of their hut and... someone had killed the child by shooting it." When the mother came into view, one of Medina's men "shot her with an M16 and she fell. When she fell, she dropped the baby." The GI next "opened up on the baby with his M16." The infant was also killed. Carter also saw an officer grab a woman by the hair and shoot her with a .45-caliber pistol: "He held her by the hair for a minute and then let go and she fell to the ground. Some enlisted man standing there said, 'Well, she'll be in the big rice paddy in the sky.'"...

Those Vietnamese who were not killed on the spot were being shepherded by the first platoon to a large drainage ditch at the eastern end of the hamlet. After Grzesik left, Meadlo and a few others gathered seven or eight villagers in one hut and were preparing to toss in a hand grenade when an order came to take them to the ditch. There he found Calley, along with a dozen other first platoon members, and perhaps seventy-five Vietnamese, mostly women, old men and children....

From Chapter Four:
THE DAY—PART II[2]

Calley then turned his attention back to the crowd of Vietnamese and issued an order: "Push all those people in the ditch." Three or four GIs complied. Calley struck a woman with a rifle as he pushed her down. Stanley remembered that some of the civilians "kept trying to get out. Some made it to the top...." Calley began the shooting and ordered Meadlo to join in. Meadlo told about it later: "So we pushed our seven to eight people in with the big bunch of them. And so I began shooting them all. So did Mitchell, Calley... I guess I shot maybe twenty-five or twenty people in the ditch... men, women and children. And babies." Some of the GIs switched from automatic fire to single-shot to conserve ammunition. Herbert Carter watched the mothers "grabbing their kids and the kids grabbing their mothers. I didn't know what to do."

Calley then turned to Meadlo and said, "Meadlo, we've got another job to do." Meadlo didn't want any more jobs. He began to argue with Calley. Sledge watched Meadlo once more start to sob. Calley turned next to Robert Maples and said, "Maples, load your machine gun and shoot these people." Maples replied, as he told the C.I.D., "I'm not going to do that." He remembered that "the people firing into the ditch kept reloading magazines into their rifles and kept firing into the ditch and then killed or at least shot everyone in the ditch." William C. Lloyd of Tampa, Florida, told the C.I.D. that some grenades were also thrown into the ditch. Dennis Conti noticed that "a lot of women had thrown themselves on top of the children to protect them, and the children were alive at first. Then the children who were old enough to walk got up and Calley began shooting the children."

One further incident stood out in many GIs' minds: seconds after the shooting stopped, a bloodied but unhurt two-year-old boy miraculously crawled out of the ditch, crying. He began running toward the hamlet. Someone hollered, "There's a kid." There was a long pause. Then Calley ran back, grabbed the child, threw him back in the ditch and shot him.

---

1. From *My Lai 4: A Report on the Massacre and Its Aftermath* (New York: Random House, 1970) by Seymour Hersh, pages 47–51, 55–57, 57–58. Reprinted by permission of International Creative Management, Inc. Copyright © 1970 by Seymour Hersh.
2. Hersh, *My Lai 4*, pages 63–64.

BOB WOODWARD and CARL BERNSTEIN

In their bestselling book that brought down a president, the two authors described themselves: "Bernstein looked like one of those counterculture journalists that Woodward despised. Bernstein thought that Woodward's rapid rise at the *Post* had less to do with his ability than his Establishment credentials."

Bob Woodward came from a strict, conservative, and comfortable middle-class suburban household. He was an Ivy League graduate, fairly apolitical and not fired up by any rebellious reformer's zeal.

Carl Bernstein came from a liberal, politically active, loosely knit family. He was a dropout who started his newspaper career when he was sixteen years old. Distinguished by his long hair and sloppy dress, he often seemed beyond the control of editors.

Woodward and Bernstein were very different—they were like Neil Simon's Odd Couple. But the Watergate twins, as they came to be called, were destined to be forever joined by the political scandal of the century.

BOB WOODWARD

Bob Woodward was born into a prominent midwestern family in Geneva, Illinois, on March 26, 1943, and raised in nearby Wheaton. His father, Alfred E.

Woodward, was Wheaton's leading attorney and Chief Judge of the Du Page County Circuit Court. The judge was a soft-spoken but firm man who had a strong influence on Bob. Bob's mother, Jane Upshur Woodward, was the subject of a huge local scandal, which led to her divorce from the judge while Bob was approaching adolescence. He was the eldest of six children.

Bob attended public schools in Wheaton and then went to Yale University at his father's urging. He enlisted in the Naval ROTC in exchange for a scholarship. After graduating from Yale with a somewhat undistinguished record, he joined the Navy to fulfill his ROTC requirements. He served four years as a communications officer on an aircraft carrier and then on a destroyer. For his fifth and final year of service he was assigned work as a communications liaison officer between the White House and the Pentagon.

Following his Navy tour, in an effort to please his father, he enrolled in Harvard Law School. He quickly tired of the legal studies and, at the age of twenty-seven, dropped out to become a journalist. Journalism was something he felt he could do, and he wanted to get his career underway.

Anxious to start at a leading newspaper in his chosen field, Woodward offered to work for the *Washington Post* without pay. When he failed to get a paid position after a two-week trial period, the *Post* helped him find work at a weekly newspaper, the *Sentinel*, in nearby Montgomery County, Maryland. For a year, he kept calling the *Post* for a job and, after writing an exposé about a bankrupt Montgomery County savings and loan association that was picked up by the *Post*, he was finally hired in 1971.

At age twenty-eight, he started out on the overnight police beat, handling the routine assignments, but also producing self-assigned investigative articles he would research and write on his own time. Nine months later, he was assigned to the Watergate story, an assignment that brought him a Pulitzer Prize and two bestselling nonfiction books, *All the President's* Men and *The Final Days*.

After the Watergate experience, he stayed on with the *Post*, first as an editor on the metropolitan desk, and later as assistant managing editor of the paper. As one of America's leading investigative journalists, he developed a unique relationship with the *Post*. He would investigate powerful people and institutions and publish his findings both as newspaper stories and as books. He developed a reputation for what is called "access" or "insider" journalism because of the way he was able to gain the confidence of leading figures of the period. He is the only contemporary author or co-author to have written eight number one national nonfiction best sellers. These include *All the President's Men* (1974), the original story of Watergate that he wrote with Carl Bernstein; *The Final Days* (1976), a description of the last one hundred days of the Nixon presidency (also written with Bernstein); *The Brethren: Inside the Supreme Court* written with Scott Armstrong (1979); *Wired: The Short Life and Fast Times of John Belushi* (1984); *Veil: The Secret Wars of the CIA 1981–1987* (1987); *The Commanders* (1991), on military decision making during the Gulf War; *The Agenda: Inside the Clinton White House* (1994); *The Choice* (1996), an analysis of the 1996 presidential campaign; and *Shadow: Five Presidents and the Legacy of Watergate 1974-1999* (1999). He also wrote a lengthy, seven-part series about Dan Quayle in 1992 that was criticized for its perceived favorable presentation of the former vice president.

CARL BERNSTEIN

Carl Bernstein was born into a politically active family on February 14, 1944 in Washington, D.C. His father, Alfred David Bernstein and his mother, Sylvia Walker, leftist sympathizers and one-time Communists, were both dedicated to civil rights issues and were in the forefront of the Progressive Movement. His mother once took him on a march to plead for clemency for the convicted spies Ethel and Julius Rosenberg. The family took part in a demonstration in front of the White House on June 19, 1953, the day the Rosenbergs were executed.

Carl's father helped organize the United Public Workers of America, a leftist union representing federal employees. Bernstein recalls attending sit-ins at segregated Washington lunch counters where he was spat upon and called a "nigger lover."

The Bernsteins were under FBI surveillance for thirty-five years and ended up with a twenty-five-hundred–page FBI file. The FBI even monitored the guests at Carl's bar mitzvah. His early experiences of being under FBI scrutiny and seeing his parents persecuted during the McCarthy era contributed to Bernstein's subsequent anti-establishment attitude.

He started school in 1951 at the Cooperative Jewish Children's School of Greater Washington and later attended public schools in Washington and Silver Springs, Maryland. He was an unenthusiastic student with his public school experience marked by failing grades, suspensions, and expulsions. "I was a terrible student. The only thing I could do in school was write. I'd pass the essay exams and flunk the true and false." He finally found his calling in a tenth-grade journalism course. He worked on the high school paper and was named editor of the *Lincoln Torch*, a Jewish youth group newspaper.

When he was sixteen, and still in high school, his father helped him get a job as a copyboy with the *Washington Star*. He then went to the University of Maryland as a commuting student, but he dropped out in 1965 to become a full-time journalist with the *Star*. He fulfilled his military obligations by serving in the National Guard and the Army. He later received an LL.D. degree from Boston University in 1975.

A gifted writer with a penchant for feature writing and investigative reporting, Bernstein rose quickly from copyboy to reporter at the *Star*. In 1965, he left the *Star* to spend a year with the *Daily Journal* in Elizabeth, New Jersey. He quickly gained a reputation as an outstanding reporter, winning several statewide awards for journalism. Tiring of the routine assignments at the *Journal*, Bernstein used his clippings to get a job with the *Washington Post*. During his interview, a *Post* editor, aware of his parents' activism, asked Bernstein, "Are you political?" He replied that the only two organizations he ever belonged to were B'nai Brith Youth and the Newspaper Guild. He got the job and started at the *Post* in October 1966. At twenty-two he was on the staff of one of the nation's leading newspapers.

Once again, he quickly made a name for himself as a top feature writer, producing magazine-type articles about Washington neighborhoods and their problems. He also gained notoriety for his self-assigned investigative pieces on police negligence, slum landlords, drugs, and fraudulent career schools. In 1972, he hustled himself onto the Watergate story that eventually brought him, with Woodward, a Pulitzer Prize and two best-selling books, *All the President's Men* and *The Final Days*.

In the aftermath of the Watergate affair, Bernstein became involved in the celebrity circuit and dated, among others, Bianca Jagger, Elizabeth Taylor, and Margaret Jay, then wife of Britain's ambassador to the United States. During the Jay affair, Bernstein himself was married to Nora Ephron, a writer and author. They divorced, and Ephron retaliated by writing *Heartburn*, a defamatory book that described Bernstein as a philanderer. The book was turned into a movie in 1986 starring Jack Nicholson and Meryl Streep.

He left the *Washington Post* in 1976 to begin studying the turbulent McCarthy era and the government's case against his father, and to start writing his memoirs.

In 1979, he was named Washington Bureau Chief for ABC. In 1981, he moved to New York City where he worked as a correspondent for ABC News until 1984. While with ABC, he exposed a secret agreement between the United States, Egypt, China, and Pakistan to supply arms to the Mujahadeen rebels fighting the Soviet Union in Afghanistan. He subsequently worked as a correspondent and contributor to *Time* and *Vanity Fair*.

In 1988 he published his autobiography, *Loyalties: A Son's Memoir*, which was one part McCarthy-era history, one part Bernstein family history, and one part his personal account of his relationship with his father, whose approval he was still seeking.

In 1992, he wrote a cover story for *Time* about a secret alliance between Ronald Reagan and Pope John Paul II that helped keep Poland's Solidarity movement alive. He followed that story up with additional research that led to *His Holiness: John Paul II and the Hidden History of Our Time,* written with Marco Politi and published in 1996.

He has also written articles for a variety of publications including the *New Republic, Rolling Stone,* the *New York Times,* and Germany's *der Spiegel.* While with the *Washington Post,* he was an occasional music critic and Bernstein still enjoys writing about rock and roll.

WATERGATE

At nine o'clock Saturday morning, June 17, 1972, Bob Woodward received a call from the city editor of the *Washington Post.* There had been a burglary at the Democratic headquarters in Washington, D.C. When he arrived in the *Post's* city room he was assigned to the main story on the burglary. He also noticed that Carl Bernstein was working on the story. While he had never worked on a story with Bernstein before, he had heard about his ability to push his way into a good story to get a byline on it.

On Sunday morning, June 18th, the city editor called Bernstein and Woodward into the office and told them to follow up the burglary story. On Monday morning, June 19th, their first Watergate story with their joint byline appeared on the front page of the *Washington Post.* Woodward was twenty-nine, Bernstein was twenty-six, and neither one was considered among the top journalists at the *Post.* Ben Bradlee, the *Post's* executive editor at the time, would later say that if he had known the story would be so important, he would have selected his best senior reporters to cover it.

So began a two-year odyssey that would change the lives of everyone involved, and forever join the fame and fortune of Woodward and Bernstein.

Despite their many personal differences, Woodward and Bernstein shared four attributes. They were young, they were single, they were ambitious, and neither one of them would take no for an answer. They were both able to devote their lives to the story. For the next two years, they were in the *Post* newsroom nearly every day of the week. They didn't take vacations, and they were able to pursue all leads and tips at any time of day or night. It was a fortuitous combination that led to the political story of the century.

Both reporters were bright and used various techniques to unravel the Watergate enigma including developing theoretical hypotheses they would test. They used two main investigative techniques: first, follow the money (a critical aspect of Nixon's 1972 reelection campaign), and second, interview low-level contacts and later talk to the key players (also Jessica Mitford's approach to sources).

Their efforts persuaded the rest of the press, especially Seymour Hersh at the *New York Times*, was persuaded that Watergate wasn't the "third-rate burglary attempt" that Ron Ziegler, Nixon's press secretary, had described. Hersh was inspired to undertake his own investigation of Watergate.

In 1973, their persistent reports, enhanced by an anonymous source called "Deep Throat," exposed the full dimension of the Watergate burglary and its direct ties to the White House. The media reports led to the appointment of the U.S. Senate Select Watergate Committee, chaired by Senator Sam Ervin. After the discovery of the Watergate tapes came the Watergate cover-up trials, the campaign finance violations prosecutions, and the presidential impeachment investigation. Finally, at 9:00 p.m., on August 8, 1974, President Richard Nixon addressed the nation from the Oval Office. He first explained his reasons and then announced, "Therefore, I shall resign the presidency, effective at noon tomorrow." Twenty-two of the president's men would eventually go to jail.

Thus ended one of the most torturous periods in American presidential history. It was a climax that Woodward and Bernstein had anticipated, but nonetheless came as a shock when Nixon resigned. Their words led to the first resignation of a president in American history.

Woodward and Bernstein both took a leave of absence from the *Post* to advise on the movie production of *All the President's Men* and to write their new book on the last one hundred days of the Nixon presidency, *The Final Days*.

The impact of the 225 stories Woodward and Bernstein wrote during their two-year pursuit of Watergate shaped history for years to come. They also inspired another generation of investigative reporters. Journalism schools across the country were swamped with applications from young people wanting to make a difference.

Bob Woodward and Carl Bernstein showed America that two young people with dedication, hard work, and the truth could take on the most powerful men in the world and win. Their first co-written article in the *Washington Post* follows.

SOURCES. Woodward, Bob, *The Commanders*, Simon & Schuster, New York, 1991; Bernstein, Carl, *Loyalties: A Son's Memoir*, Simon & Schuster, New York, 1989; Bernstein, Carl and Marco Politi, *His Holiness: John Paul II and the Hidden History of Our Time*, Doubleday, New York, 1996; Bernstein, Carl and Bob Woodward, *All the President's Men*, Simon & Schuster, New York 1974; Havill, Adrian, *Deep Truth: The Lives of Bob Woodward and Carl Bernstein*, Carol Publishing Group, New York, 1993; Woodward, Bob, *The Agenda: Inside the Clinton White House*, Simon & Schuster, New York, 1994; Woodward, Bob, *Veil: The Secret Wars of the CIA 1981–1987*, Simon & Schuster, New York, 1987; Woodward, Bob and Scott Armstrong, *The Brethren: Inside the Supreme Court*, Simon & Schuster, New York, 1979; Woodward, Bob and Carl Bernstein, *The Final Days*, Simon & Schuster, New York, 1976.

GOP Security Aide Among Five Arrested in Bugging Affair, Washington Post (June 17, 1972)[1]

Bob Woodward and Carl Bernstein

One of the five men arrested early Saturday in the attempt to bug the Democratic National Committee headquarters is the salaried security coordinator for President Nixon's reelection committee.

The suspect, former CIA employee James W. McCord Jr., 53, also holds a separate contract to provide security services to the Republican National Committee, GOP national chairman Bob Dole said yesterday.

Former Attorney General John N. Mitchell, head of the Committee for the Re-Election of the President, said yesterday McCord was employed to help install that committee's own security system.

In a statement issued in Los Angeles, Mitchell said McCord and the other four men arrested at Democratic headquarters Saturday "were not operating either in our behalf or with our consent" in the alleged bugging attempt.

Dole issued a similar statement, adding, "We deplore action of this kind in or out of politics." An aid to Dole said he was unsure at this time exactly what security services McCord was hired to perform by the National Committee.

Police sources said last night that they were seeking a sixth man in connection with the attempted bugging. The sources would give no other details.

Other sources close to the investigation said yesterday that there still was no explanation as to why the five suspects might have attempted to bug

Democratic headquarters in the Watergate at 2600 Virginia Avenue, NW, or if they were working for other individuals or organizations.

"We're baffled at this point... the mystery deepens," a high Democratic Party source said.

Democratic National Committee Chairman Lawrence F. O'Brien said the "bugging incident... raised the ugliest questions about the integrity of the political process that I have encountered in a quarter century.

"No mere statement of innocence by Mr. Nixon's campaign manager will dispel these questions."

The Democratic presidential candidates were not available for comment yesterday.

O'Brien, in his statement, called on Attorney General Richard G. Kleindienst to order an immediate, "searching professional investigation" of the entire matter by the FBI.

A spokesman for Kleindienst said yesterday, "The FBI is already investigating.... Their investigative report will be turned over to the criminal division for appropriate action."

The White House did not comment.

McCord, 53, retired from the Central Intelligence Agency in 1970 after 19 years of service and established his own "security consulting firm," McCord Associates, at 414 Hungerford Drive, Rockville.... He lives at 7 Winder Ct., Rockville.

McCord is an active Baptist and colonel in the Air Force Reserve, according to neighbors and friends.

In addition to McCord, the other four suspects, all Miami residents, have been identified as: Frank Sturgis (also known as Frank Florini), an American who served in Fidel Castro's revolutionary army and later trained a guerrilla force of anti-Castro exiles; Eugenio R. Martinez, a real estate agent and notary public who is active in anti-Castro activities in Miami; Virgilio R. Gonzales, a locksmith; and Bernard L. Barker, a native of Havana said by exiles to have worked on and off for the CIA since the Bay of Pigs invasion in 1961.

All five suspects gave the police false names after being arrested Saturday. McCord also told his attorney that his name is Edward Martin, the attorney said.

Sources in Miami said yesterday that at least one of the suspects—Sturgis—was attempting to organize Cubans in Miami to demonstrate at the Democratic National Convention there next month.

The five suspects, well-dressed, wearing rubber surgical gloves and unarmed, were arrested about 2:30 a.m. Saturday when they were surprised by Metropolitan police inside the 29-office suite of the Democratic headquarters on the sixth floor of the Watergate.

The suspects had extensive photographic equipment and some electronic surveillance instruments capable of intercepting both regular conversation and telephone communication.

Police also said that two ceiling panels near party chairman O'Brien's office had been removed in such a way as to make it possible to slip in a bugging device.

McCord was being held in D.C. jail on $30,000 bond yesterday. The other four were being held there on $50,000 bond. All are charged with attempted burglary and attempted interception of telephone and other conversations.

McCord was hired as "security coordinator" of the Committee for the Re-Election of the President on Jan. 1, according to Powell Moore, the Nixon committee's director of press and information.

Moore said McCord's contract called for a "take-home salary of $1,200 per month and that the ex-CIA employee was assigned an office in the committee's headquarters at 1701 Pennsylvania Avenue, NW."

Within the last one or two weeks, Moore said, McCord made a trip to Miami Beach—where both the Republican and Democratic National Conventions will be held. The purpose of the trip, Moore said, was "to establish security at the hotel where the Nixon Committee will be staying."

In addition to McCord's monthly salary, he and his firm were paid a total of $2,836 by the Nixon Committee for the purchase and rental of television and other security equipment, according to Moore.

Moore said that he did not know exactly who on the committee staff hired McCord, adding that it "definitely wasn't John Mitchell." According to Moore, McCord has never worked in any previous Nixon election campaigns "because he didn't leave the CIA until two years ago, so it would have been impossible." As of late yesterday, Moore said, McCord was still on the Re-Election Committee payroll.

In his statement from Los Angeles, former Attorney General Mitchell said he was "surprised and dismayed" at reports of McCord's arrest.

"The person involved is the proprietor of a private security agency who was employed by our committee months ago to assist with the installation of our security system," said Mitchell. "He has, as we understand it, a number of

business clients and interests and we have no knowledge of these relationships."

Referring to the alleged attempt to bug the opposition's headquarters,
Mitchell said: "There is no place in our campaign, or in the electoral process,
for this type of activity and we will not permit it nor condone it."

About two hours after Mitchell issued his statement, GOP National Chairman Dole said, "I understand that Jim McCord... is the owner of the firm with
which the Republican National Committee contracts for security services... if
our understanding of the facts is accurate," added Dole, "we will of course dis-
continue our relationship with the firm."

Tom Wilck, deputy chairman of communications for the GOP National Committee, said late yesterday that Republican officials still were checking to find
out when McCord was hired, how much he was paid and exactly what his
responsibilities were.

McCord lives with his wife in a two-story $45,000 house in Rockville.

After being contacted by *The Washington Post* yesterday, Harlan A.
Westrell, who said he was a friend of McCord's, gave the following background
on McCord:

He is from Texas, where he and his wife graduated from Baylor University.
They have three children, a son who is in his third year at the Air Force Academy, and two daughters.

The McCords have been active in the First Baptist Church of Washington.

Other neighbors said that McCord is a colonel in the Air Force Reserve, and
also has taught courses in security at Montgomery Community College. This
could not be confirmed yesterday.

McCord's previous employment by the CIA was confirmed by the intelligence agency, but a spokesman there said further data about McCord was not
available yesterday.

In Miami, *Washington Post* Staff Writer Kirk Schartenberg reported that
two of the other suspects—Sturgis and Barker—are well known among Cuban
exiles there. Both are known to have had extensive contracts with the Central
Intelligence Agency, exile sources reported, and Barker was closely associated
with Frank Bender, the CIA operative who recruited many members of Brigade
2506, the Bay of Pigs invasion force.

Barker, 55, and Sturgis, 37, reportedly showed up uninvited at a Cuban
exile meeting in May and claimed to represent an anticommunist organization
of refugees from "captive nations." The purpose of the meeting, at which both

men reportedly spoke, was to plan a Miami demonstration in support of President Nixon's decision to mine the harbor of Haiphong.

Barker, a native of Havana who lived both in the U.S. and Cuba during his youth, is a U.S. Army veteran who was imprisoned in a German POW camp during World War II. He later served in the Cuban Buro de Investigationes—secret police—under Fidel Castro and fled to Miami in 1959. He reportedly was one of the principal leaders of the Cuban Revolutionary Council, the exile organization established with CIA help to organize the Bay of Pigs invasion.

Sturgis, an American soldier of fortune who joined Castro in the hills of Oriente Province in 1958, left Cuba in 1959 with his close friend, Pedro Diaz Lanz, then chief of the Cuban air force. Diaz Lanz, once active in Cuban exile activities in Miami, more recently has been reported involved in such right-wing movements as the John Birch Society and the Rev. Billy James Hargis' Christian Crusade.

Sturgis, more commonly known as Frank Florini, lost his American citizenship in 1960 for serving in a foreign military force—Castro's army—but, with the aid of then-Florida Sen. George Smathers, regained it.

Contributing to this story were Washington Post *staff writers E. J. Bachinski, Bill Gold, Claudia Levy, Kirk Scharfenberg, J. Y. Smith and Martin Weil.*

---

1. Copyright © 1972, *The Washington Post*. Reprinted with permission.

Frances Moore Lappé

The events of the 1960s—the Vietnam War, poverty, and racial inequality—became a personal challenge for one teenage girl in Texas. With an unbridled optimism she would never lose, Frances Moore Lappé decided she wanted to "change the world." After graduating from college, she spent time at the library at University of California, Berkeley (UCB) doing research that would lead to a one-page handout explaining why there was enough food in the world to feed everyone. That handout grew into a book, *Diet for a Small Planet*, published in 1971. More than three million copies of the book have been sold worldwide, and it has changed the way we eat and perceive our environment, and had made us think about what we can do to improve the world.

Frances Moore Lappé was born to John and Ina Skifvars Moore on February 10, 1944, in Pendleton, Oregon. They soon moved to Texas where Frances attended public schools. Even as a high school teenager in Fort Worth, Texas, she was a self-described incurable globalist: "I was always frustrated by looking at anything but the big picture." She wanted to save the world through the U.S. Foreign Service. Although she gave up the Foreign Service after six weeks at American University, she never wavered from her ultimate goal.

Lappé transferred to Earlham College, a small Quaker school in Richmond, Indiana, where she received her bachelor's degree in history in 1966, a year dominated by the war in Vietnam, the civil rights movement, and the War on Poverty. Eager to fulfill her ambition, she worked as a community organizer with a national nonprofit organization for welfare recipients in Philadelphia. By 1968, she was frustrated by her inability to see how her work—helping people get welfare—related to the root causes of hunger and poverty. She left to do graduate studies in community organizing through the School of Social Work at UCB.

In 1969, at the age of twenty-five, she dropped out of graduate school. Instead of following the traditional classroom path to knowledge, she decided to let her passion dictate her studies. She holed up in a quiet corner of the agricultural library at UCB reading books that attempted to explain the causes of poverty and hunger. She let the questions that arose determine the path of her research. Her studies led her to focus on food and hunger, and she began experimenting with her own diets of natural foods.

It was during the course of this research that she encountered information and data that would change her life. She was surprised to find that half of America's harvest acreage went to feed livestock: It took sixteen pounds of grain and soybeans to produce just one pound of beef. But the resulting meat was not necessary to get the protein a person needs daily. From these discoveries, Lappé formed the nucleus of a theory that would help people understand that they were part of a system that was creating hunger out of plenty.

Eager to share her discoveries, Lappé reduced her ideas to a one-page handout. She rewrote it as a five-page handout, and eventually expanded it into a seventy-page booklet she planned to publish herself. Instead, a friend persuaded her to submit it to Ballantine Books in New York.

In 1971, Ballantine published *Diet for a Small Planet* and Lappé's life changed forever. (Along the way she had married Marc Lappé, moved to Hastings-on-Hudson in New York, and had two children, a son, Anthony, and a daughter, Anna.) *Diet for a Small Planet* turned into a bestseller. Lappé was asked to speak on the talk show circuit, where she would say: "We could choose a diet that was both healthier for us and placed a lighter burden on the earth's resources."

Her next major life-changing experience came in November 1974, when she attended the World Food Conference in Rome. She was surprised to see how interested the so-called experts were in her self-taught theories. But she was disappointed to discover that these experts were locked into the fruitless belief that greater production would solve the problem of hunger. Recognizing that hunger was an economic and political problem, not a production problem, she decided it could only be solved if people took more responsibility for themselves. As a result, she revised her first edition of *Diet* to make its political message much clearer.

In 1975, she met Joseph Collins of the Institute for Policy Studies in Washington and discovered that he shared her theories about the political and economic causes of hunger. This meeting led to Lappé's next life-changing experience. They agreed to collaborate on a book outlining those causes, *Food First: Beyond the Myth of Scarcity*, and with the publisher's advance they would establish a nonprofit organization to sponsor research and public education on world hunger. The Institute for Food and Development Policy was established in 1975 and moved to San Francisco in January 1977. During this period Lappé and her husband separated.

Six months after the move to California, Lappé expanded her experiences by traveling to Third World countries to study the problems of hunger first hand. Her studies helped the Food First Institute identify the root causes of hunger and poverty around the world, as well as in the United States.

Lappé's next major life change occurred in 1990, when she and her new husband, Paul Martin DuBois, launched the Center for Living Democracy, a natural progression from Food First. It was not enough for Lappé to be a social critic; she wanted people to understand the world can change if they become personally involved. The Center, headquartered in Brattleboro, Vermont, is a nonprofit that goes beyond the study of politics of hunger. It is designed to help people make true democracy a practical and rewarding approach to solving society's problems by showing them that solutions are possible. The Center for Living Democracy teaches ordinary citizens how to take more responsibility for their own lives and how to resist becoming victims of outside market forces like advertising.

Diet for a Small Planet, revised several times since its first edition in 1971, has been translated into six languages. It has shown world leaders how to maximize the earth's potential to meet nutritional needs and how to minimize the disruption of the earth to meet those needs. It has disproven the simplistic theories of hunger that suggested increased production was a solution. *Diet* launched a vegetarian revolution, alerted the public to environmental issues, and provided an early warning about pesticides in foods. Moreover, it taught millions of readers that by changing the way we eat we could change ourselves and change the world.

The Institute for Food and Development Policy, nicknamed Food First, is now the nation's leading think tank on food policy and hunger issues. The Center for Living Democracy publishes Lappé and DuBois's *The Quickening of America*, a training tool used by educators, community groups, and public agencies. Lappé tours the country providing examples of how Americans bring democracy to life, and conducts intensive workshops providing skills needed for successful problem solving. The Center's Interracial Democracy Program studies and publicizes the nature of interracial dialogue initiatives nationwide. (Information about the Center is available at *www.livingdemocracy.org*.)

The Center launched a news service in 1995. Lappé is editor-in-chief of the American News Service (ANS), which reports the successes of ordinary people employing innovative methods to solve problems in their communities. ANS stories have appeared in more than three hundred newspapers nationwide, reaching a total readership of more than 250 million. ANS is the only news service covering America's search for solutions, and seeks to establish a new role model for journalists as individuals sensitive to the communities' needs, practicing what is called "hope journalism"—reports of "constructive solution-oriented activities, that will inform, intrigue, and inspire."

Frances Moore Lappé has become one of the world's leading experts on hunger, inspiring untold numbers of people around the world. In 1981, she was named to the Nutrition Hall of Fame Center for Science and Public Interest. She received the *Mademoiselle Magazine* Award in 1997, and the World Hunger Award in 1982. In 1987, she was given the Right Livelihood Award, Sweden's "alternative Nobel Prize," which honors significant contributions in the areas of human rights, the environment, peace, and disarmament. She has also received fourteen honorary doctorates from colleges across the country.

Lappé is the author or co-author of twelve books on hunger, social change and institutional reform that have been translated into twenty-two languages, and is a regular contributor to the nation's leading newspapers and magazines.

Lappé's personal philosophy is that "we are social creatures" and that "people are much happier when they feel their life has a bigger meaning than survival of themselves and their families."

The following excerpts from *Diet for a Small Planet* reveal how Lappé got started on the path of public service and how our cultural eating habits, wasteful cash crops, and the myth of protein impact on the world's food supply.

SOURCES. Lappé, Frances Moore, *Diet for a Small Planet*, Ballantine Books, New York, 1971, 1982; Lappé, Frances Moore and Joseph Collins with Cary Fowler, *Food First: Beyond the Myth of Scarcity*, Houghton Mifflin, Boston, 1977; Lappé, Frances Moore and Paul Martin DuBois, *The Quickening of America*, Jossey-Bass Publishers, San Francisco, 1994.

Diet for a Small Planet
Frances Moore Lappé

THE BEGINNING
(From the Foreword)[1]

Several years ago I became intrigued with the debate over the "world food problem." In a world where the majority is hungry, there seemed to me no more urgent question. According to the books I read at that time, man was reaching the very limits of the earth's capacity to produce food. Although there was much disagreement about alternatives for expanding the earth's capacity, the focus was always clear: *it was the earth's natural limitations that man had to worry about.*

Naively I set out to determine for myself just how near the "limit" we were. Although, of course, I failed, the venture did payoff: my assumptions were severely jolted. First, I was astounded by how little of the earth's surface is really well suited to producing food.

I had always assumed that only three elements were needed for agriculture: sun, water, and soil. And since these elements are almost omnipresent on the planet, I thought that agricultural potential must also be. Then I realized that we probably came to hold the distorted view because all we know is our own country. But how exceptional America is! We are endowed with *all* the complex requirements for high agricultural productivity, more so than any other nation in the world.

At about the same time I came across the fact that a very large portion of these superb agricultural resources are funneled into the production of meat. I wondered whether this was really the most productive use of our rich agricultural land.

Suddenly I began to see the world's problems with food as my point of reference. Other facts began to strike me that I had previously taken for granted. I thought about products like coffee and tea. Don't they grow on agricultural land, land that might otherwise be growing nutritious food? Why do these patterns of land use exist if man needs food, and good land is scarce?

All this went through my mind. The questions I had originally asked with such a sense of urgency began to fade in importance. I now saw that in a world where only a minor portion of the land is really well suited to agriculture, man is using much of the best land with dubious efficiency. And I saw that much agricultural land which might be growing food is being used instead to "grow" money (in the form of coffee, tea, etc.). But all this had nothing to do with the earth's *natural* limits, the issue that at first had so concerned me. Maybe, I finally concluded, instead of studying geography to understand the earth's food-producing potential, I should be examining what man is doing with the food he *presently* produces....

CULTURAL EATING HABITS
(From Part One: Earth's Labor Lost)[2]

When your mother told you to eat everything on your plate because people were starving in India, you thought it was pretty silly. You knew that the family dog would be the only one affected by what you did or didn't waste. Since then you've probably continued to think that making any sort of *ethical* issue about eating is absurd. You eat what your family always ate, altered only perhaps by proddings from the food industry. It's probably a pretty unconscious affair, and you like it that way. But eating habits can have a meaning, a meaning that not only feels closer to you than an abstract ethic but brings you pleasure too....

The act of putting into your mouth what the earth has grown is perhaps your most direct interaction with the earth. But, depending on the eating habits of a culture, this interaction can have very different consequences—for mankind, and for the earth. What I will be suggesting in this book is a guideline for eating from the earth that both maximizes the earth's potential to meet man's nutritional needs and, at the same time, minimizes the disruption of the earth necessary to sustain him. It's as simple as that....

CASH CROPS[3]

Beginning over three hundred years ago the wealthy Western powers established the plantation system in their subject lands. The plantation's sole purpose was to produce wealth for the colonizers, not food for men. Thus, most of the crops selected by the colonizers—tobacco, rubber, tea, coffee, cocoa, cotton, and other fibers—have negligible nutritional value. The name subsequently given to them, "cash crops," is quite an appropriate label.

Cash crops became established in world trade as the only proper exports from the Third World; so that even after emancipation from formal colonial control, Third World countries were economically "hooked" on cash crops as their only means of survival. Coffee alone is the economic lifeblood of *forty* developing countries—as in the African country of Rwanda, where coffee represents 87.5 percent of earnings from foreign exchange.

Obviously cash crops usurp land, often the best agricultural land, that could be growing food for an undernourished local population. Over two hundred fifty thousand square miles are presently planted with non-nutritious cash crops—more than one and one-half times the entire area of California and equal to two-thirds of all the arable land in Latin America. And, more land is put under the system every day. The Food and Agriculture Organization of the U.N. reports that *nonedible* agricultural production is growing at a faster rate than edible food production in the developing countries.

The rich West points to the demands of international trade as the reason for the bind in which the Third World finds itself. True enough. But the real question remains unanswered: who is responsible for creating this pattern of land use and the subsequent rules of international trade?...

THE POISONED FOOD CHAIN[4]

By now most of us are familiar with the facts of environmental damage wrought by chlorinated pesticides like DDT: In predatory birds like pelicans and falcons, DDT and related pesticides like Dieldrin can disrupt reproductive processes, and in ocean-going fish like salmon, DDT can cause damage to the nervous system. What may be less familiar to you, and of greater importance to us here, is just *why* these particular species are being affected. A major reason is that these animals are at the top of long food chains in which pesticides accumulate as one organism is eaten by another. This process of accumulation results from the fact that organochlorine pesticides like DDT and Dieldrin are retained in animal and fish fat and are difficult to break down. Thus, as big fish eat smaller fish, or as cows eat grass (or feed), whatever pesticides they eat are largely retained and passed on. So if man is eating at the "top" of such food chains, he becomes the final consumer and thus the recipient of the highest concentration of pesticide residues.

But unlike most other predators (or "carnivores," if you like), man has a choice of what and how much he eats....

PROTEIN ISN'T EVERYTHING
(From Part Two: Bringing
Protein Theory Down to Earth)[5]

Many people who might otherwise rely more on plant sources for protein continue to eat great quantities of meat because they believe that only "good red meat" can supply the many vitamins and minerals that their bodies need. Are they right?

A national food survey in Britain in 1966 showed that although 40 percent of the protein in a typical British diet comes from plant sources, *plants provide, on the average, more than twice the amount of vitamins and minerals provided by meat and fish*. Seven nutrients were considered: vitamin A, thiamine, riboflavin, niacin, vitamin C, calcium, and iron. Plant sources were the greatest contributors of all nutrients except riboflavin and calcium. But dairy produce and eggs, *not meat*, provided the bulk of the daily requirements of these two nutrients. This general pattern emerged in spite of the fact that green vegetables, which are valuable sources of many of these nutrients, comprise a relatively minor part of the British diet.

A breakdown of sources of vitamins and minerals in the American diet reveals a similar pattern. Although plant sources provide only 31 percent of the protein in our national diet, they provide 50 percent of the vitamin A, 59 percent of the thiamine, 53 percent of the niacin, 94 percent of the vitamin C, and 62 percent of the iron. As in the British study, dairy products contribute the largest percentage of both riboflavin and calcium.

Other important nutrients not covered by the British survey include phosphorus, potassium, and magnesium. Although meat is a good source for both phosphorus and potassium there are nonmeat sources which are even better.... In the case of magnesium, meat is actually among the poorer sources. Rich sources include cocoa, nuts, soybeans, whole grain, and green leafy vegetables.

In fact, the only required nutrient thought to be limited strictly to animal sources is cobalamin (vitamin B12). But there are potentially significant exceptions to this rule. A type of blue-green algae, *Spirulina maxima* (a popular food in parts of Africa), and two other algae all contain cobalamin. Thus, it is possible, at least theoretically, to fill all man's nutritional needs from plant sources. For most of you, however, the important fact is that there is no danger of cobalamin deficiency as long as you eat dairy products or eggs.

Thus, we can safely conclude that a varied plant protein diet supplemented with dairy products and eggs can supply sufficient protein while at the same time surpassing meat in the provision of some of the other basic nutrients. All this is not meant to belittle the nutritional value of meat. My aim is only to provide a more realistic view of the wide variety of nutritious food sources to replace the culturally fixed idea of the absolute supremacy of meat.

1. Frances Moore Lappé, *Diet for a Small Planet*, Friends of the Earth/Ballantine, New York, 1971, pages xi–xiii.
2. Lappé, *Diet for a Small Planet*, page 3.
3. Lappé, *Diet for a Small Planet*, pages 16–17.
4. Lappé, *Diet for a Small Planet*, page 19.
5. Lappé, *Diet for a Small Planet*, pages 54–55.

About the Author

Dr. Carl Jensen is a professor emeritus of Communication Studies at Sonoma State University, California, and former director of Project Censored, an internationally recognized media research project. Founded by Jensen in 1976, Project Censored is America's longest-running research project, which annually explores news media censorship.

Jensen has been involved with the media for more than forty-five years as a daily newspaper reporter, weekly newspaper publisher, public relations practitioner, advertising executive, and educator. He spent fifteen years with Batten, Barton, Durstine, and Osborn, the international advertising agency, where he was an award-winning copywriter, account supervisor, and vice president.

Specializing in mass communications, Jensen received his B.A., M.A., and Ph.D. degrees in sociology from the University of California, Santa Barbara, in 1971, 1972, and 1977, respectively. From 1973 to 1996, he taught media studies, sociology, and journalism courses at Sonoma State University where he founded Sonoma State University's B.A. degree in Communication Studies as well as the Journalism Certificate Program. Jensen founded the Lincoln Steffens Journalism Award for Investigative Reporting in Northern California in 1981.

He has written and lectured extensively about press censorship, the First Amendment, and the mass media. His 1996 Project Censored Yearbook received the first national Firecracker Award from the American Wholesale Book Sellers Association for the best alternative nonfiction book of the year.

He also wrote *20 Years of Censored News* (Seven Stories Press, 1997) and the introductory biography of Upton Sinclair for the reprint of *The Millennium: A Comedy of the Year 2000* (Seven Stories Press, 2000) by Upton Sinclair. Jensen was consulting editor for *Ready Reference: Censorship*, a three-volume encyclopedia set covering major aspects of censorship issues in both American and world history, published by Salem Press, Pasadena, in 1997.

Jensen has been cited by the national Association for Education in Journalism and Mass Communication for his "innovative approach to constructive media criticism and for providing a new model for media criticism." The Giraffe Project honored Jensen "for sticking his neck out for the common good" and for being a "role model for a caring society." The Media Alliance presented Jensen with the Media Alliance Meritorious Achievement Award in the "Unimpeachable Source" category. The Society of Professional Journalists in Los Angeles awarded him its 1990 Freedom of Information Award.

In 1992, Jensen was named the outstanding university professor of journalism in California by the California Newspaper Publishers Association and was awarded the 1992 Hugh M. Hefner First Amendment Award in education from the Playboy Foundation for his achievement in defending the First Amendment. In 1996, Jensen received the James Madison Freedom of Information Award for Career Achievement from the Northern California Chapter of the Society of Professional Journalists, the University President's Award of Appreciation for "Dedicated Service to Sonoma State University," and was cited for outstanding achievement by the Sonoma State University Academic Senate.

Jensen is married and has four children, three grandchildren, and one great grandchild. He and his wife Sandra; Elske, their great Great Dane; and their cat, Miro, live in beautiful downtown Cotati, in Northern California.